中國貴金屬紀念幣年鑑

Almanac of Chinese Precious Metal Commemorative Currencies

1996～1998

主 编

尹成友　王震云

副主编

杨福基　李守荣

李小平　周战地　王　喆

中国金融出版社

CHINA FINANCIAL PUBLISHING HOUSE

责任编辑：查子安　彭元勋
装帧设计：北京楚星美术设计有限公司
平面制作：王　永　刘晓明　张睿洲　孟艳梅　李晓丽
责任印制：郝云山

图书在版编目（CIP）数据

中国贵金属纪念币年鉴.1996~1998/尹成友，王震云主编.－北京：中国金融出版社，1999
ISBN 7-5049-2253-6
Ⅰ.中…
Ⅱ.①尹…②王…
Ⅲ.纪念币，贵金属－中国－1996~1998－年鉴
Ⅳ.G894-54
中国版本图书馆CIP数据核字(1999)第54567号

出版发行　中国金融出版社
社址　北京广安门外小红庙南里3号
邮编　100055
经销　新华书店
制版　北京楚星美术设计有限公司
印刷　利丰雅高制作（深圳）有限公司
开本　889毫米×1194毫米 1/16
印张　25.5
版次　2000年4月第1版
印次　2000年4月第1次印刷
印数　平装3000册　　精装1000册
定价　平装298.00元　　精装320.00元

《中国贵金属纪念币年鉴》编委会

《中国贵金属纪念币年鉴》编辑部

Almanac of Chinese Precious Metal Commemorative Currencies

前　言

为弘扬中华民族灿烂的钱币文化，拓展和繁荣海内外钱币文化市场，1979年经国务院批准和授权，中国人民银行向国内外发行金银纪念币，以增进与世界各国的经济、文化交流。中国现代金银纪念币以其丰富的选题内容、独特的民族风格、生动鲜明的艺术形象、精良的铸造技术和异彩纷呈的种类，形成当代中国钱币文化中一道亮丽的风景线，引起社会各界的热烈反响和关注。

金银纪念币作为金属铸币中的特殊币种，是国家法定货币，《中华人民共和国人民币管理条例》将其定性为贵金属纪念币。伴随着中国的改革开放，中国现代金币事业得到迅猛发展，金银纪念币以其鲜明的文化特色展现着其独特的魅力，成为世界钱币文化宝库中光彩夺目的重要组成部分。

中华民族传统文化源远流长，中国钱币文化在传播中华民族传统文化方面，以其新颖独特的方式产生了深远的影响。殷商之际，先民首创人类金属铸币之先河，几千年来，中国钱币文化自成体系，有着悠久深厚的历史文化内涵。中国现代金银纪念币更是集丰富的历史文化和民族艺术精华之大成，是当代中国钱币文化的精华之所在。

1996年至1998年所发行的金银纪念币题材丰富，内容广泛，不仅涉及中华民族几千年的历史文化和古今中外重大历史事件，而且关联到文物、古迹、自然风景、体育运动、名画等，其寓意深刻、选材精心，是中国现代金银纪念币制作、发行日臻完善的精华。

为了配合金银纪念币产品的市场化，在以往编印年鉴的基础上，经过精心策划，并经中国金币总公司和中国金融出版社及有关单位的通力合作，《中国贵金属纪念币年鉴》(1996～1998)终于付梓出版。这是钱币文化界的一件幸事，也是中国现代金银纪念币的一件盛事。《中国贵金属纪念币年鉴》是以往出版的《中国金银币年鉴》的延续。《中国贵金属纪念币年鉴》（1996 ~ 1998）着重突出和展示了香港回归祖国、澳门回归祖国、中国人民解放军建军70周年、中国工农红军长征胜利60周年、重庆直辖市成立、中国熊猫金币发行15周年等重大历史事件，以及孙中山、周恩来、刘少奇、齐白石等著名人物和中国古代历史文化系列等内容的金银纪念币，深刻地体现了民族特色和时代感。年鉴中均附有与主题相关的大量图片和文字资料，展示了图文并茂的现代艺术风格，具备较强的艺术性、知识性、趣味性和资料性，各界人士可以通过鉴赏《中国贵金属纪念币年鉴》感受到不断发展和提高的中国现代金银纪念币的铸造水平，同时也为广大钱币爱好者和专业经销机构销售、鉴赏、研究中国现代金银纪念币提供了最完备、最权威的工具书。

最后，真诚感谢中国人民银行总行领导和货币金银局领导为中国现代金银纪念币的发行和年鉴的出版工作给予的支持和指导；真诚感谢各造币厂的领导、设计师和全体参与金银纪念币制作人员所付出的辛勤劳动。

FOREWARD

To popularize the glorious Chinese coin culture and, to expand both domestic and international markets for coins, and for the sake of increasing the economic and cultural exchanges between China and the world, the People's Bank of China was authorized to issue gold and silver commemorative coins in 1979, with the approval of the State Council of the People's Republic of China. Chinese modern gold and silver commemorative coins have become an conspicuous scene in modern Chinese coin culture for their rich themes, unique national style, vivid artistic figures, striking quality and extraordinary variety, and have been warmly welcomed and concerned.

As special kinds of coins, gold and silver commemorative coins are the legal tender of the state. *The Regulations of the People's Republic of China Governing the Renminbi* identifies them as precious metal commemorative currencies. With the reform and opening of China, Chinese modern gold and silver coinage has developed rapidly. It is the distinctive cultural features that make Chinese gold and silver commemorative coins an important part of the coin culture in the world.

Chinese traditional culture has a long history. In respect regarding spreading Chinese traditional culture, Chinese coin culture has a profound influence by its unique way. It was Chinese people who invented metal coin in the Shang Dynasty. During the past thousands of years, Chinese coin culture had formed its own system, which has profoundly historic and cultural traits. Combining the long history and the cream of the national art, Chinese modern commemorative gold and silver coins are the key aspect in Chinese modern coin culture.

The themes expressed on the gold and silver commemorative coins issued in 1996 ~ 1998 are very rich, which, not only concerns the history, culture and important events in the world, but also involves cultural relics, historic sites, scenery, sports and famous painting, etc. They are pregnant with meaning and are carefully selected, the cream of the increasingly perfect production and issue of Chinese modern commemorative gold and silver coins.

In order to cooperate with the marketnization of gold and silver commemorative coins, we are now compiling the present book on the ground of the experience of the past years through meticulous plan and under the cooperation of China Gold Coin Inc. and China Financial Publishing House and other related units. It is a great event for the circle of coin culture, and Chinese gold and silver commemorative coins as well. *Almanac of Chinese Precious Metal Commemorative Currencies* (1996 ~ 1998) is the continuance of *Almanac of Chinese Coins* published in the past. *Almanac of Chinese Precious Metal Commemorative Currencies* (1996 ~ 1998) stresses such important historic events as the return of Hong Kong to China, the 70th anniversary of the founding of the People's Liberation Army, the 60th anniversary of the victory of the Long March of the Chinese Workers' and Peasants' Red Army, the Founding of Chongqing Municipal City, the 15th anniversary of the issue of Chinese panda gold coin, etc. Such famous figures as Sun Yat-sen, Zhou Enlai, Liu Shaoqi, Qi Baishi, together with the series of Chinese ancient historic culture also found their expressions on the coins. All of these profoundly reflect the national features and the spirit of our age. A vast amount of related pictures and texts are attached to the main themes, both of which are excellent showing the modern artistic style of this volume. Its artistry, knowledge, tastes and data deserve reading. Personages of various circles will see the increasingly developed quality of Chinese modern commemorative gold and silver coins in this book. It is also the most complete and authoritative reference book for the coin collectors and specialized distributors to sell, appreciate and study Chinese modern gold and silver commemorative coins.

At last, we should like to thank the leaders of the Head Quarters of the People's Bank of China and the Currency, Gold & Silver Bureau for their support and instructions. We would also like to thank the leaders, designers and all the producers of the mines for their industrious work.

目　录

一九九六年

一九九七年

一九九八年

CONTENTS

1996

1997

1998

1996

中國貴金屬紀念幣年鑒

Almanac of Chinese Precious Metal Commemorative Currencies

1996 Issue of the
Chinese Panda
Gold and Silver Coin
Series

中國貴金屬紀念幣圖鑒

一、1996年版中国熊猫金银币

一九九六年

中国贵金属纪念币年鉴

自1982年中国人民银行发行熊猫系列金银币以来，按惯例每年更换一组版面，图案各异，生动传神地展现出熊猫的千姿百态。

熊猫，又称大熊猫，或"大猫熊"，是一种古老的动物，其祖先可以追溯到一千二百万年以前，并一直生存至今，被称为"活化石"。现在，大熊猫只分布在中国四川、甘肃、西藏及陕西等地，是中国独有的珍稀野生动物，在对外文化交流活动中有"国宝"的美誉。

1996年版中国熊猫金银币共有16个品种，其中金币6种，银币4种，双金属币4种，铂币2种。正面图案均为国号、年号、北京天坛祈年殿。背面图案：普制金币、铂币分别为熊猫攀树图及面额，普制银币分别为母子熊猫食竹图、小溪边的熊猫及面额，精制金币分别为大熊猫、熊猫食竹图及面额，精制银币分别为熊猫食竹图、三只熊猫嬉戏图及面额，双金属币分别为熊猫食竹图、母子熊猫图及面额。

1996年版中国熊猫金银币由中国人民银行发行，分别由上海造币厂、沈阳造币厂、深圳国宝金币制造厂、中国金币总公司铸造，中国金币总公司总经销。

Since the 1982 issue of the series of Chinese panda gold and silver coins by the People's Bank of China, it has become a custom to change a group of layouts annually to display the panda's various postures vividly.

Panda, also called 'giant panda', is a kind of ancient animal whose ancestor could be traced back to 12 million years ago and has survived until nowadays, so it is called 'live fossil'. Panda is only distributed over Sichuan, Gansu, Tibet and Shaanxi, China, which is a unique endangered wild animal species of China and, is called 'national treasure' of China in the activities of international cultural exchange.

The 1996 issue of the Chinese panda gold and silver coins contains 16 kinds: 6 kinds of gold coins, 4 kinds of silver coins, 4 kinds of bi-metallic coins and 2 kinds of platinum coins. The common obverse depict the picture of the title of PRC, issuing year and the Hall of Prayer for Good Harvests of the Temple of Heaven in Beijing. The reverses of the bu. gold and platinum coins depict the picture of pandas climbing the tree and face value, and that of the bu. silver coins depict the pictures of mother and baby pandas eating bamboo, pandas by the brook and face value respectively, and that of the proof silver coins depict the pictures of panda eating bamboo, three playing pandas and face value respectively, and that of the bi-metallic coins depict the pictures of pandas eating bamboo, mother and baby pandas and face value respectively.

The 19… issue of Chinese panda gold and silver coins was issued by the People's Bank of China, minted by Shanghai M… Shenyang Mint, Shenzhen Panda Gold Coin Mint, and China Gold Coin Inc. respectively, distributed by Chi… …n Inc..

共同正面

原　大 Full Size

放　大

面额（元）	100	100
直径（毫米）	32	32
含纯金（盎司）	1	1
成色（%）	99.9	99.9
质量	普制	精制
年号	1996	1996
发行量（枚）		1500
铸造单位	上海造币厂 沈阳造币厂	沈阳造币厂

Face Value (Yuan)	100	100
Diameter (mm)	32	32
Pure Gold Content (oz)	1	1
Fineness (%)	99.9	99.9
Quality	Bu.	Proof
Issuing Year	1996	1996
Mintage (Pieces)		1500
Minted by	Shanghai Mint Shenyang Mint	Shenyang Mint

共同正面

放 大

原 大 Full Size

面额（元）	50	25	10	5
直径（毫米）	27	22	18	14
含纯金（盎司）	1/2	1/4	1/10	1/20
成色（%）	99.9	99.9	99.9	99.9
质量	普制	普制	普制	普制
年号	1996	1996	1996	1996
发行量（枚）				
铸造单位	上海造币厂 沈阳造币厂			

Face Value (Yuan)	50	25	10	5
Diameter (mm)	27	22	18	14
Pure Gold Content (oz)	1/2	1/4	1/10	1/20
Fineness (%)	99.9	99.9	99.9	99.9
Quality	Bu.	Bu.	Bu.	Bu.
Issuing Year	1996	1996	1996	1996
Mintage (Pieces)				
Minted by	Shanghai Mint Shenyang Mint			

正 面

原 大 Full Size

面额（元）	100	Face Value (Yuan)	100
直径（毫米）	80	Diameter (mm)	80
含纯银（盎司）	12	Pure Silver Content (oz)	12
成色（%）	99.9	Fineness (%)	99.9
质量	精制	Quality	Proof
年号	1996	Issuing Year	1996
发行量（枚）	800	Mintage (Pieces)	800
铸造单位	上海造币厂	Minted by	Shanghai Mint

共同正面

放　大

原　大 Full Size

面额（元）	10	10	5
直径（毫米）	40	40	33
含纯银（盎司）	1	1	1/2
成色（%）	99.9	99.9	99.9
质量	普制	精制	普制
年号	1996	1996	1996
发行量（枚）		8000	
铸造单位	上海造币厂 沈阳造币厂 深圳国宝金币制造厂	沈阳造币厂	沈阳造币厂 深圳国宝金币制造厂

Face Value (Yuan)	10	10	5
Diameter (mm)	40	40	33
Pure Silver Content (oz)	1	1	1/2
Fineness (%)	99.9	99.9	99.9
Quality	Bu.	Proof	Bu.
Issuing Year	1996	1996	1996
Mintage (Pieces)		8000	
Minted by	Shanghai Mint Shenyang Mint Shenzhen Panda Gold Coin Mint	Shenyang Mint	Shenyang Mint Shenzhen Panda Gold Coin Mint

共同正面

原 大 Full Size

放 大

面额（元）	10	5
直径（毫米）	18	14
含纯铂（盎司）	1/10	1/20
成色（%）	99.95	99.95
质量	精制	精制
年号	1996	1996
发行量（枚）	2500	5000
铸造单位	中国金币总公司	

Face Value (Yuan)	10	5
Diameter (mm)	18	14
Pure Platinum Content (oz)	1/10	1/20
Fineness (%)	99.95	99.95
Quality	Proof	Proof
Issuing Year	1996	1996
Mintage (Pieces)	2500	5000
Minted by	China Gold Coin Inc.	

正　面

原　大 Full Size

面额（元）	500	Face Value (Yuan)	500
直径（毫米）	80	Diameter (mm)	80
含纯金（盎司）	5	Pure Gold Content (oz)	5
含纯银（盎司）	2	Pure Silver Content (oz)	2
成色（%）	[illegible].99	Fineness (%)	99.99
质量	精制	Quality	Proof
年号	1996	Issuing Year	1996
发行量（枚）	199	Mintage (Pieces)	199
铸造单位	上海造币厂	Minted by	Shanghai Mint

正　面

正　面

正　面

原　大 Full Size

放　大

面额（元）	50	25	10
直径（毫米）	36	30	23
含纯金（盎司）	1/2	1/4	1/10
含纯银（盎司）	1/5	1/8	1/28
成色（%）	99.9	99.9	99.9
质量	精制	精制	精制
年号	1996	1996	1996
发行量（枚）	2500	2500	2500
铸造单位	沈阳造币厂		

Face Value (Yuan)	50	25	10
Diameter (mm)	36	30	23
Pure Gold Content (oz)	1/2	1/4	1/10
Pure Silver Content (oz)	1/5	1/8	1/28
Fineness (%)	99.9	99.9	99.9
Quality	Proof	Proof	Proof
Issuing Year	1996	1996	1996
Mintage (Piece)	2500	2500	2500
Minted by	Shenyang Mint		

The Commemorative
Coins of the
15th Anniversary of the
Issue of the Chinese
Panda Gold Coins

中國貴金屬紀念幣章鑒

二、中国熊猫金币发行
15 周年纪念币

一九九六年

中国贵金属纪念币年鉴

为纪念中国熊猫金币发行15周年，中国人民银行特发行中国熊猫金币发行15周年纪念币。该套币由上海造币厂铸造，中国金币总公司总经销。

中国熊猫金币始发于1982年，第一套熊猫金币共4种，此后每年均发行，从未间断。各年度熊猫金币正面图案均为国名、北京天坛祈年殿、年号，90年代以后其设计由一环式改为双环式。背面图案采用的是中国珍稀野生动物大熊猫图案，每年更换一次，迄今为止，已采用了熊猫30多种不同的姿态作为图案，如熊猫食竹、母子熊猫悄悄话、三只熊猫树下嬉戏等。熊猫金币的质量分为精制、普制两种。熊猫金币规格齐全，除了国际上通用的1盎司、1/2盎司、1/4盎司、1/10盎司、1/20盎司5种常规规格外，还有12盎司、5盎司两种非常规规格。

中国熊猫金币在国际上具有极高的收藏价值和投资价值，这不仅表明中国传统文化所蕴藏的深厚潜力，同时也展现了中国贵金属币跻身于世界先进行列的自信心和创造力。

该套纪念币共3个品种，其中1/4盎司、1/10盎司、1盎司普制金币各1种。正面图案均为国号、年号、北京天坛祈年殿及纪念文字，背面图案均为熊猫攀树及面额。

The Chinese panda gold coins were first issued at the beginning of 1982. To commemorate the 15th anniversary of the issue of the Chinese panda gold coins, the People's Bank of China especially issued the commemorative coins of the 15th anniversary of the issue of the Chinese panda gold coins, which were minted by Shanghai Mint and distributed by China Gold Coin Inc..

The first set in the series of Chinese panda gold coins contains 4 kinds, and from then on the People's Bank of China has been issuing the Chinese panda gold coins every year without interruption. Every year the gold panda coins' obverses all depict the same picture of the title of PRC, issuing year and the Hall of Prayer for Good Harvests of the Temple of Heaven in Beijing. Since 1990's, their designs have been changed from one-circle type to bi-circle type. The reverses depict the pictures of the Chinese endangered wild animal-giant panda. The pictures change annually, and over 30 kinds of postures of panda have been used as the pictures up to now, such as the pictures of pandas eating bamboo, whisper between the mother and baby pandas and three pandas playing under the tree, etc. There are two kinds of qualities: proof and bu. The panda gold coins have a complete range of specifications: besides the general 1 oz., 1/2 oz., 1/4 oz., 1/10 oz., and 1/20 oz. specifications, there are two non-standard specifications: 12 oz. and 5 oz.

The Chinese panda gold coins are very worthy collecting and investing, which not only evinces the profound potentiality contained by Chinese traditional culture, but also shows the confidence and ingenuity of Chinese precious coins surpassing the world's most advanced level.

The commemorative coins of the 15th anniversary of the issue of Chinese panda gold coins contain 3 kinds: 1/4 oz., 1/10 oz., and 1 oz., bu. gold coins. The common obverse depicts the picture of the title of PRC, issuing year, the Hall of Prayer for Good Harvests of the Temple of Heaven in Beijing and commemorative words, and the common reverse depicts the picture of pandas climbing the tree and face value.

共同正面

原　大 Full Size

放　大

面额（元）	100	25	10
直径（毫米）	32	22	18
含纯金（盎司）	1	1/4	1/10
成色（%）	99.9	99.9	99.9
质量	普制	普制	普制
年号	1996	1996	1996
发行量（枚）	3800	8000	20000
铸造单位		上海造币厂	

Face Value (Yuan)	100	25	10
Diameter (mm)	32	22	18
Pure Gold Content (oz)	1	1/4	1/10
Fineness (%)	99.9	99.9	99.9
Quality	Bu.	Bu.	Bu.
Issuing Year	1996	1996	1996
Mintage (Pieces)	3800	8000	20000
Minted by		Shanghai Mint	

45th Anniversary of the
Establishment of Chinese
Aviation Industry
Commemorative Coins

中國貴金屬紀念幣圖鑒

三、中国航空工业创建45周年纪念币

一九九六年

为纪念中国航空工业创建45周年，推动中国航空事业的发展，中国人民银行发行中国航空工业创建45周年纪念币。该套纪念币由上海造币厂铸造，中国金币总公司总经销。

中国航空工业的发展始于1951年4月，当时成立了航空工业管理委员会，并在重工业部设立航空工业管理局。45年来，中国航空工业致力于军用飞机、民用飞机、部分战术导弹和其他机电产品的研制，不断满足中国国防和国民经济建设的需要，同时也向国外出口产品。歼八Ⅱ型飞机是中国80年代研制的单座高空高速歼击机，用于执行国土防空和争夺前线制空权等任务，最大飞行时速1200千米／小时，最大航程2200千米，最长持续飞行时间2小时35分。初教五飞机是1954年7月中国航空工业试制成功的新中国第一架飞机。

该套纪念币为1盎司普制银币2种。正面图案均为国徽、国号、年号。背面图案：其中一种为歼八Ⅱ型飞机图案、长城、纪念文字及面额，一种为初教五飞机图案、长城、纪念文字及面额。

To commemorate the 4.' anniversary of the establishment of Chinese aviation industry and to motivate its further development, the People's Bank of China issued the commemorative coins of the 45th anniversary of the establishment of Chinese aviation industry, which were minted by Shanghai Mint and distributed by China Gold Coin Inc..

Chinese aviation industry began in April 1951. At that time, the Aviation Industry Management Committee was established and the Aviation Industry Bureau of Administration was also established which belonged to the Heavy Industry Ministry. During the past 45 years, Chinese aviation industry has devoted itself to the research and produce of military airplanes, civil airplanes, some tactical missiles and other mechanical and electrical products, to continuously satisfy the demands of Chinese national defense and the development of national economy. Meanwhile, it also exports its products. Annihilate 8 II fighter plane, a high-altitude, high speed, single-seat fighter, was developed in the 1980's, which is used to carry out the tasks of territory air defense and fighting for the front air domination. Its maximum speed i... 200 km/h, maximum voyage 2,200 km, and maximum sustained flying time 2 hours and 35 minutes. C... ...ane was the first successfully trial-produced plane of the People's Republic of China.

...of the Establishment of Chinese aviation industry commemorative coins contain 2 kinds of 1 oz. ... ...h the common obverse depicting the picture of the national emblem, title of PRC and the iss... the reverses depicts the picture of Annihilate 8 II fighter plane, the Great Wall, commemorative wor... ...lue, and that of the other depicts the picture of Chujiao 5 plane, the Great Wall, commemorative words ... value.

共同正面

原　大 Full Size

放　大

面额（元）	10	10
直径（毫米）	40	40
含纯银（盎司）	1	1
成色（%）	99.9	99.9
质量	普制	普制
年号	1996	1996
发行量（枚）	20000	20000
铸造单位	上海造币厂	上海造币厂

Face Value (Yuan)	10	10
Diameter (mn	40	40
Pure Silver C... (oz)	1	1
Fineness (%)	99.9	99.9
Quality		Bu.
Issuing Yea	...96	1996
Mintage (P...	...00	20000
Minted by	... Mint	Shanghai Mint

40th Anniversary of the Establishment of Chinese Aerospace Industry Commemorative Coins

中國貴金屬紀念幣鑒

四、中国航天工业创建 40 周年纪念币

一九九六年

为纪念中国航天工业创建40周年，推动中国航天事业的进一步发展，中国人民银行发行中国航天工业创建40周年纪念币。该套币由上海造币厂铸造，中国金币总公司总经销。

中国航天工业的发展始于1956年导弹工业的筹建，起步较晚。但中国广大航天科学工作者根据中国国情，在自力更生的前提下，在短短40年的时间里，就在应用卫星、运载火箭技术方面走在了世界前列，使中国成为世界上少数几个航天技术大国之一。

截止到1996年7月，中国已成功研制了系列战略火箭和长征系列运载火箭，成功发射国内外各类卫星35颗，在中远程导弹、系列运载火箭的研制、设计方面接近世界先进水平。中国运载火箭已进入基本型系列化的阶段，在实施“军民结合”、走向世界的战略转变中，积极开拓国内、国外市场。长征二E火箭，即长二捆火箭，用于执行发射中低地轨道有效载荷任务，代表了中国航天工业的先进水平。1990年7月，长征二E火箭首次发射成功，将中国火箭近地轨道运载能力提高至9200公斤。1992年8月，长征二E火箭将澳星B_1送入预定轨道，标志着中国已具备了发射90年代大型商用通信卫星的能力。

中国的卫星研制始于60年代，1970年4月24日中国成功地发射了第一颗人造卫星，卫星的研制逐步从试验、试用阶段发展到应用阶段，并具备了一定规模。卫星应用技术已在通信广播、气象与环境探测、国民普查与资料探测、军事应用等方面作出了巨大贡献，为中国社会主义建设的各个领域提供了重要的参考资料和决策依据。

该套纪念币为1盎司普制银币2种。该币正面图案均为国徽、国号、年号、长城。背面图案：一种为长征二E火箭、纪念文字及面额，一种为人造卫星、纪念文字及面额。

To commemorate the 40th anniversary of the establishment of Chinese aerospace industry and to motivate its further development, the People's Bank of China issued the commemorative coins of the 40th anniversary of the establishment of Chinese aerospace industry, which were minted by Shanghai Mint and distributed by China Gold Coin Inc..

Chinese aerospace industry got off to a late start, which began in 1956 when the preparations were started for the construction of the missile industry. But, according to the condition of China, Chinese aerospace scientists have enabled our applications satellite and carrier rocket technologies to rank among the world's most advanced technology, which took only 40 years. China has become one of the few countries possessing aerospace technology.

Up to July 1996, China has successfully developed series of strategic rockets and the Long March series of carrier rockets, and lunched 35 domestic and foreign satellites of various kinds. China has approached the world's most advanced level in the development and design of long-range, medium-range missiles and series of carrier rockets. Chinese carrier rockets have entered a stage of serialization of basic types. In the transition of military-civilian combination and heading for the world, Chinese carrier rockets have been opening up both domestic and foreign markets actively. Long March 2E carrier rocket represents the advanced level of Chinese aerospace industry, which carries out the task of useful load in the low earth orbit during the launching. In July 1990, Long March 2E was first launched successfully which raised the diode current capacity in Leo to 9200 kg. In August 1992, it delivered the B_1 satellite made in Australia to the fixed orbit, which marked that China has possessed the ability of launch large-scale commercial communication satellite of the 1990's.

Chinese satellite's development began in the 1960's. China successfully launched her first man-made satellite on April 24th, 1970. The development of satellite has developed from the stage of test and probation to the stage of application and, has possessed a fair-sized scale. The satellite applied technology has made a great contribution to communication, broadcasting, weather and environment exploration, national survey and data exploration, and military application, all of which provided important reference and decision-making basis to every field of Chinese socialist construction.

The commemorative coins of the 40th anniversary of the establishment of Chinese aerospace industry contain 2 kinds of 1 oz. bu. silver coins. The common obverse depicts the picture of the national emblem, title of PRC, issuing year and the Great Wall. One of the reverses depicts the picture of the Long March 2E rocket, commemorative words and face value, and that of the other depicts the picture of the man-made satellite, commemorative words and face value.

共同正面

放　大

原　大 Full Size

面额（元）	10	10
直径（毫米）	40	40
含纯银（盎司）	1	1
成色（%）	99.9	99.9
质量	普制	普制
年号	1996	1996
发行量（枚）	20000	20000
铸造单位	上海造币厂	

Face Value (Yuan)	10	10
Diameter (mm)	40	40
Pure Silver Content (oz)	1	1
Fineness (%)	99.9	99.9
Quality	Bu.	Bu.
Issuing Year	1996	1996
Mintage (Pieces)	20000	20000
Minted by	Shanghai Mint	

Fifth Set in the Series of
Chinese Ancient Scientific
and Technical
Inventions And Discoveries
Gold and Silver Coins

中國貴金屬紀念幣圖鑒

五、中国古代科技发明发现系列金银币(第5组)

一九九六年

为弘扬中国古代文明，中国人民银行自1992年开始发行中国古代科技发明发现系列金银币，1996年发行该套系列金银币第5组，由沈阳造币厂铸造，中国金币总公司总经销。

该组币图案以船舵、马具、索桥、乐器、天文钟为题材，展现了中华民族的灵巧智慧和源远流长的中华文明。该组币共发行10个品种，包括1/2盎司精制金币5种、20克精制银币5种。其正面图案均为中国长城、国号、年号，背面图案分别为船舵、马具、索桥、乐器、天文钟及面额。

中国是世界上造船航海历史最悠久的国家之一。在相当长一段历史时期中，中国的造船技术一直处于世界领先地位。大约在公元2～4世纪，中国开始出现真正的轴向转动舵，这对于提高船舵的操纵性能具有重大意义。大约在12世纪，中国的轴向转动舵技术经过印度洋传到地中海。

和中国古代车辆驾驶技术的高度发展相适应，一些马具也是首先由中国发明的。马鞍，春秋时已出现，汉代时已经做得很讲究。唐代更以制作精美的马鞍作为对边防将士的赏赐，以示矢志疆场。制造蹄铁和装蹄、削蹄是一门专门技术，它在中国大约已有两千多年的历史，马镫也是中国人民对世界的一大贡献。

索桥首创于中国，中国西南、西北地区的一些河流，谷深水急，无法筑墩建桥。中国古代人民就发明了用竹、藤、铁等作为索桥。北魏时新疆地区有了铁索桥，这是世界上最早的铁索桥。西方到16世纪时才出现这类桥。

中国的乐器，源远流长。以汉族乐器来说，远古时就有了磬、埙、笛等，先秦时期已有钟、编钟、铙、鼓等，后来又创制了锣、拍板、大鼓等，同时又陆续将一些少数民族的乐器和个别外来乐器加以吸收和改进。长期以来，这些已经变成了汉民族的传统乐器，如钹、唢呐等。汉族乐器，据《辞海》不完全统计有近200种之多，《中国少数民族乐器志》所载的有502种。

世界上最古老的天文钟诞生在中国，是中国北宋天文学家苏颂、韩公廉等人建造的大运仪象台。它高约十二米，分作三层。上层放浑仪，用来观测日月星辰的位置；中层放浑象，它是一个球体，在球面上布列天体的星宿位置；下层设木阁，又分成五层，每层有门，到一定时刻门中有木人出来报时。这是远远早于欧洲同类装置的一项重大发明。

To carry forward Chinese ancient civilization, the People's Bank of China has been issuing the series of Chinese ancient scientific and technical inventions and discoveries commemorative gold and silver coins since 1992. The 1996 issue was the fifth set, which was minted by Shenyang Mint and distributed by China Gold Coin Inc..

This set of coins take the rudder, harness, rope bridge, musical instruments, and astronomical clock as the themes, which exhibit Chinese people's dexterity, wisdom and long stream of civilization. This set contains 5 kinds of 1/2 oz. proof gold coins and 5 kinds of 20g proof silver coins. The common obverse depict the picture of the Great Wall, title of PRC and the issuing year, while the reverses depict the pictures of rudder, harness, rope bridges, musical instruments, astronomical clock and face value respectively.

China is one of the countries in the world that have the longest history of shipbuilding and navigation. Chinese shipbuilding technology had been in the highest flight during a certain period in the history. In the ca. 2 ~ 4 century A.D., the first real axial rudder emerged in China, which was of great importance to improve the serviceability of rudder. About the 12th century, Chinese axial rudder technology was spread to the Mediterranean by India.

Conforming to the highly developed chariot driving skill of ancient China, some harnesses were also first invented by Chinese people. Saddle, appeared in the Spring and Autumn period, and had been made very finely in the Han Dynasty. Moreover, delicate saddles were awarded to frontier officers and soldiers for their devotion to the frontier in the Tang Dynasty. It is a kind of expertise to make horseshoe, to horseshoe and to cut the hoof. China has had this expertise for about over two thousands of years. Stirrup is also a great contribution of China to the world.

Rope bridges were first invented in China. In the southwest and nor. ıwest of China, some rivers are so torrential that constructing piers is impossible. So the Chinese people invented rope bridges made by bamboo, rattan and iron. Xinjiang region had iron rope bridges, the earliest iron rope bridges ˙ › the world, in the Northern Wei Dynasty, while the West didn't have this kind of bridges until the 16th century.

Chinese musical instruments goes back to ancient times. In the case of the musical instruments of Han nationality, *qing* (chime stone), *xun* (an ancient egg-shaped, holed wind instrument) and flute were invented in the remote antiquity; bell, suspended bell, cymbal (clapperless bell) and drum emerged in the pre-Qin period; gang, clappers and tom-tom were invented afterward. Meanwhile, China incorporated and ameliorated some of the minorities' instruments and one or two exotic instruments in succession, which have become the traditional musical instruments of the Han nationality, such as *bo* (big cymbal) and *suona* horn (a woodwind instrument). According to incomplete statistics of *Ci Hai*, there are nearly 200 kinds of traditional musical instruments of the Han nationality, while the *Zhongguo Shaoshu Minzu Yueqi Zhi* (Chinese Minorities' Musical Instruments Records) says there are 502 kinds of instruments.

The world's oldest astronomical clock was born in China, that is the Big Astronomical Observatory made by Su Song and Han Gonlian, astronomers of the Northern Song Dynasty. Its height was about 12 meters. It was divided into three floors: shen yi was on the upper floor, which was used to observe the location of the hosts of heaven; hun xiang (armillary sphere) was on the second floor, which was a sphere with the location of the hosts of heaven on the surface; the lower floor was a wood cabinet with five floors, each floor had a door, and at a certain time a puppet went outside the door to announce the hour. This great invention was much earlier than that of Europe.

共同正面

原 大 Full Size

面额（元）	50	50	50	50	50
直径（毫米）	27	27	27	27	27
含纯金（盎司）	1/2	1/2	1/2	1/2	1/2
成色（%）	99.9	99.9	99.9	99.9	99.9
质量	精制	精制	精制	精制	精制
年号	1996	1996	1996	1996	1996
发行量（枚）	1200	1200	1200	1200	1200
铸造单位			沈阳造币厂		

Face Value (Yuan)	50	50	50	50	50
Diameter (mm)	27	27	27	27	27
Pure Gold Content (oz)	1/2	1/2	1/2	1/2	1/2
Fineness (%)	99.9	99.9	99.9	99.9	99.9
Quality	Proof	Proof	Proof	Proof	Proof
Issuing Year	1996	1996	1996	1996	1996
Mintage (Pieces)	1200	1200	1200	1200	1200
Minted by			Shenyang Mint		

原　大 Full Size

共同正面

面额（元）	5	5	5	5	5
直径（毫米）	36	36	36	36	36
含纯银（克）	20	20	20	20	20
成色（%）	90	90	90	90	90
质量	精制	精制	精制	精制	精制
年号	1996	1996	1996	1996	1996
发行量（枚）	15000	15000	15000	15000	15000
铸造单位	沈阳造币厂				

Face Value (Yuan)	5	5	5	5	5
Diameter (mm)	36	36	36	36	36
Pure Silver Content (g)	20	20	20	20	20
Fineness (%)	90	90	90	90	90
Quality	Proof	Proof	Proof	Proof	Proof
Issuing Year	1996	1996	1996	1996	1996
Mintage (Pieces)	15000	15000	15000	15000	15000
Minted by	Shenyang Mint				

Series of Chinese Twelve
Animals of Lunar Calendar
— The Year of the Rat
Gold and Silver Coins

中國貴金屬紀念幣圖鑑

六、中国十二生肖系列 —— 丙子（鼠）年金银币

一九九六年

1996年，是中国传统十二生肖纪年中之丙子(鼠)年，中国人民银行为此发行丙子(鼠)年金银币，分别由上海造币厂、沈阳造币厂、中国金币总公司铸造，中国金币总公司总经销。

1975年，湖北省云梦睡虎出土的秦简之《日书》中首次出现鼠与地支“子”相配的记载。有关学者认为，地支记时之子时(现代时间23～24时)，正系鼠最为活跃之时，故中国先民以鼠与地支“子”相配。

鼠昼伏夜出，聪敏机灵。在中国先民心目中，鼠为神性动物。在中国古代神话与民俗故事中，鼠往往具有勤劳善良的品质，并多以人类朋友的形象出现。中国传统民俗年画“老鼠嫁女”，更充满吉祥、喜庆、欢乐气氛，生活气息浓郁，至今仍深受国人青睐。

中国现代杰出国画艺术大师齐白石先生画过多幅关于老鼠的作品，如《老鼠与玉米》、《老鼠与果实》、《老鼠与油灯》、《老鼠自称》等。其画鼠作品独具匠心，笔法、构思简洁凝炼，巧拙兼济，形象生动，写尽老鼠机警、伶俐之特性，意境绝佳。

中国丙子(鼠)年金银币共有10个品种。其中1/2盎司精制金币(梅花型)1种，2/3盎司精制银币(梅花型)1种，背面图案为齐白石所绘的《老鼠与玉米》及面额；5盎司精制金银币各1种，背面图案为齐白石所绘《老鼠与果实》及面额；12盎司精制金银币各1种，背面图案均为齐白石所绘《老鼠自称》及面额；1公斤精制金币(梅花型)1种，背面图案为齐白石所绘《老鼠与油灯》及面额。上述金币、银币正面图案均为国号、年号、成都望江楼。另有1盎司精制金银币各1种，1盎司铂币1种，正面图案为国徽、国号、年号，背面图案为齐白石所绘《老鼠与油灯》及面额。

1996 was the Chinese traditional year of the rat of the Twelve Year Animal Cycle. The People's Bank of China issued the year of the rat gold and silver coins, which were minted by Shanghai Mint, Shenyang Mint and China Gold Coin Inc. respectively, distributed by China Gold Coin Inc..

Rishu (Day book), the bamboo-strip almanacs of the Qin period that was uncovered at Shuihudi of Yunmeng of Hubei province, first documented the match between rat and one of the twelve *dizhi* (earthly branches)-*zi*. Some scholars believe that because the rat is most active at the hour of *zi* (23:00 pm ~ 24:00 pm), Chinese ancient people matched the rat with *zi*.

Rat hides by day and comes out at night and is very clever. In Chinese ancients' mental view, rat was a supernatural being. In Chinese mythology and folklore, rat often had the industrious and kindhearted characters, and often appeared as the humankind's friend. Chinese traditional folk Spring Festival picture *Rat Married His Daughter* is full of lucky, joyous and happy air, and has the rich flavor of life, so it finds favor in people's eyes.

Mr. Qi Baishi, the modern outstanding master of traditional Chinese painting had many paintings with the theme of rat, for example, *Rat and Maize, Rat and Fruit, Rat and Oil Lamp* and *Rat Weighs Up Itself*. His paintings showed originality. The technique of drawing and plan were concise. They vividly revealed the rat's alert and clever characters and had excellent artistic conceptions.

The year of the rat gold and silver coins contain 10 kinds. The 1/2 oz. proof gold (plum blossom type) coin and the 2/3 oz. proof silver coin (plum blossom type) have the common reverse depicting the painting *Rat and Maize* drawn by Qi Baishi and face value. The 5 oz. proof gold and silver coins have the common reverse depicting the painting *Rat and Fruit* drawn by Qi Baishi and face value. The 12 oz. proof gold and silver coins have the common reverse depicting the painting *Rat Weighs Up Itself* drawn by Qi Baishi and face value. The 1kg proof gold coin (plum blossom type) has the reverse depicting the painting *Rat and Oil Lamp* drawn by Qi Baishi and face value. The above gold and silver coins have the common obverse depicting the picture of the title of PRC, issuing year and the Wangjiang Tower in Chengdu. The rest three kinds contain 1 oz. proof gold, 1 oz. proof silver and 1 oz. platinum with the common obverse depicting the picture of the national emblem, title of PRC and the issuing year, and with the common reverse depicting the painting *Rat and Oil Lamp* drawn by Qi Baishi and face value.

正　面

原　大 Full Size

面额（元）	2000
直径（毫米）	100
含纯金（公斤）	1
成色（%）	99.9
质量	精制
年号	1996
发行量（枚）	15
铸造单位	上海造币厂

Face Value (Yuan)	2000
Diameter (mm)	100
Pure Gold Content (kg)	1
Fineness (%)	99.9
Quality	Proof
Issuing Year	1996
Mintage (Pieces)	15
Minted by	Shanghai Mint

正　面

原　大 Full Size

放　大

面额（元）	100
直径（毫米）	27
含纯金（盎司）	0.458
成色（%）	91.6
质量	精制
年号	1996
发行量（枚）	2300
铸造单位	沈阳造币厂

Face Value (Yuan)	100
Diameter (mm)	27
Pure Gold Content (oz)	0.458
Fineness (%)	91.6
Quality	Proof
Issuing Year	1996
Mintage (Pieces)	2300
Minted by	Shenyang Mint

共同正面

正 面

原 大 Full Size

原 大 Full Size

面额（元）	1000	500	100
直径（毫米）	70	60	32
含纯金（盎司）	12	5	1
成色（%）	99.9	99.9	99.9
质量	精制	精制	精制
年号	1996	1996	1996
发行量（枚）	99	99	1800
铸造单位	上海造币厂	沈阳造币厂	上海造币厂

Face Value (Yuan)	1000	500	100
Diameter (mm)	70	60	32
Pure Gold Content (oz)	12	5	1
Fineness (%)	99.9	99.9	99.9
Quality	Proof	Proof	Proof
Issuing Year	1996	1996	1996
Mintage (Pieces)	99	99	1800
Minted by	Shanghai Mint	Shenyang Mint	Shanghai Mint

共同正面

原　大 Full Size

面额（元）	100	50
直径（毫米）	80	70
含纯银（盎司）	12	5
成色（%）	99.	99.9
质量	精	精制
年号	1	1996
发行量（枚）	1	1000
铸造单位		沈阳造币厂

Face Value (Yuan)	100	50
Diameter (mm)	80	70
Pure Silver Content (oz)	12	5
Fineness (%)	99.9	99.9
Quality	Proof	Proof
Issuing Year	1996	1996
Mintage (Pieces)	500	1000
Minted by	Shanghai Mint	Shenyang Mint

正　面

原　　大 Full Size

正　面

放　　大

原　　大 Full Size

面额（元）	10	10
直径（毫米）	32	36
含纯银（盎司）	1	0.6
成色（%）	99.9	90
质量	精制	精制
年号	1996	1996
发行量（枚）	8000	6800
铸造单位	上海造币厂	沈阳造币厂

Face Value (Yuan)	10	10
Diameter (mm)	32	36
Pure Silver Content (oz)	[illegible]	0.6
Fineness (%)	[illegible]	90
Quality	[illegible]	Proof
Issuing Year	[illegible]	1996
Mintage (Pieces)	[illegible]	6800
Minted by	[illegible]t	Shenyang Mint

正　面

放　大

原　大 Full Size

面额（元）	100	Face Value (Yuan)	100
直径（毫米）	32	Diameter (mm)	32
含纯铂（盎司）	1	Pure Platinum Content (oz)	1
成色（%）	99.95	Fineness (%)	99.95
质量	精制	Quality	Proof
年号	1996	Issuing Year	1996
发行量（枚）	300	Mintage (Pieces)	300
铸造单位	中国金币总公司	Minted by	China Gold Coin Inc.

The 26th Summer Olympic
Games of 1996
(Sailboard Athlete)
Commemorative Coin

中國貴金屬紀念幣圖鑒

七、1996年第26届夏季奥运会（帆板运动员）纪念币

一九九六年

中国贵金属纪念币年鉴

第26届夏季奥运会于1996年7月19日~8月4日在美国亚特兰大举行。为纪念第26届夏季奥运会，中国人民银行曾于1995年发行第26届夏季奥运会纪念币1套(其中金币2种，银币5种)。在第26届夏季奥运会上，香港运动员李丽珊在1996年7月19日举行的女子帆板比赛项目中获得冠军，这是香港运动员首次在奥运会上获得金牌。中国人民银行为此增发第26届夏季奥运会纪念币1种，该纪念币为27克精制银币，其正面图案为国徽、国号及年号，背面图案为帆板运动员及面额。

帆板运动是一个介于帆船和冲浪板之间的新兴项目，1967年出现于美国，1984年被列入奥运会比赛项目。帆板运动是世界体育史上发展最快、最热门的项目之一。

The 26th Summer Olympic Games was held in Atlanta, U.S., during July 19-August 4, 1996. To commemorate this game, the People's Bank of China had issued a set of commemorative coins (2 gold and 5 silver) in 1995. In the 26th Summer Olympic Games Li Lishan from Hong Kong won the championship of women sailboard game on July 19, which was the first time that Hong Kong athlete won a championship in Olympic Games. The People's Bank of China especially issued the 26th Summer Olympic Games commemorative coin for this. It is a 27g proof silver coin with the obverse depicting the picture of the national emblem, title of PRC and the issuing year, and with the reverse depicting the sailboard athlete and face value.

Sailboard is a kind of burgeoning sport combined the sailboat and surfboard together, which appeared in the U.S. in 1967 and was placed on the Olympic games in 1984. Sailboard is one of the most popular sports in the world sports history that grows fastest.

正　面

原　大 Full Size

放　大

面额（元）	10
直径（毫米）	38.6
含纯银（盎司）	0.803
成色（%）	92.5
质量	精制
年号	1996
发行量（枚）	30000
铸造单位	上海造币厂

Face Value (Yuan)	10
Diameter (mm)	38.6
Pure Silver Content (oz)	0.803
Fineness (%)	92.5
Quality	Proof
Issuing Year	1996
Mintage (Pieces)	30000
Minted by	Shanghai Mint

The 130th Anniversary of the Birth of Sun Yat-sen Commemorative Coins

中國貴金屬紀念幣圖鑒

八、孙中山诞辰130周年纪念币

一九九六年

为纪念孙中山诞辰130周年，缅怀伟大的革命先行者，中国人民银行发行孙中山诞辰130周年纪念币，由深圳国宝金币制造厂铸造，中国金币总公司总经销。

孙中山(1866年11月12日～1925年3月12日)，中国伟大的资产阶级民主主义革命家，中华民国的创始人。孙中山名文，字德明，号日新、逸仙，1897年在日本进行革命活动时，化名中山樵，以后遂名中山。

1894年"兴中会"在檀香山的成立，标志着孙中山资产阶级民主革命思想的初步形成及其革命活动的正式开始。1905年，孙中山顺应时势在日本东京联合各革命团体创立的"中国同盟会"，成为中国历史上第一个资产阶级政党。1912年，中华民国南京临时政府成立，孙中山被推举为临时大总统，颁布多项改革法令和政策。袁世凯盗取辛亥革命的胜利果实后，孙中山重新举起民主革命的旗帜，积极主张武力讨袁。1919年孙中山将中华革命党改组为中国国民党。

俄国十月革命的胜利和中国共产党的诞生，使孙中山的革命思想发生了质的转变。孙中山改组了国民党，确立了"联俄、联共、扶助农工"三大政策，将旧三民主义发展为新三民主义，使中国国民党成为工人、农民、小资产阶级和民族资产阶级的革命联盟。1925年孙中山因病在北京逝世，享年59岁。

孙中山诞辰130周年纪念币共2个品种，其中1/2盎司精制金币1种，1盎司精制银币1种，正面图案均为广州中山纪念堂，背面图案均为松柏环绕的孙中山肖像及面额。

To commemorate the 130th anniversary of the birth of Sun Yat-sen, the great pioneer revolutionary of China, the People's Bank of China issued the 130th anniversary of the birth of Sun Yat-sen commemorative coins, minted by Shenzhen Panda Gold Coin Mint and distributed by China Gold Coin Inc..

Sun Yat-sen (December 12,1866 ~ March 12,1925) was a great bourgeois-democratic revolutionary and the founder of the Republic of China. His first name was Wen, given name Deming, alias Rixin and Yet-sen. When he conducted the revolution in Japan in 1897, he took the anonym Zhongshanqiao hence he was called Sun Zhongshan.

The Revive China Society was found in Honolulu in 1894 which marked the preliminary formation of the bourgeois-democratic revolutionary ideology of Sun Yat-sen and the real beginning of his revolutionary activity. In 1905, Sun Yat-sen united the other revolutionary societies to found the United League of China in Tokyo, the first bourgeois party in Chinese history. In 1912 the Republic of China was founded, and Sun Yat-sen was elected the temporary president of the Nanjing temporary government. He issued several reform decrees and policies. After Yuan Shikai usurped the fruit of the Revolution of 1911, Sun Yat-sen raised up the revolutionary flag again to crusade against Yuan by force. In 1919 Sun Yat-sen reorganized the Chinese Revolution Party to the Chinese Kuomintang.

The victory of the Russian October Revolution and the birth of Chinese Communist Party changed Sun Yat-sen's revolutionary ideology radically. He reorganized the Kuomintang and established the Three Polices: 'Ally with Russia', 'Ally with the Communist Party' and 'Assist the peasants and workers'. He developed the old Three Principles of the People into the new Three Principles of the People and made the Kuomintang become a united revolutionary league comprising workers, peasants, petty bourgeois and national bourgeois. Sun Yat-sen passed away at the age of 59 in Beijing because of illness.

The 130th anniversary of the birth of Sun Yat-sen commemorative coins contain 1/2 oz. proof gold and 1 oz. proof silver with the common obverse depicting the picture of the Sun Yat-sen Memorial Hall in Guangzhou and with the common reverse depicting the portrait of Sun Yat-sen wreathed by the pine and cypress and face value.

正　面

原　大 Full Size

放　大

面额（元）	50
直径（毫米）	27
含纯金（盎司）	1/2
成色（%）	99.9
质量	精制
年号	1996
发行量（枚）	3000
铸造单位	深圳国宝金币制造厂

Face Value (Yuan)	50
Diameter (mm)	27
Pure Gold Content (oz)	1/2
Fineness (%)	99.9
Quality	Proof
Issuing Year	1996
Mintage (Pieces)	3000
Minted by	Shenzhen Panda Gold Coin Mint

正 面

原 大 Full Size

放 大

面额（元）	10	Face Value (Yuan)	10
直径（毫米）	40	Diameter (mm)	40
含纯银（盎司）	1	Pure Silver Content (oz)	1
成色（%）	99.9	Fineness (%)	99.9
质量	精制	Quality	Proof
年号	1996	Issuing Year	1996
发行量（枚）	20000	Mintage (Pieces)	20000
铸造单位	深圳国宝金币制造厂	Minted by	Shenzhen Panda Gold Coin Mint

1996 Issue of the
Avalokitesvara Buddha
Gold and Silver Coin
Series

中國貴金屬紀念幣圖鑒

九、1996年版观世音菩萨金银币

一九九六年

为使世界了解中国佛教文化，中国人民银行发行观世音菩萨金银币，由上海造币厂铸造，中国金币总公司总经销。

观世音是梵文Avalokites' Vara的意译，据说其可以"观察"世界上的一切声音，所以名为"观世音"菩萨。唐代避李世民之讳，改称观音。

佛经记载，观世音为了教化不同层次、不同环境的众生，可以变化出三十二种化身及观音本相共三十三身。后来佛教根据观音三十三身的说法，绘制了三十三种观音的画像，即"三十三观音"。比较典型的观音形象有杨柳观音、千手观音、洒水观音、合什观音、莲座观音、玉露观音、送子观音、玉瓶观音等多种形象。

浙江省境内的普陀山是中国四大佛教名山之一。据说五代时和尚慧锷建"不肯去"观音院，开创佛寺之始。从此，普陀山成为供奉观音的道场。

1996年版观世音菩萨金银币共发行7个品种。其中1盎司普制银币1种，1/2盎司精制银币2种，1/10盎司普制金币1种，1/20盎司普制金币1种，1盎司加厚精制银币2种。其正面图案均为国号、年号、普陀山，背面图案分别为莲花观音像、金莲观音像、玉瓶观音像及面额。

In order to let the world understand Chinese Buddhist culture , the People's Bank of China issued the Avalokitesvara Buddha gold and silver coins, which were minted by Shanghai Mint and distributed by China Gold Coin Inc..

Guanshiyin is a Chinese transliteration of the Sanskrit word Avalokitesvara. It is said that He could 'observe' all of the sound in the world, and so He is called 'observe the sound in the world' Buddha (Chinese *Guanshiyin*). In the Tang Dynasty, He was renamed 'observe the sound' (Chinese *Guanyin*) to avoid the taboo on the personal name of Emperor Li Shimin.

According to the Buddhist scripture, Avalokitesvara could appear as 32 kinds of nirmanakaya (metamorphosic body) and His true body totaling 33 bodies in order to moralize all living creatures of various levels and circumstances. Subsequently Buddhists had drawn 33 kinds of portraits of Avalokitesvara according to this, called '33 Avalokitesvara'. The typical images of Avalokitesvara contain 'Willow Avalokitesvara', 'Sahasrabhuja-avalokitesvara (Thousand-arm Avalokitesvara)', 'Water Spraying Avalokitesvara', 'Anjali-avalokitesvara (saluted Avalokitesvara by putting palms together)', 'Lotus Throne Avalokitessvara', 'Jade Dew Avalokitesvara', 'Birth Giving Avalokitesvara' and 'Jade Flask Avalokitesvara', etc.

The Putuo Mount situated in Zhejiang province is one of the Chinese Four Famous Buddhist Mounts. It is said that a monk named Hui-e built an Avalokitesvara temple named 'Not Willing to Go' in the Five Dynasties, which marked the beginning of temple construction on the Putuo Mount. Since then the Putuo Mount has become the rite of making offerings to Avalokitesvara.

1996 issue of the Avalokitesvara Buddha gold and silver coins series contain 7 kinds of coins: 1 oz. bu. silver, 2 kinds of 1/2 oz. proof silver, 1/10 oz. bu. gold, 1/20 oz. bu. gold and 2 kinds of 1 oz. additional thickness proof silver. Their obverses all depict the picture of the national emblem, issuing year and the Putuo Mount, and the reverses depict the picture of Lotus Avalokitesvara, Gold Lotus Avalokitesvara, Jade Flask Avalokitesvara respectively and face value.

共同正面

原　大 Full Size

放　大

面额（元）	10	5
直径（毫米）	18	14
含纯金（盎司）	1/10	1/20
成色（%）	99.9	99.9
质量	普制	普制
年号	1996	1996
发行量（枚）	10000	35000
铸造单位	上海造币厂	

Face Value (Yuan)	10	5
Diameter (mm)	18	14
Pure Gold Content (oz)	1/10	1/20
Fineness (%)	99.9	99.9
Quality	Bu.	Bu.
Issuing Year	1996	1996
Mintage (Pieces)	10000	35000
Minted by	Shanghai Mint	

共同正面

原 大 Full Size

面额（元）	10	5	5
直径（毫米）	40	33	33
含纯银（盎司）	1	1/2	1/2
成色（%）	99.9	99.9	99.9
质量	普制	精制	精制
年号	1996	1996	1996
发行量（枚）	30000	5000	5000
铸造单位	上海造币厂		

注：另有两种1盎司精制加厚银币，其图案、面额、直径、成色、铸造单位分别与1/2盎司银币相同。

Face Value (Yuan)	10	5	5
Diameter (mm)	40	33	33
Pure Silver Content (oz)	1	1/2	1/2
Fineness (%)	99.9	99.9	99.9
Quality	Bu.	Proof	Proof
Issuing Year	1996	1996	1996
Mintage (Pieces)	30000	5000	5000
Minted by	Shanghai Mint		

Note: There are another two items of 1oz. piedfort silver coin proof, which designs, face value, diameters, fineness and the minting institution are the same as the item of half ounce silver coin.

1996 Issue of Unicorn
Gold and Silver Coin Series

中國貴金屬紀念幣圖鑑

十、1996年版麒麟金银币

一九九六年

为了弘扬中国传统文化，中国人民银行自1994年开始发行麒麟金银币。1996年版麒麟金银币分别由上海造币厂、中国金币总公司铸造，中国金币总公司总经销。

麒麟是人们传说中的一种罕见的神灵吉祥之物。古代以麟出现为祥瑞，因此又称麟为“祥麟”。古代传说麟是龙子，即龙与母牛交配而产，麒麟的形态是“麇身、牛尾、狼蹄、一角”。大凡遇麟出现，是被当作大瑞现象报告给官府的，朝廷还要举行仪式或以某种形式来承应天赐祥瑞的。在中国最早的诗歌总集《诗经》中有《麟之趾》一诗，用麟的形象来赞美宽厚仁爱的文王，可见麟不仅神灵之极，而且仁厚之至。这种对麟的赞美在我们今天的语言中还可看出痕迹，如“凤毛麟角”、“麒麟儿”等。

1996年版麒麟金银币共有15个品种，其中1盎司、1/2盎司、1/4盎司、1/10盎司、1/20盎司、5盎司、1公斤精制金币各1种，1/20盎司普制金币1种，20克普制银币1种，1盎司、5盎司、20盎司精制银币各1种，1盎司、1/4盎司精制铂币各1种，1/20盎司普制铂币1种。1996年版麒麟金银币正面图案均为国号、年号、麒麟，背面图案分别为西方独角兽及花束、西方独角兽头像、西方独角兽及少女像和面额。

To enhance Chinese traditional culture, the People's Bank of China has been issuing the unicorn gold and silver coins since 1994. 1996 issue of unicorn gold and silver coins were minted by Shanghai Mint and China Gold Coin Inc. respectively, and were distributed by the latter.

Unicorn, in Chinese legend, is a kind of unusually magic and auspicious animal. In the ancient time, people took the appearance of unicorn as a kind of auspicious sign, so they also called unicorn 'auspicious unicorn'. In the ancient legend, unicorn was the son of dragon and cow. Its shape was 'the body of an elk, the tail of an ox, the hoofs of a wolf and a single horn'. Once the unicorn appeared it would be taken as a great auspicious sign to be reported to the government. The court would perform a ceremony or other forms to thank the heaven bestowing the auspicious sign. *Book of Poetry*, the earliest anthology of verse of China, has a verse titled *The Good Unicorn*, which praises the clement and kindhearted King Wen as the image of unicorn, thus shows the unicorn is not only very magic but also very clement and kindhearted. This kind of praise of the unicorn can still be traced to nowadays language, such as 'precious and rare as phoenix feathers and unicorn horns' and 'the son of unicorn' etc.

1996 issue of unicorn gold and silver coins contains 15 kinds of coins: 1 oz., 1/2 oz., 1/4 oz., 1/10 oz., 1/20 oz., 5 oz. and 1 kg proof gold coins, 1/20 oz. bu. gold coin, 20g bu. silver coin, 1 oz., 5 oz. and 20 oz. proof silver coins, 1 oz. and 1/4 oz. proof platinum coins and 1/20 oz. bu. platinum coin. All the above have the common obverse depicting the picture of the title of PRC, issuing year and the unicorn. The reverses depict the pictures of western unicorn and bouquet, head portrait of western unicorn, portraits of western unicorn and maid respectively and face value.

正 面

原 大 Full Size

面额（元）	2000	Face Value (Yuan)	2000
直径（毫米）	100	Diameter (mm)	100
含纯金（公斤）	1	Pure Gold Content (kg)	1
成色（%）	99.9	Fineness (%)	99.9
质量	精制	Quality	Proof
年号	1996	Issuing Year	
发行量（枚）	18	Mintage (Pieces)	
铸造单位	上海造币厂	Minted by	Shanghai Mint

共同正面

原　大 Full Size

面额（元）	[illegible]	100
直径（毫米）	[illegible]	32
含纯金（盎司）	[illegible]	1
成色（%）	99.9	99.9
质量	精制	精制
[illegible]	1996	1996
[illegible]量（枚）	108	1250
铸造单位	上海造币厂	

Face Value (Yuan)	500	100
Diameter (mm)	60	32
Pure Gold Content (oz)	5	1
Fineness (%)	99.9	99.9
Quality	Proof	Proof
Issuing Year	1996	1996
Mintage (Pieces)	108	1250
Minted by	Shanghai Mint	

共同正面

原 大 Full Size

面额（元）	50	25	10	5	5
直径（毫米）	27	22	18	14	14
含纯金（盎司）	1/2	1/4	1/10	1/20	1/20
成色（%）	99.9	99.9	99.9	99.9	99.9
质量	精制	精制	精制	精制	普制
年号	1996	1996	1996	1996	1996
发行量（枚）	1000	3000	5000	5000	
铸造单位	上海造币厂				

Face Value (Yuan)	50	25	[illegible]	5	5
Diameter (mm)	27	22	[illegible]	14	14
Pure Gold Content (oz)	1/2	[illegible]	10	1/20	1/20
Fineness (%)	99.9	[illegible]	99.9	99.9	99.9
Quality	Proof	Proof	Proof	Proof	Bu.
Issuing Year	1996	1996	1996	1996	1996
Mintage (Pieces)	1000	3000	5000	5000	
Minted by	Shanghai Mint				

正　面

原　大 Full Size

面[illegible]	150
[illegible]	100
[illegible]	20
[illegible]	99.9
[illegible]	精制
[illegible]	1996
[illegible]行量（枚）	500
铸造单位	上海造币厂

Face Value (Yuan)	150
Diameter (mm)	100
Pure Silver Content (oz)	20
Fineness (%)	99.9
Quality	Proof
Issuing Year	1996
Mintage (Pieces)	500
Minted by	Shanghai Mint

共同正面

原　大 Full Size

面额（元）	50	10	5
直径（毫米）	70	40	36
含纯银（盎司）	5	1	
含纯银（克）			20
成色（%）	99.9	99.9	99.9
质量	精制	精制	普制
年号	1996	1996	1996
发行量（枚）	999	8000	
铸造单位	上海造币厂		

Face Value (Yuan)			5
Diameter (mm)	70		6
Pure Silver Content (oz)	5		
Pure Silver Content (g)			
Fineness (%)	99.9	9	
Quality	Proof	Proo	
Issuing Year	1996	1996	
Mintage (Pieces)	999	8000	
Minted by	Shanghai Mint		

共同正面

原 大 Full Size

面额（元）	100	25	5
直径（毫米）	32	22	14
含纯铂（盎司）	1	[illegible]	1/20
成色（%）	99.95	[illegible]	99.95
质量	[illegible]	[illegible]	普制
年号	[illegible]	[illegible]	1996
[illegible]	[illegible]	500	8000
	中国金币总公司		

Face Value (Yuan)	100	25	5
Diameter (mm)	32	22	14
Pure Platinum Content (oz)	1	1/4	1/20
Fineness (%)	99.95	99.95	99.95
Quality	Proof	Proof	Bu.
Issuing Year	1996	1996	1996
Mintage (Pieces)	500	500	8000
Minted by	China Gold Coin Inc.		

60th Anniversary of the Victory of the Long March of the Chinese Workers' and Peasants' Red Army Commemorative Coins

中國貴金屬紀念幣鑒

十一、中国工农红军长征胜利 60周年纪念币

一九九六年

为纪念中国工农红军长征胜利60周年，缅怀革命先烈，中国人民银行发行中国工农红军长征胜利60周年纪念币。该套纪念币由沈阳造币厂铸造，中国金币总公司总经销。

第二次国内革命战争时期，由于王明“左”倾机会主义路线的错误领导，中央红军未能打破国民党军队的第五次“围剿”，南方各根据地的红军，均先后被迫退出根据地进行长征。1934年10月10日，中央红军主力从中央革命根据地出发长征，连续突破了国民党军队的四道封锁线，转到了湘江以西地区。遵义会议后，中央红军在毛泽东的亲自指挥下，四渡赤水，强渡乌江，抢占大渡河，爬雪山，过草地，于1935年到达陕西吴起镇，同红十五军团会合。1936年6月，红军第二方面军与第四方面军在甘孜会师，并共同继续北上。1936年10月，红军第二方面军、第四方面军与第一方面军在甘肃会宁胜利会师，这标志着红军长征的胜利结束。

该套纪念币共有3个品种。其中1/2盎司金币1种，正面图案为国号、年号、瑞金苏维埃礼堂旧址，背面图案为长征途中的毛泽东肖像及纪念文字和面额；1盎司精制银币2种，正面图案：一种为国号、年号、遵义会议旧址，一种为国号、年号、延安宝塔山，背面图案分别为毛泽东骑马的肖像、红军胜利会师图及纪念文字和面额。

To commemorate the 60th anniversary of the victory of the Long March of the Chinese Workers' and Peasants' Red Army and to recall the revolutionary martyr, the People's Bank of China issued the 60th anniversary of the victory of the Long March of the Chinese Workers' and Peasants' Red Army commemorative coins, which were minted by Shenyang Mint and distributed by China Gold Coin Inc..

In the Second Revolutionary Civil War, the Central Red Army did not defeat the fifth 'encircle and suppress' by the Kuomintang army due to the fault leading of Wang Ming's 'Left' opportunism. The Red Armies in the southern bases were forced to withdraw from their bases to march successively. The main force of the Central Red Army began their Long March on October 10,1934. They broke through four defense lines of the Kuomintang army successively and shifted to the region west of the Xiang River. After the Zunyi Meeting, the Central Red army, under the command of Mao Zedong, crossed the Chi River four times, forced its way across the Wu River and Dadu River, climbed snow-topped mountains and plodded through grasslands and finally arrived at Wuqi town of Shaanxi joining forces with the Fifteenth Army Group of the Red Army. The Second and the Fourth Front Army of the Red Army joined forces at Ganzi in June 1936 and then, kept moving toward the north together. In October 1937, the Second, the Fourth and the First Front Army successfully joined together at Huining of Gansu, which marked the successful end of the Long March of the Red Army.

This set contains three kinds of coins: 1/2 oz. gold coin with the obverse depicting the picture of the title of PRC, issui[illegible]ear and the site of the former Soviet Hall in Ruijin, and with the reverse depicting the picture of the portrait o[illegible] Zedong on the way of the Long March, commemorative words and face value; 2 kinds of 1 oz. proof silver co[illegible] one of the obverses depicting the picture of the title of PRC, issuing year and the site of Zunyi Meeting[illegible]of the other depicting the picture of the title of PRC, issuing year and the Pagoda Mount in Yan'an, [illegible]verses depicting the picture of the portrait of Mao Zedong riding on a horse, the drawing of the Red Arm[illegible]fully Joining Forces, commemorative words respectively and face value.

正 面

原 大 Full Size

放 大

面额（元）	50	Face Value (Yuan)	50
直径（毫米）	27	Diameter (mm)	27
含纯金（盎司）	1/2	Pure Gold Content (oz)	1/2
成色 （%）	99.9	Fineness (%)	99.9
质量	精制	Quality	Proof
年号	1996	Issuing Year	1996
发行量（枚）	6000	Mintage (Pieces)	6000
铸造单位	沈阳造币厂	Minted by	Shenyang Mint

正 面

正 面

原 大 Full Size

原 大 Full Size

面额（元）	10	10
直径（毫米）	40	40
含纯银（盎司）	1	1
成色（%）	99.9	99.9
质量	精制	精制
年号	1996	1996
发行量（枚）	20000	20000
铸造单位	沈阳造币厂	

Face Value (Yuan)	10	10
Diameter (mm)	40	40
Pure Silver Content (oz)	1	1
Fineness (%)	99.9	99.9
Quality	Proof	Proof
Issuing Year	1996	1996
Mintage (Pieces)	20000	20000
Minted by	Shenyang Mint	

The Centenary of Chinese
Postal Service
Commemorative Coins

中國貴金屬紀念幣彙鑒

十二、中国邮政 100 周年纪念币

一九九六年

中国贵金属纪念币年鉴

为纪念中国邮政创立100周年，推进中国邮政事业的发展，中国人民银行发行中国邮政100周年纪念币。该套纪念币由沈阳造币厂铸造，中国金币总公司总经销。

100年前的1896年3月20日，清朝光绪皇帝在大臣张之洞奏请开办国家邮政的奏折上御批“依议钦此”，于是大清邮政成立，中国近代邮政由此诞生。中国邮政自开办之日起就隶属海关，帝国主义列强对中国主权、邮权恣意侵犯。

1949年中华人民共和国成立后，中国邮权才彻底收回。从大清邮政、中华邮政至人民邮政，中国邮政事业走过了艰难创业、苦心经营、曲折前进、蓬勃发展的历程。时至今日，已形成了一个覆盖全国、联通世界的庞大邮政网络，与近200个国家和地区建立了直接通邮关系，邮政局所的覆盖面、干线邮路的总长度以及通邮规模都得到了很大的提高。改革开放以来，商业信函、礼仪信函、特快专递等新业务发展迅速，邮政网的技术装备水平也得到显著提高。

该套纪念币共2个品种，其中1/4盎司普制金币1种，1盎司普制银币1种。金银币正面图案均为国号、年号、“特1”国徽邮票图案及纪念文字，背面图案均为清朝“团龙邮票”图案及面额。

To commemorate the centenary of the establishment of Chinese postal service and to propel Chinese postal service forward, the People's Bank of China issued the centenary of Chinese postal service commemorative coins, which were minted by Shenyang Mint and distributed by China Gold Coin Inc..

100 years ago, on March 20,1896, Emperor Guangxu of the Qing Dynasty approved minister Zhang Zhidong's memorial for running national postal service, so the Postal Service of the Qing Dynasty was set up, which was the start of Chinese modern postal service. Chinese postal service had been under the control of the customs since its establishment. The imperialist powers had willfully trampled upon Chinese postal service and sovereignty.

Chinese postal service had not been regained until the founding of the People's Republic of China in 1949. Chinese postal service has undergone the stages of hard start, painstaking operation, tortuous advance and flourishing development. Up to now, a massive postal net covering the whole nation and linking with the world has come into being. The net has direct links with over 200 countries. The range of the post offices, the total length of the main postal routes and the scope of the postal communication have been greatly increased. The new businesses such as the commercial letters, ceremony and propriety letters and express mail have grown rapidly and, the level of the technical equipments of the postal net has also been raised remarkably.

The commemorative coins of the centenary of Chinese postal service contain two kinds: 1/4 oz. bu. gold and 1 oz. bu. silver. Their obverses all depict the picture of the title of PRC, issuing year, the picture of the 'Special 1' national emblem stamp and commemorative words, and their reverses all depict the picture of the 'Circular Dragon Stamp' and face value.

正　面

原　　大 Full Size

放　大

面额（元）	25
直径（毫米）	22
含纯金（盎司）	1/4
成色（%）	99.9
质量	普制
年号	1996
发行量（枚）	3000
铸造单位	沈阳造币厂

Face Value (Yuan)	25
Diameter (mm)	22
Pure Gold Content (oz)	1/4
Fineness (%)	99.9
Quality	Bu.
Issuing Year	1996
Mintage (Pieces)	3000
Minted by	Shenyang Mint

正　面

放　大

原　大 Full Size

面额（元）	10
直径（毫米）	40
含纯银（盎司）	1
成色（%）	99.9
质量	普制
年号	1996
发行量（枚）	30000
铸造单位	沈阳造币厂

Face Value (Yuan)	10
Diameter (mm)	40
Pure Silver Content (oz)	1
Fineness (%)	99.9
Quality	Bu.
Issuing Year	1996
Mintage (Pieces)	30000
Minted by	Shenyang Mint

Second Set in the Series
of the Return
of Hong Kong to China
Commemorative Coins

中國貴金屬紀念幣圖鑒

十三、香港回归祖国纪念币
（第 2 组）

一九九六年

中国贵金属纪念币年鉴

1997年7月1日，中国政府对香港恢复行使主权。为纪念香港回归祖国这一重大历史事件，经国务院批准，中国人民银行决定在全球限量发行香港回归祖国金银纪念币1套，共3组，第1组和第2组分别于1995年12月、1996年7月发行。香港回归祖国纪念币(第2组)由上海造币厂铸造，中国金币总公司总经销。

香港，包括香港岛、九龙、新界本土及离岛(135个岛屿)四部分。地处珠江三角洲南部，珠江出海口东侧，陆地面积1092平方公里，人口642万多人，是世界上人口最密集的地方之一。

香港历来是中国神圣领土的一部分。英国侵略者从19世纪40年代初到19世纪90年代末不断扩大对华掠夺，通过签订不平等条约——《南京条约》、《北京条约》、《展拓香港界址专条》，占领了香港。

1984年12月，中英两国正式签署了关于香港问题的《联合声明》，确认了中国将在1997年收回香港，恢复行使主权，按照邓小平提出的“一国两制”方针解决香港问题。

1990年4月，《中华人民共和国香港特别行政区基本法》正式颁布，确定了中英两国政府在过渡时期承担的义务和责任及未来香港发展的基本构架。

香港回归祖国纪念币(第2组)共3个品种，其中1/2盎司精制金币、5盎司精制金币、1盎司精制银币各1种。其正面图案均为国号、年号、天安门华表及牡丹花，背面图案均为中华人民共和国香港特别行政区基本法文本、九龙风景图及中英文“平稳过渡，长期繁荣”字样和面额。

On July 1, 1997, Chinese government resumed the exercise of sovereignty over Hong Kong. To commemorate this important historical event, the People's Bank of China decided to issue a series of commemorative coins of the return of Hong Kong to China on a global scale with limited quantities upon the approval of the State Council. This seri[illegible] consist[illegible] of 3 sets. The first and second sets were issued in December 1995 and July 1996 respectively. The [illegible] minted by Shanghai Mint and distributed by China Gold Coin Inc..

[illegible]ng consists of four parts: Hong Kong island, Kowloon, New Territories and Lee Islands (135 islands). It is [illegible] outh of the Zhu River Delta and to the east of the issue of the Zhu River. Its area is 1,092 square kilom[illegible]lation 6.42 million, one of the world's most populous areas.

Ho[illegible]en a part of Chinese sacred territory from time immemorial. The British invaders had insistently expanded th[illegible]ir plunder upon China from the 1840's to 1890's. They seized hold of Hong Kong through the unfair treaties -- the *Treaty of Nanjing*, the *Treaty of Peking* and the *Convention for the Expansion of Hong Kong*.

In December 1984, China and U.K formally signed the *Joint Declaration of the Government of PRC and the government of U.K. On the Question of Hong Kong*, which affirmed that China would resume the exercise of sovereignty over Hong Kong and resolve the questions of Hong Kong under the 'one country, two systems' principle proposed by Mr. Deng Xiaoping.

In April 1990, the Basic Law of Hong Kong Special Administrative Region of the People's Republic of China was enacted, which defines the obligations undertaken by China and U.K. during the transition period and the basic framework of Hong Kong's future development.

The second set contains 1/2 oz. proof gold, 5 oz. proof gold and 1 oz. proof silver. The obverses all depict the picture [illegible]he title of PRC, issuing year, the Ornamental Columns Erected in front of the Gate of Heavenly Peace and p[illegible] The reverses all depict the picture of the text of the Basic Law of Hong Kong Special Administrative Regio[illegible]he People's Republic of China, the landscape of Kowloon, Chinese-English words ' Peaceful Transition, Lon[illegible] Prosperity' and face value.

共同正面

放大

原 大 Full Size

面额（元）	500	50
直径（毫米）	60	27
含纯金（盎司）	5	1/2
成色 （%）	99.99	99.9
质量	精制	精制
年号	1996	1996
发行量（枚）	228	11800
铸造单位	上海造币厂	

Face Value (Yuan)	500	50
Diameter (mm)	60	27
Pure Gold Content (oz)	5	1/2
Fineness (%)	99.99	99.9
Quality	Proof	Proof
Issuing Year	1996	1996
Mintage (Pieces)	228	11800
Minted by	Shanghai Mint	

放 大

正 面

原 大 Full Size

面额（元）	10
直径（毫米）	40
含纯银（盎司）	1
成色（%）	99.9
质量	精制
年号	1996
发行量（枚）	88000
铸造单位	上海造币厂

Face Value (Yuan)	10
Diameter (mm)	40
Pure Silver Content (oz)	1
Fineness (%)	99.9
Quality	Proof
Issuing Year	1996
Mintage (Pieces)	88000
Minted by	Shanghai Mint

Second Set in the Series of
The Romance
of the Three Kingdoms
Gold and Silver Coins

中國貴金屬紀念幣圖鑒

十四、中国古典文学名著《三国演义》金银币（第2组）

一九九六年

为了弘扬中国传统文化，中国人民银行于1995年开始发行中国古典文学名著《三国演义》金银币。1996年发行《三国演义》金银币第2组，该组金银币由上海造币厂铸造，中国金币总公司总经销。

该组金银币共7个品种，1/2盎司、5盎司精制金币各1种，27克精制银币4种，5盎司精制银币1种。正面图案均为作者罗贯中肖像、国号、年号；背面图案分别为官渡之战图、三英战吕布图、曹操、曹丕、曹植、司马懿及面额。

《三国演义》是元明之际罗贯中编著的一部长篇历史小说，是中国四大古典文学名著之一。《三国演义》通行本一百二十回，描写了公元184年(东汉中平元年)到公元280年(西晋太康元年)近百年间的历史。书中以魏、蜀、吴的兴衰为重点，揭示了东汉末年政治腐败、社会凋敝的现实，展现了当时各种封建势力与政治集团之间的激烈斗争，寄托着作者的政治思想。

《三国演义》艺术成就也很高。它有声有色地描写了一系列战争，对于各次战争的特定环境、战争双方的力量对比、战略部署和战术运用等，都交待得十分清楚，并描绘了许多生动的战争场面。作者也善于刻画人物，塑造了许多性格鲜明、影响深远的艺术形象。

曹操，字孟德，东汉末杰出的政治家和军事家。曹操在镇压黄巾起义中扩充了实力，先后削平了吕布、袁绍、刘表、袁术等割据势力，统一了北部中国。后封魏王。曹操既有才干和谋略，又非常奸险和残暴。同时，他又是一个诗人，其诗苍凉悲壮，沉雄多气，尤擅乐府。

曹丕是曹操次子，字子桓，继曹操为魏王，即魏文帝，他推行九品中正制，确立士族特权。同时，曹丕又是邺下文人领袖，发展了抒情小赋，诗歌多表现征夫思妇之哀，于文学多有贡献。

曹植是曹操第三子，曹丕之弟，字子建。早年他以才华深得曹操的赏识与庞爱。曹丕做皇帝后，对他横加压抑与迫害，他在愤懑与苦闷中死去。曹植的文学成就很高，是汉末最负盛名的作家。

司马懿，本是曹丕的侍从之臣，是一个很有谋略的人物，深得曹丕信任。公元249年，司马懿发动政变，掌握了魏国军政大权。由于他奠定的基础，他的后世司马炎才得以建立晋朝。

官渡之战是曹操战胜袁绍统一北方的关键性战役。公元199年，袁绍率兵十余万攻曹，曹操以两万兵力与袁军在官渡相持，次年，曹利用敌军轻敌无备，偷袭其后方，焚烧其辎重，乘袁军慌乱，迅猛出击，歼灭了袁军主力，奠定了统一北方的基础。这是一次以弱胜强、以少胜多的著名战役。

三英战吕布见于《三国演义》第5回。叙述关羽斩华雄之后，董卓屯兵虎牢关，袁绍派兵迎敌。刘备、关羽、张飞亦随公孙策前往。董卓勇将吕布连伤数员大将，张飞、关羽与之酣战，不能获胜，后刘备也参战，吕布终于抵抗不住，拨马而逃。三英战吕布突出了刘、关、张的英雄形象。

To popularize Chinese traditional culture, the People's Bank of China has been issuing the famous classical literature work *The Romance of the Three Kingdoms* gold and silver coins since 1995. The second set was minted by Shanghai Mint and distributed by China Gold Coin Inc.. It contains 7 kinds of coins: 1/2 oz. and 5 oz. proof gold coins, 4 kinds of 27g proof silver coins and 5 oz. proof silver coin. The obverses all depict the picture of the portrait of the author Luo Guanzhong, title of PRC and the issuing year. The reverses depict the pictures of the Guandu Warfare, the Three Heroes Combating with Lu Bu, the portraits of Cao Cao, Cao Pi, Cao Zhi and Sima Yi respectively and face value.

The Romance of the Three Kingdoms, written by Luo Guanzhong during the period between the late Yuan Dynasty and early Ming Dynasty, was a historical novel. It is one of the Four Famous Classical Literature Works of China. It consists of 120 chapters narrating the history from 184 A.D. (the first year of Zhong Ping of the Eastern Han Dynasty) to 280 A.D. (the first year of Tai Kang of the Western Jin Dynasty). The novel focuses on the prosperity and the depression and fall of the kingdoms of Wei, Shu and Wu, reveals the political corruption and social decline at the end of the Eastern Han Dynasty, shows the intense struggle among the feudal powers and the political groups. The author placed his political ideology on his novel.

The artistic merits of *The Romance of the Three Kingdoms* are brilliant, too. It vividly describes a series of wars, and for each war it depicts every detail of the certain circumstances, the relative strength of the two belligerent parties, the strategic plans, the tactical application and many lively scenes of the war. The author also had genius for portraying distinctive characters that have a profound influence.

Cao Cao, given name Mengde, was an outstanding politician and strategist towards the end of the Eastern Han Dynasty. He enforced his strength in the course of suppressing the Huangjin Uprising and then wiped out the separatist powers of Lu Bu, Yuan Shao, Liu Biao and Yuan Shu, finally unified North China. After that he was conferred King Wei. Cao Cao was not only capable and astute, but also treacherous and brutal. Meanwhile, he was also a poet whose poems were solemn, stirring and powerful. Yuefu songs were his best works.

Cao Pi, Emperor Wen of the Kingdom Wei, given name Zihuan, the second son of Cao Cao, succeeded to the throne after Cao Cao's death. He pursued the Nine Ranks policy, which established the privileges of the ... atum. At the same time, he was also the leader of the literati in Ye city. He developed the lyrics, which conveyed the grief of the soldiers and their wives. He had made a great contribution to Chinese literature.

Cao Zhi, given name Zijian, was the third son of Cao Cao and younger brother of Cao Pi. Cao Cao had appreciated his talent and doted on him very much when Cao Zhi was young. When Cao Pi ascended the throne, Cao Zhi suffered great inhibition and persecution by his brother and he died in depression and resentment at last. Cao Zhi was an accomplished and the most famous literati at the end of the Eastern Han Dynasty.

Sima Yi, an astute man, was once an attendant of Cao Pi and was very trusted by the latter. In 249 A.D. he launched a palace coup d'état and took over the military and political power of Wei. It was on this base that his descendant Sima Yan founded the Jin Dynasty.

The Guandu Warfare was a key point that made Cao Cao defeat Yuan Shao and unite the North China. In 199 A.D. Yuan Shao led one hundred thousands of soldiers to attack Cao Cao. The two sides was locked in a stalemate at Guandu with the latter heading twenty thousands of soldiers. The next year, Cao Cao, observed that the enemy underestimated him and didn't take precautions, attacked his opponent's rear on the sneak and burned the impedimenta. His army hit out quickly and wiped out the main force of the enemy, which laid the foundation of uniting the North China. This was a famous war in which pit few against many and defeat the strong by the weak.

Chapter 5 of *The Romance of the Three Kingdoms* describes the combat between the three heroes and Lu Bu. After Guan Yu beheaded Hua Xiong, Dong Zhuo stationed troops at Hulao Pass, and Yuan Shao sent troops to meet the enemy head-on. Liu Bei, Guan Yu and Zhang Fei also went there accompanying Gongsun Ce. Dong Zhuo sent his braise general Lu Bu hurting several generals. Zhang Fei and Guan Yu fought with him for hours but could not defeat him. So Liu Bei joined them to fight with Lu Bu, the latter finally could not resist and ran away. This story stressed the heroic images of Liu, Guan and Zhang.

共同正面

放　大

原　大 Full Size

面额（元）	500	50
直径（毫米）	60	27
含纯金（盎司）	5	1/2
成色（%）	99.9	99.9
质量	精制	精制
年号	1996	1996
发行量（枚）	99	2000
铸造单位	上海造币厂	

Face Value (Yuan)	500	50
Diameter (mm)	60	27
Pure Gold Content (oz)	5	1/2
Fineness (%)	99.9	99.9
Quality	Proof	Proof
Issuing Year	1996	1996
Mintage (Pieces)	99	2000
Minted by	Shanghai Mint	

正 面

原 大 Full Size

面额（元）	50	Face Value (Yuan)	50
直径（毫米）	70	Diameter (mm)	70
含纯银（盎司）	5	Pure Silver Content (oz)	5
成色 （%）	99.9	Fineness (%)	99.9
质量	精制	Quality	Proof
年号	1996	Issuing Year	1996
发行量（枚）	500	Mintage (Pieces)	500
铸造单位	上海造币厂	Minted by	Shanghai Mint

共同正面

原　大 Full Size

面额（元）	10	10	10	10
直径（毫米）	38.6	38.6	38.6	38.6
含纯银（盎司）	0.803	0.803	0.803	0.803
成色（%）	92.5	92.5	92.5	92.5
质量	精制	精制	精制	精制
年号	1996	1996	1996	1996
发行量（枚）	7000	7000	7000	7000
铸造单位	上海造币厂			

Face Value (Yuan)	10	10	10	10
Diameter (mm)	38.6	38.6	38.6	38.6
Pure Silver Content (oz)	0.803	0.803	0.803	0.803
Fineness (%)	92.5	92.5	92.5	92.5
Quality	Proof	Proof	Proof	Proof
Issuing Year	1996	1996	1996	1996
Mintage (Pieces)	7000	7000	7000	7000
Minted by	Shanghai Mint			

Second Set in the Series
of China Silk Road
Gold and Silver Coins

中國貴金屬紀念幣圖鑒

十五、中国丝绸之路金银币
（第2组）

一九九六年

中国贵金属纪念币年鉴

为展现中国古代人民同亚洲、欧洲、非洲人民之间的政治、经济、文化交流的历史，弘扬中国古代文明，中国人民银行自1995年开始发行中国丝绸之路金银币，1996年发行了中国丝绸之路金银币第2组。该组金银币由上海造币厂铸造，中国金币总公司总经销。该套金银币共5个品种，其中1/3盎司精制金币1种和20克精制银币4种。正面图案均为国徽、国号、年号，背面图案分别为取经图、飞天图、塑像图、载乐图、通商图及面额。

举世闻名的丝绸之路，是历史上横跨欧亚大陆的重要交通线。在相当长的一段时间里，这条交通线沟通了欧、亚、非之间的政治、经济和文化的联系，成为中国人民同中亚、西亚、欧洲以及非洲人民友好交往的桥梁。中国丝绸之路金银币背面图案表现了丝绸之路沿途典型的人文景观和历史画面。其中汉代取经图描述了汉代蔡培西行印度取回佛经的历史事迹；飞天图则是中国石窟壁画艺术的杰出代表作；塑像图则展示了石窟艺术的又一重要部分——风格多样的泥塑作品；载乐图则利用骆驼上的乐队这一画面形象地记载了西方音乐传入中国的情形；通商图则印证了中西的商贸历史。

To illustrate the history of political, economical and cultural exchanges between Chinese people and Asian, European and African people, and to enhance Chinese ancient civilization, the People's Bank of China has been issuing the China Silk Road gold and silver coins since 1995. The 1996 issue is the second set in this series, which was minted by Shanghai Mint and distributed by China Gold Coin Inc.. This set consists of 5 kinds: 1/3 oz. proof gold coin and 4 kinds of 20g proof silver coins. The obverses all depict the picture of the national emblem, title of PRC and the issuing year. The reverses depict the pictures of Going On A Pilgrimage for Buddhist Scriptures, Flying *Apsaras*, Statues, Playing Music, Trading respectively and face value.

The world-famous Silk Road had been an important traffic line connecting Asia and Europe in the history. During a long period this line had provided the political, economical and cultural links among Asia, Europe and Africa, and served as a bridge of friendship between the people of China and the people of Central Asia, Western Asia, Europe and Africa.

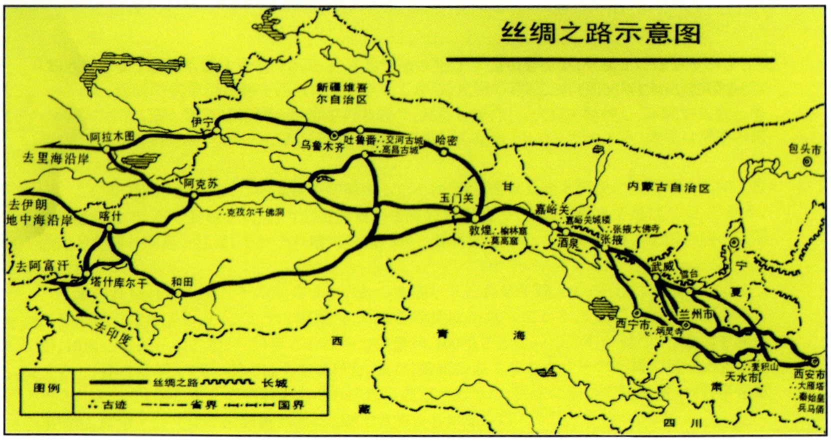

The reverses of these coins depict the typical human scenes and historical pictures along the Silk Road. Among them, the picture of Going On A Pilgrimage For Buddhist Scripture of the Han Dynasty tells the story of Cai Pei going to India and getting back the Buddhist scripture; the picture of the Flying *Apsaras* is the outstanding representative work of the art of Chinese frescoes in the grottos; the picture of Statues shows another important aspect of the art of the grottos—various styles of clay sculptures; the picture of Playing Music records the state of affairs when the western music was introduced into China using the scene of a band on the camel; the picture of Trading corroborates the history of the trade between China and the West.

正　面

原　大 Full Size

放　大

面额（元）	50	Face Value (Yuan)	50
直径（毫米）	23	Diameter (mm)	23
含纯金（盎司）	1/3	Pure Gold Content (oz)	1/3
成色（%）	91.6	Fineness (%)	91.6
质量	精制	Quality	Proof
年号	1996	Issuing Year	1996
发行量（枚）	10000	Mintage (Pieces)	10000
铸造单位	上海造币厂	Minted by	Shanghai Mint

共同正面

原 大 Full Size

面额（元）	5	5	5	5
直径（毫米）	36	36	36	36
含纯银（克）	20	20	20	20
成色（%）	90	90	90	90
质量	精制	精制	精制	精制
年号	1996	1996	1996	1996
发行量（枚）	15000	15000	15000	15000
铸造单位	上海造币厂			

Face Value (Yuan)	5	5	5	5
Diameter (mm)	36	36	36	36
Pure Silver Content (g)	20	20	20	20
Fineness (%)	90	90	90	90
Quality	Proof	Proof	Proof	Proof
Issuing Year	1996	1996	1996	1996
Mintage (Pieces)	15000	15000	15000	15000
Minted by	Shanghai Mint			

The 9th Asian International Philately Exhibition of 1996 Commemorative Coins

中國貴金屬紀念幣圖鑑

十六、1996 年第九届亚洲国际集邮展览纪念币

一九九六年

为纪念1996年第九届亚洲国际集邮展览，推动中国及亚洲集邮事业的发展，中国人民银行发行'96第九届亚洲国际集邮展览纪念币。该套纪念币由沈阳造币厂铸造，中国金币总公司总经销。

第九届亚洲国际集邮展览于1996年5月18日~25日在中国北京国际展览中心隆重举行。这是中国首次举办的大型国际邮展。邮展采用国际通常做法，分竞赛性和非竞赛性展品展出，竞赛类展品共1346框，其中有12部获大金奖，8部获金奖，多部作品获镀金奖、银奖等。非竞赛类展品共183框。此外还有集邮文献近百部。邮展期间设置了专门的销售厅，为广大集邮爱好者提供邮政服务和邮品销售。中国参赛的147部展品中，2部获大金奖，1部获金奖。

1996年第九届亚洲国际集邮展览纪念币为1盎司普制银币2种。一种为邮票加字银币，正面图案为国号、年号、"特1"国徽邮票及"中国邮政一百周年纪念"字样，背面图案为清朝"团龙邮票"图案、"'96中国—第九届亚洲国际集邮展览纪念"字样及面额。另一种为熊猫加字银币，正面图案为国号、年号、北京天坛祈年殿及"'96中国—第九届亚洲国际集邮展览纪念"字样，背面图案为熊猫母子图及面额。

To commemorate the 9th Asian International Philately Exhibition of 1996 and to push forward the development of the philatelic undertakings of China and Asia, the People's Bank of China issued the 9th Asian International Philately Exhibition of 1996 commemorative coins, which were minted by Shenyang Mint and distributed by China Gold Coin Inc..

The 9th Asian International Philately Exhibition was held ceremoniously at the Beijing International Exhibition Center from May 18 to May 25, 1996. This had been the first time that China held such a large-scale international philately exhibition. The exhibition adopted the international practices dividing the items on display into competitive and non-competitive items. The competitive items consist of 1,346 frames, among which 12 won the big gold medals, 8 won gold medals and several works won gilded medals or silver medals. The non-competitive items consist of 183 frames. Besides, there were nearly a hundred of philatelic documents on display. During the exhibiting time there was a special sales hall providing the stamp-collectors postal service and selling of the stamp items. Among the 147 Chinese competitive items, 2 won the big gold medals and 1 won gold medal.

The 9th Asian International Philately Exhibition of 1996 commemorative coins contain two kinds of 1 oz. bu. silver coins. One is a stamp plus words silver coin with the obverse depicting the picture of the title of PRC,issuing year ,'Special 1'national emblem stamp and the Chinese words'The Centenary of Chinese Postal Service',and with the reverse depicting the picture of 'Circular Dragon' stamp of the Qing Dynasty ,the Chinese words ''96 China-9th Asian International Philately Exhibition Souvenir'and face value. Another is a panda plus words silver coin with the obverse depicting the picture of the title of PRC, issuing year, the Hall of Prayer for Good Harvests of the Temple of Heaven in Beijing and the Chinese words ''96 China-9th Asian International Philately Exhibition Souvenir', and with the reverse depicting the picture of the mother and baby pandas and face value.

正 面

原 大 Full Size

正 面

原 大 Full Size

面额（元）	10	10
直径（毫米）	40	40
含纯银（盎司）	1	1
成色 （%）	99.9	99.9
质量	普制	普制
年号	1996	1996
发行量（枚）	20000	20000
铸造单位	沈阳造币厂	

Face Value (Yuan)	10	10
Diameter (mm)	40	40
Pure Silver Content (oz)	1	1
Fineness (%)	99.9	99.9
Quality	Bu.	Bu.
Issuing Year	1996	1996
Mintage (Pieces)	20000	20000
Minted by	Shenyang Mint	

1996 Beijing International
Coin Exposition
Commemorative Coins

中國貴金屬紀念幣章鑒

十七、1996年北京国际钱币博览会纪念币

一九九六年

中国贵金属纪念币年鉴

为纪念1996年北京国际钱币博览会，促进中国及世界钱币事业的发展，中国人民银行发行1996年北京国际钱币博览会纪念币。该套纪念币由沈阳造币厂铸造，中国金币总公司总经销。

1996年北京国际钱币博览会于1996年11月6日～11日在中国北京国际贸易中心隆重举行，这是首次在中国举办的大型国际钱币专业博览会。此次博览会是由中国金币总公司、中国印钞造币总公司和中国钱币学会联合举办的，共有包括中国在内的20多个国家和地区的70家造币厂以及金银纪念币、钱币、邮票经销公司参展。此次大会是中国钱币界的一次盛会，对促进中国钱币市场的发展和国内外钱币文化的交流具有重要意义。

1996年北京国际钱币博览会纪念币为1盎司普制银镶金币1种，这是中国首次发行银镶金这种形式的纪念币，其正面图案为北京天坛祈年殿、国号、年号及“’96北京国际钱币博览会纪念”的字样，背面图案为大熊猫、镶嵌的金质小熊猫及面额。

To commemorate the 1996 Beijing International Coin Exposition and to push forward the numismatic undertaking of China and the world, the People's Bank of China issued the 1996 Beijing International Coin Exposition commemorative coins, minted by Shenyang Mint and distributed by China Gold Coin Inc..

The 1996 Beijing International Numismatic Exposition was held ceremoniously at the Beijing International Trade Center from November 6 to 11, 1996. This had been the first time that China held such a large-scale international numismatic professional exposition. China Gold Coin Inc., China Banknote Printing & Minting Corp. and China Numismatic Society together held this exposition. 70 mints, gold and silver commemorative coins companies, coin companies and stamp companies from over 20 countries and regions including China took part in this exposition. This exposition was a grand gathering of Chinese numismatic circle, which was important to promote the development of Chinese numismatic market and the numismatic cultural exchange between China and abroad.

1996 Beijing International Numismatic Exposition commemorative coin is a 1 oz. bu. silver coin inlayed with gold, which had been the first time that this kind was issued. The obverse depicts the picture of the Hall of Prayer for Good Harvests of the Temple of Heaven in Beijing, title of PRC, issuing year and the Chinese words ''96 Beijing International Numismatic Exposition Souvenir', the reverse depicts the picture of giant panda, inlayed gold small panda and face value.

正　面

原　大 Full Size

放　大

面额（元）	10
直径（毫米）	40
银镶金（盎司）	1
成色（%）	99.9
质量	普制
年号	1996
发行量（枚）	20000
铸造单位	沈阳造币厂

Face Value (Yuan)	10
Diameter (mm)	40
Pure Silver Content (oz)	1
Fineness (%)	99.9
Quality	Bu.
Issuing Year	1996
Mintage (Pieces)	20000
Minted by	Shenyang Mint

The Scenery of the Three Gorges
of the Yangtze River
Gold and Silver Coins

中國貴金屬紀念幣圖鑒

十八、长江三峡风光金银币

一九九六年

为使世人更多地了解长江三峡的壮丽风光，中国人民银行于1996年发行长江三峡风光金银币，该套金银币由上海造币厂铸造，中国金币总公司总经销。

长江三峡风光金银币图案取材于长江三峡的自然人文景观。

三峡是长江风景旅游线上风景最为奇秀、最为集中的山水画廊，它西起重庆奉节的白帝城，东到湖北宜昌的南津关，全长192公里。长江三峡由瞿塘峡、巫峡和西陵峡三段峡谷组成。三峡之美，在于"雄、险、奇、幽"四字。瞿塘峡以雄伟险峻著称。巫峡以幽深秀丽驰名，特别是巫山十二峰，久享盛名，其中神女峰最为俏丽。西陵峡滩多水急，则以险闻名。

错开峡在大溪镇下游不远的长江南岸，相互对错，高入云端。中国古代著名的大禹治水，传说禹匆忙中开错了峡道，后经西王母的女儿瑶姬帮助才开凿成功，讲的就是错开峡。

白帝庙在奉节县城东4公里，扼瞿塘峡西口长江北岸，相传为西汉末公孙述所建，三国时刘备即在此托孤于诸葛亮。今存寺庙系康熙后重修的，主要建筑有明良殿、武侯祠、观星楼等。庙前平台可远眺江景，雄奇无比。

屈原祠位于归州镇东1.5公里的向家坪，为清代所建。该建筑坐南朝北，依山而建，四周林木环绕，风景旖旎，人文景观丰富。有山门、配房、碑廊、屈原纪念馆及屈原墓等建筑。

昭君宅在湖北兴山县境内的宝坪村。村内有楠木井、娘娘牛、梳妆台、望月楼等遗迹。王昭君在竟宁元年(公元前33年)自愿出嫁匈奴，为民族间的亲善友好作出了贡献。

张飞庙位于云阳县城对岩的飞凤山下，始建于蜀汉末年，又名张桓侯祠。主要建筑有结义楼、望云轩、正殿、旁殿、助风阁、得月亭和杜鹃亭等，是巴蜀胜境之一。

长江三峡风光金银币共2个品种，其中1/2盎司精制金币1种，2盎司精制银币1种(由4枚银币相连组成)。1/2盎司精制金币正面图案为国号、年号、错开峡，背面图案为三峡大坝图及面额；2盎司精制银币正面图案分别为国号、年号与白帝庙、屈原祠、昭君宅、张飞庙，背面图案为四枚银币相连组成的长江三峡全景图及面额。该套金银币均为长方形，这是中国人民银行首次发行方型金银币。

To let the world know more about the glorious scenery of the Three Gorges of the Yangtze River, the People's Bank of China issued the scenery of the Three Gorges of the Yangtze River gold and silver coins, minted by Shanghai Mint and distributed by China Gold Coin Inc..

The gold and silver coins of the scenery of the Three Gorges of the Yangtze River draw materials from the natural and human sceneries of the Three Gorges.

The Three Gorges is a landscape gallery that comprises the most beautiful and the most condense sceneries along the Yangtze River. It runs from the west Baidi City of Fengjie of Chongqing to the east Nanjin Pass of Yichang of Hubei, with total length of 192 kilometers. The Three Gorges is made up of the Qutang Gorge, Wu Gorge and Xiling Gorge. 'Grandeur, perilousness, marvelousness, deepness and sereneness' are the features of the Three Gorges. The Qutang Gorge is famous for its grandeur and precipitousness. The Wu Gorge is renowned for its deepness and beautifulness, especially the Twelve Peaks of the Wu Mount, one of which, the Goddess Peak, is the most beautiful. The Xiling Gorge is famous for its perilousness with many shoals and rapids.

The Staggering Gorge (*Cuokai* Gorge) lies in the south bank of the Yangtze River not long from the lower reaches of the Daxi Town. The two sides of the gorge stagger and reach to the sky. Chinese legend said that when the famous hero Dayu was harnessing the river, he opened up the wrong gorge in haste. He didn't succeed until he got the help from Yaoji, a daughter of Xi Wang Mu (Queen Mother of the West). This gorge is the Staggering Gorge.

The Baidi Temple is 4 kilometers east from the Fengjie County, holds the western entrance of the Qutang Gorge in the north bank of the Yangtze River. According to legend, Gongsun Shu at the end of the Western Han Dynasty built it. It is where Liu Bei entrusted his son to Zhuge Liang in the Three Kingdoms Period. The temple was renovated after Emperor Kangxi and survives to now. The main buildings consist of the Mingliang Hall, Wuhou Memorial Hall and the Tower For Observing Stars. Standing in the platform in front of the temple can command an open view of the marvelous Yangtze River of the distance.

The Qu Yuan Memorial Temple, built in the Qing Dynasty, lies in Xiangjia Level Ground 1.5 kilometers east of the Guizhou Town. It is at the foot of the mountain facing north, surrounded by trees. The human scenes are abundant here, such as the gate of the temple, the wings, the porch of steles, the Qu Yuan Memorial Hall and the tomb of Qu Yuan.

The House of Zhaojun is in the Baoping village of the Xingshan County of Hubei Province. There are many sites like the *Phoebe nanmu* Well, Lady Cattle, Dressing Table, Tower for Seeing the Moon. Wang Zhaojun voluntarily got married with the chief of the Huns in the first year of Jingning (33 B.C.), which contributed to the good will between the two nationalities.

The Zhang Fei Temple lies at the foot of the Feifeng Mount, Duiyan of the Yunyang County. It was built at the end of the Shu Kingdom period, also called Zhang Huan Marquis Temple. The main buildings consist of the Sworn Tower, House for Seeing the Clouds, Main Hall, Side Hall, Wind-adding Pavilion, Booth of Getting the Moon and Cuckoo Booth. It is one of the scenic spots of the Ba-Shu Region.

The Three Gorges of the Yangtze River scenery gold and silver coins contain 2 kinds: 1/2 oz. proof gold and 2 oz. proof silver (made of 4 conjoint silver coins). The former has the obverse depicting the picture of the title of PRC, issuing year and the Staggering Gorge (*Cuokai* Gorge); and the reverse depicting the picture of the Three Gorges Dam and face value. The latter has the obverse depicting the pictures of the title of PRC, issuing year and the Baidi Temple, the Qu Yuan Temple, the House of Zhaojun and the Zhang Fei Temple, respectively. And the reverse depicting the picture of the panorama of the Three Gorges made up of 4 conjoint silver coins and face value. These coins are all rectangular. This was the first time using rectangular shape in the issues of the People's Bank of China.

正　面

放　大

原　大 Full Size

面额（元）	50
规格（毫米）	29 × 19
含纯金（盎司）	1/2
成色（%）	99.9
质量	精制
年号	1996
发行量（枚）	6000
铸造单位	上海造币厂

Face Value (Yuan)	50
Size (mm)	29 × 19
Pure Gold Content (oz)	1/2
Fineness (%)	99.9
Quality	Proof
Issuing Year	1996
Mintage (Pieces)	6000
Minted by	Shanghai Mint

正　面

原　大 Full Size

面额（元）	20（× 4）	Face Value (Yuan)	20(× 4)
规格（毫米）	36 × 55(× 4)	Size (mm)	36 × 55 (× 4)
含纯银（盎司）	2(× 4)	Pure Silver Content (oz)	2(× 4)
成色（%）	99.9	Fineness (%)	99.9
质量	精制	Quality	Proof
年号	1996	Issuing Year	1996
发行量（枚）	8000(× 4)	Mintage (Pieces)	8000(× 4)
铸造单位	上海造币厂	Minted by	Shanghai Min

1996 Asian Winter Games
Commemorative Medal

中國貴金屬紀念幣彙鑒

十九、1996年亚洲冬运会纪念章

一九九六年

为纪念1996年第三届亚洲冬季运动会，推动亚洲各国冰雪运动的发展，中国金币总公司发行1996年冬季运动会纪念章1套，该套纪念章由上海造币厂铸造。此套纪念章为5盎司精制金章1种，正面图案为第三届亚洲冬季运动会会徽，背面图案为第三届亚洲冬季运动会吉祥物。

1996年第三届亚洲冬季运动会于1996年2月4日~11日在中国黑龙江省哈尔滨市举行。亚洲17个国家和地区的400余名运动员参加了8个大项43个小项的角逐，这是亚洲有史以来参赛人数最多、规模最大的一次冰雪盛会。 在这届亚洲冬季运动会上，共有两队打破一项世界纪录，54人次打破13项亚洲纪录，181人次打破亚洲冬季运动会纪录，是冬运会历史上成绩最显著的一届。东道主中国代表团以15枚金牌列金牌总数第一，首次参赛的哈萨克斯坦代表团以14枚金牌位居第二，日本和韩国各获8枚金牌，并列金牌总数第三。

To commemorate the third Asian Winter Games of 1996 and to push forward the development of the ice and snow sports of the Asian countries, China Gold Coin Inc. issued the 1996 Asian Winter Games commemorative medal, minted by Shanghai Mint. It is a 5 oz. proof gold medal, with the obverse depicting the emblem of the third Asian Winter Games and with the reverse depicting the picture of the mascot of the third Asian Winter Games.

[illegible] third Asia[illegible] Winter Games was held in Harbin, Heilongjiang Province from February 4 to 11, 1996. Over 400 [illegible]letes fr[illegible] 7 Asian countries and regions participated 8 events comprising 43 items, the biggest ice and snow gathe[illegible] had the most participants in Asian history. Two teams broke a world's record, 54 person-times broke 1[illegible] of Asian records and totally 181 person-times broke the Asian Winter Games records. It achieved the most [illegible]kable success in the history of the winter games. Chinese delegation, the host, rank first with 15 gold medal[illegible] Kazakhstan delegation, the first time participated the games, rank second with 14 gold medals; Japan and Korea tied for third place with 8 gold medals.

正　面

原　大 Full Size

放　大

直径（毫米）	60
含纯金（盎司）	5
成色（%）	99.9
质量	精制
年号	1996
发行量（枚）	100
铸造单位	上海造币厂

Diameter (mm)	60
Pure Gold Content (	5
Fineness (%)	99.9
Quality	Proof
Issuing Year	1996
Mintage (Pieces)	100
Minted by	Shanghai Mi

The Centenary of the
Birth of Mao Zemin
Commemorative Medal

中國貴金屬紀念幣圖鑒

二十、毛泽民诞辰100周年纪念章

一九九六年

中国贵金属纪念币年鉴

毛泽民是中国共产党财政金融工作的先驱，党内最早的理财专家之一。在22年的革命生涯中，他主要担负财政方面的领导工作。为纪念毛泽民的革命功绩，缅怀革命伟人，中国金币总公司于1996年发行毛泽民诞辰100周年银质纪念章，该纪念章由沈阳造币厂铸造。

毛泽民(1896～1943年)，毛泽东的大弟弟。幼年读过几年私塾，后来在家种田。在毛泽东的影响下，毛泽民在家乡参加了农民革命活动，并于1922年加入中国共产党。后被派往安源、上海、武汉、天津等地领导工人运动。1931年，进入中央革命根据地，任中华苏维埃共和国临时中央政府国家银行行长。1937年底离开延安到达新疆迪化。当时新疆地方军阀盛世才伪装进步，表示愿与中国共产党合作，并要求中国共产党派人协助工作，于是毛泽民留在新疆主持财政工作。但毛泽民的财政整顿堵住了盛世才的贪赃之道，盛世才于1943年9月秘密杀害了毛泽民，此时毛泽民年仅47岁。

毛泽民诞辰100周年纪念章为1盎司普制银章1种，其正面图案为杜鹃花簇拥着毛泽民肖像及文字，背面图案为江西瑞金中华苏维埃国家银行旧址。

Mao Zemin was a pioneer of Chinese Communist Party's finance, one of the earliest financiers in the Party. He was the chief leader of the financial work during his 22-year long revolutionary career. To commemorate Mao Zemin's contributions to the revolutionary course and cherish the memory of our revolutionary martyrs, China Gold Coin Inc. issued the centenary of the birth of Mao Zemin commemorative silver medal, minted by Shenyang Mint.

Mao Zemin (1896 ~ 1943) was the senior younger brother of Mao Zedong. He had studied in an old-style private school for a few years when he was young, after that he went in for farming back home. Under the influence of Mao Zedong, he took part in the peasants' revolutionary movement in his hometown and joined the Communist Party in 1922. Later he was sent to An'yuan, Shanghai, Wuhan and Tianjin to lead the labor movements. He went to the Central Revolutionary Base in 1937 and was appointed the president of the Temporary National Bank of the Temporary Central Government of the Soviet Republic of China. He left Yan'an to Urumchi in the end of 1937. At that time Sheng Shicai, the warlord of Xinjiang, pretended to be progressive and expressed his wish to cooperate with the Communist Party. He invited the Party to assign an officer to assist him, so Mao Zemin stayed in Xinjiang taking charge of finance. But Mao Zemin's financial rectification plugged up the way Sheng Shicai accumulated money by unfair means, so the latter killed Mao Zemin clandestinely in September 1943, when Mao Zemin was only 47-years old.

The centenary of the birth of Mao Zemin commemorative medal is a 1 oz. bu. silver medal with the obverse depicting the picture of the portrait of Mao Zemin wreathed by azalea, and with the reverse depicting the picture of the site of the National Bank of the Soviet Republic of China in Ruijin, Jiangxi.

正　面

原　大 Full Size

放　大

直径（毫米）	40
含纯银（盎司）	1
成色（%）	99.9
质量	普制
年号	1996
发行量（枚）	10000
铸造单位	沈阳造币厂

Diameter (mm)	40
Pure Silver Content (oz)	1
Fineness (%)	99.9
Quality	Bu.
Issuing Year	1996
Mintage (Pieces)	10000
Minted by	Shenyang Mint

1996 Munich International Coin Fair Commemorative Medals

中國貴金屬紀念幣章鑒

二十一、1996年慕尼黑国际硬币展销会纪念章

一九九六年

为纪念1996年慕尼黑国际硬币展销会，中国金币总公司发行1996年慕尼黑国际硬币展销会纪念章，该纪念章由沈阳造币厂铸造。该套纪念章包括1/4盎司精制金套银纪念章和1盎司精制银章各1枚。正面图案分别为北京天坛祈年殿及慕尼黑楼景和中国长城及慕尼黑塔景，背面图案为熊猫攀树图。

To commemorate 1996 Munich International Coin Fair, China Gold Coin Inc. issued the 1996 Munich International Coin Fair commemorative medals, minted by Shenyang Mint. This set consists of 1/4 oz. proof gold medal and 1 oz. proof silver medal. The obverses depict the pictures of the Hall of Prayer for Good Harvests of the Temple of Heaven in Beijing and the Munich buildings or the Great Wall and the Munich towers respectively. The reverses all depict the picture of the panda climbing the tree.

正　面

原　大 Full Size

放　大

直径（毫米）	40
含纯银（盎司）	1
成色（%）	99.9
质量	精制
年号	1996
发行量（枚）	2500
铸造单位	沈阳造币厂

Diameter (mm)	40
Pure Silver Content (oz)	1
Fineness (%)	99.9
Quality	Proof
Issuing Year	1996
Mintage (Pieces)	2500
Minted by	Shenyang Mint

正　面

放　大

原　大 Full Size

直径（毫米）	30	Diameter (mm)	30
含纯金（盎司）	1/4	Pure Gold Content (oz)	1/4
含纯银（盎司）	1/8	Pure Silver Content (oz)	1/8
成色（%）	99.9	Fineness (%)	99.9
质量	精制	Quality	Proof
年号	1996	Issuing Year	1996
发行量（枚）	1500	Mintage (Pieces)	1500
铸造单位	沈阳造币厂	Minted by	Shenyang Mint

1996 Issue
of Saint Valentine's Day
Gold Medal

中國貴金屬紀念幣章鑒

二十二、1996年版情人节金章

一九九六年

1996年版情人节金章由中国金币总公司发行，深圳国宝金币制造厂铸造。

情人节为每年的2月14日，是欧美及大洋洲一些国家的节日。关于情人节的来历，一般的说法是：公元3世纪，罗马帝国的基督教徒瓦伦丁，因带头反抗罗马帝国统治者对基督教徒的迫害而被处死，基督教徒为了纪念他，便把他被处死的日子(2月14日)定为情人节。因此情人节又称瓦伦丁节。“瓦伦丁”便成为“情人”的代名词。在欧美国家，情人节的标志是红心和鲜花。

1996年版情人节金章重1/10盎司，限量发行5000枚。该章正面图案为双朵玫瑰花及中英文“祝福”字样、年号，背面图案为维纳斯半身像。

1996 issue of Saint Valentine's Day gold medals were issued by China Gold Coin Inc. and minted by Shenzhen Panda Gold Coin Mint.

Saint Valentine's Day is February 14, which is a holiday of some Euramerican and Oceania countries. The general wording about its origin is that: in the third century A.D., a Christian named Valentine of the Roman Empire was executed for leading the revolt against the persecution to the Christians by the Roman rulers. The Christians determine the day when he was killed (January 14) as the Lover's Day, also called Saint Valentine's Day to commemorate him. After then 'Valentine' has become the alternative of 'Lover'. In some Euramerican countries red heart and rose are the symbols of the Saint Valentine's Day.

1996 issue of Saint Valentine's Day gold medal weighs 1/10 oz., and is limited quantity to 5000. The obverse depicts the picture of bi-roses, Chinese-English words 'Bless' and the issuing year, and the reverse depicts the picture of the bust of Venus.

正　面

原　大 Full Size

放　大

直径（毫米）	18
含纯金（盎司）	1/10
成色（%）	99.9
质量	普制
年号	1996
发行量（枚）	5000
铸造单位	深圳国宝金币制造厂

Diameter (mm)	18
Pure Gold Content (oz)	1/10
Fineness (%)	99.9
Quality	Bu.
Issuing Year	1996
Mintage (Pieces)	5000
Minted by	Shenzhen Panda Gold Coin Mint

1996 Issue
of The Mother's Day
Gold Medal

二十三、1996年版母亲节金章

一九九六年

母亲节在每年5月的第二个星期日，是美国法定的全国性节日。如今，全世界已有43个国家公认这一节日，可以说，母亲节已成为一个世界性的节日了。为纪念这一世界性的节日，中国金币总公司发行1996年版母亲节金章，该章由深圳国宝金币制造厂铸造。

母亲节由一个叫安娜·贾维丝的美国小姐发起设立。1906年，其母亲突然去世。为了表达对母亲的怀念和感激，她决定实现母亲生前的愿望——创立一个母亲节。为此，她四处奔走，赢得了社会各界的普遍支持。1914年，美国国会通过决议，并由威尔逊总统亲自签署，将每年5月的第二个星期日定为母亲节。

1996年版母亲节金章重1/10盎司，发行3000枚。正面图案为康乃馨花及文字、年号，背面图案为母子雕像图。

The Mother's Day is the second Sunday of May, which is a legal national holiday in the U.S. Up to now, there have been 43 countries legalizing this holiday that it has already become a cosmopolitan holiday. To commemorate this cosmopolitan holiday, China Gold Coin Inc. issued the 1996 issue of the Mother's Day gold medal, minted by Shenzhen Panda Gold Coin Mint.

The Mother's Day was established on an American lady's initiative whose name was Anna. Her mother suddenly passed away in 1906. She decided to fulfill her mother's unrealized wish – establishing a Mother's Day – to express her love and appreciation. She appealed for this around the States and won general support from all circles of the society. In 1914, the Congress adopted a resolution, which was signed by President Wilson, established the second Sunday of May as the Mother's Day.

1996 issue of the Mother's Day gold medal weighs 1/10 oz. with the quantity of 3000 pieces. The obverse depicts the picture of the carnation, words and the issuing year. The reverse depicts the picture of the statuary of the mother and son.

正 面

原 大 Full Size

放 大

直径（毫米）	18
含纯金（盎司）	1/10
成色（%）	99.9
质量	普制
年号	1996
发行量（枚）	3000
铸造单位	深圳国宝金币制造厂

Diameter (mm)	18
Pure Gold Content (oz)	1/10
Fineness (%)	99.9
Quality	Bu.
Issuing Year	1996
Mintage (Pieces)	3000
Minted by	Shenzhen Panda Gold Coin Mint

1996 Issue of the Peony
Gold and Silver Medals

中國貴金屬紀念幣圖鑑

二十四、1996年版牡丹花金银章

一九九六年

中国贵金属纪念币年鉴

牡丹，是和平、繁荣、吉祥、富贵的象征，被中国各族人民一致推举为国花。牡丹是中国的特产。牡丹花，色泽艳丽，玉笑株香，华贵绝伦，被誉为“花中之王”。牡丹花色较多，有白、绿、红、紫、黄，又有浓淡深浅之分，花大而香，争奇斗艳，所以也有“国色天香”之称。

牡丹原为野生植物，南北朝时期成为名贵的观赏品，自隋朝开始，牡丹进入皇宫，唐开元年间大盛于长安，由于朝廷带头提倡，牡丹身价百倍。宋代牡丹中心由长安向东转移到洛阳，达到鼎盛时期。到目前为止，中国引进和培育了数百种花大色艳、色彩俱佳的名贵牡丹。

1996版牡丹花金银章包括1/10盎司普制金章和1盎司普制银章各1种，其正面图案均为牡丹花，背面图案为龙门奉先寺卢舍那大佛。该套金银章由中国金币总公司发行，沈阳造币厂铸造。

Peony, symbolizing peace, prosperity, auspiciousness and, wealth and rank, has been chosen as the national flower by the Chinese people of all nationalities at consensus. Peony is a special flower of China. It is very bright-colored, fragrant and sumptuous, and is eulogized as 'the Queen of the flowers'. Peony has various kinds of colors including white, green, red, purple, yellow, and the colors are further divided into dark and light colors. The flower is big and fragrant, so it gets another name 'national beauty and heavenly fragrance'.

Peony was once a kind of wild plant. It became a precious ornamental in the Southern and Northern Dynasties. It had entered the palace since the Sui Dynasty, and had been very popular in Chang'an during the Kaiyuan period of the Tang Dynasty. Because of the advocating of the court of the Song Dynasty, peony had raised suddenly in social status. The center of planting peony was transferred from Chang'an to Luoyang in the Song Dynasty and reached the period of full bloom. Up to now, China has introduced and cultivated hundreds of kinds of rare peonies, which are both very big and bright-colored.

1996 issue of the peony gold and silver medals contain 1/10 oz. bu. gold medal and 1 oz. bu. silver medal with the obverse depicting the picture of peony, and with the reverse depicting the picture of the statue of Vairocana in the Fengxian Temple of Longmen. This set of gold and silver medals was issued by China Gold Coin Inc. and minted by Shenyang Mint.

正　面

原　大 Full Size

放　大

直径（毫米）	18
含纯金（盎司）	1/10
成色（%）	99.9
质量	普制
年号	1996
发行量（枚）	3000
铸造单位	沈阳造币厂

Diameter (mm)	18
Pure Gold Content (oz)	1/10
Fineness (%)	
Quality	
Issuing Year	
Mintage (Pieces)	
Minted by	Shen…

正　面

原　大 Full Size

放　大

直径（毫米	40
含纯银	1
	99
	普制
	1996
	10000
	沈阳造币厂

Diameter (mm)	40
Pure Silver Content (oz)	1
Fineness (%)	99
Quality	Bu.
Issuing Year	1996
Mintage (Pieces)	10000
Minted by	Shenyang Mint

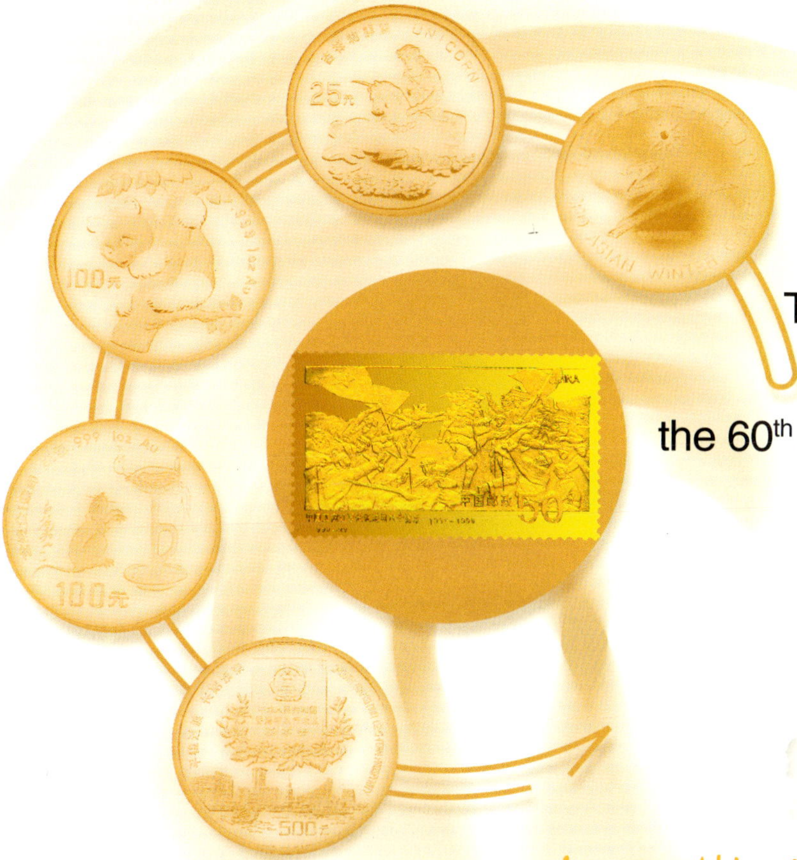

The Commemorative Gold and Silver Stamps of the 60th Anniversary of the Victory of the Long March of Chinese Workers' and Peasants' Red Army

中國貴金屬紀念幣章鑒

二十五、纪念中国工农红军长征胜利60周年金银邮票

一九九

为纪念中国工农红军长征胜利60周年，中国金币总公司与中国集邮总公司联合发行纪念中国工农红军长征胜利60周年金银邮票，由沈阳造币厂铸造。

红军长征始于1934年10月。由于王明“左”倾机会主义路线的错误领导，中央红军未能打破国民党军队的第五次“围剿”，南方各根据地的红军，均先后被迫退出根据地进行长征。

中央红军连续突破国民党军队的四道封锁线，转到了湘江以西地区。遵义会议后，中央红军在毛泽东亲自指挥下，四渡赤水，强渡乌江、大渡河，翻雪山，过草地，于1935年10月到达陕西吴起镇，同红十五军团会合。1936年6月红军第二方面军与第四方面军于甘孜会师，并共同继续北上。1936年10月，第二方面军、第四方面军在甘肃会宁同第一方面军会师，这标志着红军长征的胜利结束。

中国工农红军长征胜利60年周年金银邮票共2个品种。其中3克精制金邮票1种，5克精制银邮票1种。该套金银邮票的图案与同年由邮电部发行的中国工农红军长征胜利60周年纪念邮票的图案相同，分别为红军过草地、三军大会师。

To commemorate the 60th anniversary of the victory of the Long March of the Chinese Workers' and Peasants' Red Army, China Gold Coin Inc., together with C.N.P.C., issued the commemorative gold and silver stamps of the 60th anniversary of the victory of the Long March of the Chinese Workers' and Peasants' Red Army, minted by Shenyang Mint.

The Long March began in October 1934. The Central Red Army did not defeat the fifth 'encircle and suppress' by the Kuomintang army due to the fault leading of Wang Ming's 'Left' opportunism. The Red Armies in the southern bases were forced to withdraw from their bases to march successively.

The Central Red Army broke through four defensive lines of the Kuomintang army successively and shifted to the region west of the Xiang River. After the Zunyi Meeting, the Central Red army, under the command of Mao Zedong, crossed the Chi River four times, forced its way across the Wu River and Dadu River, climbed snow-topped mountains and plodded through grasslands and finally arrived at Wuqi town of Shaanxi joining forces with the Fifteenth Army Group of the Red Army. The Second and the Fourth Front Army of the Red Army joined forces at Ganzi in June 1936 and then, kept moving toward the north together. In October 1937, the Second, the Fourth and the First Front Army successfully joined together at Huining of Gansu, which marked the successful end of the Long March of the Red Army.

The commemorative gold and silver stamps of the 60th anniversary of the victory of the Long March of the Chinese Workers' and Peasants' Red Army contain two kinds: 3g proof gold stamp and 5g proof silver stamp. The picture of this set are the Red Army Plodding Through the Grasslands and the Three Armies Joining Forces, same as those of the commemorative stamps of the 60th anniversary of the victory of the Long March of the Chinese Workers' and Peasants' Red Army issued by the Ministry of Post and Telecommunications in the same year.

含纯金（克）	3	Pure Gold Content (g)	3
成色（%）	99.9	Fineness (%)	99.9
质量	精制	Quality	Proof
年号	1996	Issuing Year	1996
发行量（枚）	10000	Mintage (Pieces)	10000
铸造单位	沈阳造币厂	Minted by	Shenyang Mint

含纯银（克）	5	Pure Silver Content (g)	5
成色（%）	99.9	Fineness (%)	99.9
质量	精制	Quality	Proof
年号	1996	Issuing Year	1996
发行量（枚）	10000	Mintage (Pieces)	10000
铸造单位	沈阳造币厂	Minted by	Shenyang Mint

The Gold and Silver Small-Size Stamps of the Centennial Treasured Tripod Caldron

中國貴金屬紀念幣圖鑒

二十六、世纪宝鼎小型张金银邮票

一九九六年

为了传播“世纪宝鼎”的巨大影响，弘扬民族文化，中国金币总公司与中国集邮总公司联合发行世纪宝鼎小型张金银邮票，由沈阳造币厂铸造。

世纪宝鼎，是为纪念联合国成立50周年，由中国政府向联合国赠送的一只高2.1米、重1.5吨的青铜鼎。作为永久性的纪念，世纪宝鼎被安放在纽约联合国总部大厦前的草坪上。

鼎是中国文化的代表性器物，是太平安定的吉祥象征。世纪宝鼎高2.1米，象征即将来临的二十一世纪；鼎口直径1.5米；重1.5吨。鼎双耳高耸，满身商周纹饰，寓意避邪。基座高50厘米，意为联合国成立50周年；基座2米见方，四周铸有56条夔龙，表示中国有56个民族。此宝鼎造型雄伟，气势宏大，古朴祥和，美观庄重。它是中国青铜文化有史以来最大最重的一只鼎，集历代青铜鼎特色之大成，熔古代技艺与现代科技于一炉，极具独到之处。

江泽民主席称“世纪宝鼎”是“一件具有民族特色和时代特征的礼物”。

世纪宝鼎小型张金银邮票为长方形精制邮票1种，正面图案为世纪宝鼎小型张邮票图案，图案正中部分为1/4盎司金制，四周部分为3/4盎司银制。

To propagate the tremendous influence of the Centennial Treasured Tripod Caldron and to carry forward the culture of the nationalities, China Gold Coin Inc., together with C.N.P.C., issued the gold and silver small-size stamps of the Centennial Treasured Tripod Caldron, minted by Shenyang Mint.

The Centennial Treasured Tripod Caldron is a gift given by the Chinese government to the U.N. to commemorate the 50th anniversary of the founding of U.N. It is 2.1 meters high and weighs 1.5 tons, made by bronze. It is emplaced on the lawn in front of the Headquarter of U.N in New York as a permanent souvenir.

Tripod caldron (*ding*) is a representative vessel of Chinese culture auspiciously symbolizing peace and tranquility. The Centennial Treasured Tripod Caldron is 2.1 meters high symbolizing the coming 21st century; the diameter of the rim is 1.5 meters; it weighs 1.5 tons. The two ears stand tall and erect. The body is full of decorative patterns of the Shang and Zhou periods, which symbolize warding off evil. The foundation is 50 centimeters high which symbolizes the 50th anniversary of the founding of U.N; and it is 2 meters wide with 56 dragons cast around it, which means that there are 56 nationalities in China. This tripod is grandly shaped, and is of primitive simplicity. It is the biggest and heaviest tripod caldron in the history of Chinese bronze culture. It incorporates the features of the bronze tripod caldrons of the past dynasties and combines the ancient techniques and modern science and technology together, showing distinctive qualities.

President Jiang Zemin called the Centennial Treasured Tripod Caldron 'a gift with distinctive national features and with the characters of the times'.

The gold and silver small-size stamps of the Centennial Treasured Tripod Caldron is a rectangular proof stamp with the obverse depicting the same picture as that of the Centennial Treasured Tripod Caldron small-size stamp, the central part is made of 1/4 oz. gold, the rest is made of 3/4 oz. silver.

含纯金（盎司）	1/4
含纯银（盎司）	3/4
成色（%）	99.9
质量	精制
年号	1996
发行量（枚）	5000
铸造单位	沈阳造币厂

Pure Gold Content (oz)	1/4
Pure Silver Content (oz)	3/4
Fineness (%)	99.9
Quality	Proof
Issuing Year	1996
Mintage (Pieces)	5000
Minted by	Shenyang Mint

The Year of the Rat
Gold and Silver Stamps

中國貴金屬紀念幣章鑒

二十七、中国丙子（鼠）年金银邮票

一九九六年

1996年是中国传统十二生肖纪年中之丙子(鼠)年，为示纪念，中国金币总公司与中国集邮总公司联合发行中国丙子(鼠)年生肖金银邮票，由沈阳造币厂铸造。

鼠昼伏夜出，聪敏机灵。在中国先民心目中，鼠为神性动物。在中国古代神话与民俗故事中，鼠往往具有勤劳善良的品质，并多以人类朋友的形象出现。中国传统民俗年画“老鼠嫁女”，更充满吉祥、喜庆、欢乐气氛，生活气息浓郁，至今仍深受国人青睐。

中国先民认为，鼠乃祥瑞、智慧与活力之化身，鼠年满含生机、欢乐，乃是大吉大利、万事亨通、百业俱兴之年。

中国丙子(鼠)年金银邮票共2个品种，1种为2克精制金邮票，1种为3克精制银邮票，图案为鼠年生肖邮票图案。

1996 was the Chinese traditional year of the rat of the Twelve Year Animal Cycle. To commemorate this, China Gold Coin Inc., together with C.N.P.C., issued the year of the rat gold and silver stamps, minted by Shenyang Mint.

Rat hides by day and comes out at night and is very clever. In Chinese ancients' mental view, rat was a supernatural being. In Chinese mythologies and folklores, rat often had the industrious and kindhearted characters, and often appeared as the humankind's friend. Chinese traditional folk Spring Festival picture *Rat Married His Daughter* is full of lucky, joyous and happy air, and has the rich flavor of life, so it finds favor in people's eyes.

Chinese ancients believed that rat was the embodiment of auspiciousness, wisdom and vigor. The year of rat is full of life, happiness, and is a year that is lucky and prosperous, in which everything goes well and all businesses flourish.

The year of the rat gold and silver stamps contain two kinds: 2g proof gold and 3g proof silver. The picture is the same as that of the year of rat stamp.

含纯金（克）	2	
含纯银（克）		3
成色（%）	99.9	99.9
质量	精制	精制
年号	1996	1996
发行量（枚）	10000	10000
铸造单位	沈阳造币厂	

Pure Gold Content (g)	2	
Pure Silver Content (g)		3
Fineness (%)	99.9	99.9
Quality	Proof	Proof
Issuing Year	1996	1996
Mintage (Pieces)	10000	10000
Minted by	Shenyang Mint	

1997

中國貴金屬紀念幣券鑒

Almanac of Chinese Precious Metal Commemorative Currencies

1997 Issue of the
Chinese Panda
Gold and Silver Coin
Series

中國貴金屬紀念幣圖鑒

一、1997年版中国熊猫金银币

一九九七年

熊猫金银币自1982年发行以来，一直深受国内外钱币收藏家、爱好者和投资者的喜爱，1997年版熊猫金银币是此系列金银币的第16套。熊猫金银币与国外同类金银币的设计风格有所不同，虽然材质、成色、规格大致一样，但为达到收藏和投资的双重效果，熊猫币每年更换图案，千姿百态的熊猫活灵活现地展现在金银币上，为中国熊猫金银币打入国际钱币市场奠定了基础。

熊猫，又称大熊猫，或“大猫熊”，是一种最古老的动物，其祖先的生活年代可以追溯到一千二百万年以前，与它同时期的动物如剑齿虎等，都早已灭绝并已成为化石，而大熊猫却一直生存至今，被人们称为“活化石”。现在，大熊猫主要分布在中国的四川、甘肃、西藏等地，由于其稀少而倍显珍贵，已被世界环保组织列为一级保护动物。

1997年版中国熊猫金银币系列共17个品种。其中金币6种，银币3种，彩色银币2种，铂币2种，双金属币4种。1997年版熊猫彩色银币是中国人民银行首次发行的彩色银币。熊猫金银币由中国人民银行发行，分别由上海造币厂、沈阳造币厂、深圳国宝金币制造厂、中国金币总公司铸造，中国金币总公司总经销。正面图案均为北京天坛祈年殿。背面图案：金币、铂币为熊猫松竹图及面额；精制银币为母子熊猫图及面额；普制银币为熊猫松竹图、小溪边的熊猫及面额；彩色银币为彩色大熊猫行走图及面额；双金属币为双熊猫嬉戏图、熊猫攀树图及面额。

Since the 1982 issue of the Chinese panda gold and silver coins, this series has been fond of by coin collectors and investors in and out of China. 1997 issue of the panda gold and silver coins is the 16th set in the series. The design style of the panda gold and silver coins is different from that of the similar coins abroad. Though the material, quality and specification are roughly the same, the panda coins change pictures annually to achieve both the collecting and investing results. Diversiform pandas vividly appear in the gold and silver coins, which lay a foundation for Chinese panda coins entering the international coin market.

Panda, also called giant panda, is the most ancient animal whose ancestor could be traced to 12 million years ago and has survived until nowadays, while the contemporaneous animals like sabre-toothed tiger has already extinguished and become fossil, so it is called 'live fossil'. Panda is only distributed over Sichuan, Gansu, and Tibet, China. It is treasured because of its scarcity and has been listed as the first-class protected animals by the World Environmental Protection Organization.

1997 issue of Chinese panda gold and silver coins contain 17 kinds: 6 kinds of gold coins, 3 kinds of silver coins, 2 kinds of color silver coins, 2 kinds of platinum coins and 4 kinds of bi-metallic coins. It was the first time that the People's Bank of China issued the color coins. The above coins were issued by the People's Bank of China, minted by Shanghai Mint, Shenyang Mint, Shenzhen Panda Gold Coin Mint and China Gold Coin Inc. respectively, distributed by China Gold Coin Inc..The common obverse depicts the picture of the Hall for Prayer for Good Harvests of the Temple of Heaven in Beijing. The reverses of the gold and platinum coins depict the picture of the pandas with pine and bamboo, and face value; and that of proof silver coins depict the picture of the mother and baby pandas, and face value; and that of the bu. silver coins depict the picture of the pandas with pine and bamboo, the panda by the brook and face value; and that of the color silver coins depict the picture of the walking panda and face value; and that of the bi-metallic coins depict the picture of the two playing pandas, panda climbing the tree and face value.

正　面

原　大 Full Size

面额（元）	2000
直径（毫米）	90
含纯金（公斤）	1
成色（%）	99.99
质量	精制
年号	1997
发行量（枚）	58
铸造单位	上海造币厂

Face Value (Yuan)	2000
Diameter (mm)	90
Pure Gold Content (kg)	1
Fineness (%)	99.99
Quality	Proof
Issuing Year	1997
Mintage (Pieces)	58
Minted by	Shanghai Mint

共同正面

原　　大 Full Size

放　　大

面额（元）	100	50	25	10	5
直径（毫米）	32	27	22	18	14
含纯金（盎司）	1	1/2	1/4	1 /10	1/20
成色（％）	99.9	99.9	99.9	99.9	99.9
质量	普制	普制	普制	普制	普制
年号	1997	1997	1997	1997	1997
发行量（枚）					
铸造单位	上海造币厂 沈阳造币厂				

Face Value (Yuan)	100	50	25	10	5
Diameter (mm)	32	27	22	18	14
Pure Gold Content (oz)	1	1/2	1/4	1 /10	1/20
Fineness (%)	99.9	99.9	99.9	99.9	99.9
Quality	Bu.	Bu.	Bu.	Bu.	Bu.
Issuing Year	1997	1997	1997	1997	1997
Mintage (Pieces)					
Minted by	Shanghai Mint Shenyang Mint				

正　面

正　面

正　面

原　大　Full Size

面额（元）	100	10	5
直径（毫米）	80	40	33
含纯银（盎司）	12	1	1/2
成色（%）	99.9	99.9	99.9
质量	精制	普制	普制
年号	1997	1997	1997
发行量（枚）	2500		
铸造单位	上海造币厂	上海造币厂 沈阳造币厂	深圳国宝金币制造厂

Face Value (Yuan)	100	10	5
Diameter (mm)	80	40	33
Pure Silver Content (oz)	12	1	1/2
Fineness (%)	99.9	99.9	99.9
Quality	Proof	Bu.	Bu.
Issuing Year	1997	1997	1997
Mintage (Pieces)	2500		
Minted by	Shanghai Mint	Shanghai Mint Shenyang Mint	Shenzhen Panda Gold Coin Mint

共同正面

原　大 Full Size

放　大

面额（元）	10	5
直径（毫米）	18	14
含纯铂（盎司）	1/10	1/20
成色（%）	99.95	99.95
质量	普制	普制
年号	1997	1997
发行量（枚）	2500	5000
铸造单位	中国金币总公司	

Face Value (Yuan)	10	5
Diameter (mm)	18	14
Pure Platinum Content (oz)	1/10	1/20
Fineness (%)	99.95	99.95
Quality	Bu.	Bu.
Issuing Year	1997	1997
Mintage (Pieces)	2500	5000
Minted by	China Gold Coin Inc.	

正　面

原　大 Full Size

面额（元）	500
直径（毫米）	80
含纯金（盎司）	5
含纯银（盎司）	2
成色（%）	99.99
质量	精 制
年号	1997
发行量（枚）	199
铸造单位	上海造币厂

Face Value (Yuan)	500
Diameter (mm)	80
Pure Gold Content (oz)	5
Pure Silver Content (oz)	2
Fineness (%)	99.99
Quality	Proof
Issuing Year	1997
Mintage (Pieces)	199
Minted by	Shanghai Mint

正 面

正 面

正 面

原 大 Full Size

面额（元）	50	25	10
直径（毫米）	36	30	23
含纯金（盎司）	1/2	1/4	1/10
含纯银（盎司）	1/5	1/8	1 /28
成色（%）	99.9	99.9	99.9
质量	精制	精制	精制
年号	1997	1997	1997
发行量（枚）	2800	2800	2800
铸造单位	沈阳造币厂		

Face Value (Yuan)	50	25	10
Diameter (mm)	36	30	23
Pure Gold Content (oz)	1/2	1/4	1/10
Pure Silver Content (oz)	1/5	1/8	1 /28
Fineness (%)	99.9	99.9	99.9
Quality	Proof	Proof	Proof
Issuing Year	1997	1997	1997
Mintage (Pieces)	2800	2800	2800
Minted by	Shenyang Mint		

共同正面

放 大

原 大 Full Size

面额（元）	10	5
直径（毫米）	40	36
含纯银（盎司）	1	1/2
成色（%）	99.9	99.9
质量	精制	精制
年号	1997	1997
发行量（枚）	100000	100000
铸造单位	中国金币总公司	

Face Value (Yuan)	10	5
Diameter (mm)	40	36
Pure Silver Content (oz)	1	1/2
Fineness (%)	99.9	99.9
Quality	Proof	Proof
Issuing Year	1997	1997
Mintage (Pieces)	100000	100000
Minted by	China Gold Coin Inc.	

Series of Chinese Twelve
Animals of Lunar Calendar
—The Year of the Ox
Gold and Silver Coins

中國貴金屬紀念幣章鑒

二、中国十二生肖系列——丁丑（牛）年金银币

一九九七年

1997年为中国农历丁丑（牛）年，中国人民银行为此发行中国丁丑（牛）年金银币，分别由上海造币厂、沈阳造币厂、深圳国宝金币制造厂、中国金币总公司铸造，中国金币总公司总经销。

就中国十二生肖民俗而言，有关牛与地支“乙”相配之最早文献见于1975年湖北省云梦睡虎出土的秦简《日书》所载：“丑，牛也。”牛，性格驯顺，体态雄壮，力大无穷，甘于奉献，乃是中国古代“六畜”之首。早在新石器时代，中国先民即开始驯牛。随着古代农业的发展，牛更成为人们从事农耕之得力助手。

中国先民视牛为予幸福、吉祥之神兽，且象征智慧。中国古代敬神、祭祀大典，牛为必备祭礼。中国人认为牛是人类忠实的伙伴，尤敬其吃苦耐劳、坚韧不拔的奉献精神，认为牛年既是创业、奋进之年，又为事业通达、大获成功之年。

这套中国丁丑(牛) 年金银币共12个品种。1盎司精制银币2种，1盎司精制金币、铂币各1种，正面图案均为国徽、国号、年号，背面图案均为黄胄所绘牛及面额。12盎司精制金币、银币各1种，正面图案均为国号、年号、南京明远楼，背面图案均为刘继卣所绘牛及面额。1公斤精制金币(梅花型)1种，正面图案为国号、年号、南京明远楼，背面图案为马骀所绘牛及面额。1/10盎司普制金币1种，正面图案为国号、年号、南京明远楼，背面图案为小牛图及面额。5盎司精制金币、银币各1种，正面图案均为国号、年号、南京明远楼，背面图案为张大千所绘牛及面额。1/2盎司精制金币(梅花型)1种，2/3盎司精制银币(梅花型)1种，正面图案均为国号、年号、南京明远楼，背面图案均为马晋所绘牛及面额。

1997 was the Chinese traditional year of the ox of the Twelve Year Animal Cycle, the People's Bank of China issued the year of the ox gold and silver coins for this year, minted by Shanghai Mint, Shenyang Mint, Shenzhen Panda Gold Coin Mint and China Gold Coin Inc. respectively, distributed by China Gold Coin Inc..

In terms of the Chinese tradition of the Duodecimal Animal Cycle, the earliest recordation about the match between the ox and one of the twelve *dizhi* (earthly branches) *chou* was found in *Rishu* (Day book), the bamboo-strip almanacs of the Qin period which was uncovered at Shuihudi of Yunmeng, Hubei province, in 1975.It says '*chou* is ox'. The ox is tame and docile, and it has powerful carriage. It is of prodigious strength and is ready to devote itself, so it was named the head of the 'six livestock' in ancient China. As early as the Neolithic age Chinese ancients have already domesticated ox. Ox has become the farmers' right hand with the development of ancient agriculture.

Chinese ancients regarded ox as a supernatural animal that could grant them blessedness and auspiciousness, and they thought it also symbolized wisdom. Ox was always an offering in Chinese ancient grand ceremonies for godliness and offering sacrifices to ancestors. Chinese people think that ox is a faithful friend of human beings, and they especially respect its devoting sprit of hardworking, being unafraid of hardships and grittiness. They believe that the year of the ox is both a year of starting a business and bracing up, and a year of success.

This set contains 12 kinds: 2 kinds of proof silver coins, 1 oz. proof gold and platinum coins have the obverses depicting the picture of the national emblem, title of PRC and the issuing year, and the reverses depicting the picture of the drawing of ox drawn by Huang Zhou and face value. 12 oz. proof gold and silver coins have the obverses depicting the picture of the national emblem, issuing year and the Mingyuan Tower in Nanjing, and the reverses depicting the picture of the drawing of ox drawn by Liu Jiyou and face value. 1 kg proof gold coin (plum blossom type) has the obverse depicting the picture of the national emblem, issuing year and the Mingyuan Tower in Nanjing, and the reverse depicting the picture of the drawing of ox drawn by Ma Dai and face value. 1/10 oz. bu. gold coin has the obverse depicting the picture of the national emblem, issuing year and the Mingyuan Tower in Nanjing, and the reverse depicting the picture of the drawing of calf and face value. 5 oz. proof gold and silver coins have the obverses depicting the picture of the national emblem, issuing year and the Mingyuan Tower in Nanjing, and the reverses depicting the picture of the drawing of ox drawn by Zhang Daqian and face value. The 1/2 oz. proof gold (plum blossom type) and 2/3 oz. proof silver coins (plum blossom type) have the obverses depicting the picture of the national emblem, issuing year and the Mingyuan Tower in Nanjing, and the reverses depicting the picture of the drawing of ox drawn by Ma Jin and face value.

正　面

原　大 Full Size

面额（元）	1000
直径（毫米）	70
含纯金（盎司）	12
成色（%）	99.9
质量	精制
年号	1997
发行量（枚）	99
铸造单位	上海造币厂

Face Value (Yuan)	1000
Diameter (mm)	70
Pure Gold Content (oz)	12
Fineness (%)	99.9
Quality	Proof
Issuing Year	1997
Mintage (Pieces)	99
Minted by	Shanghai Mint

共同正面

原　　大 Full Size

面额（元）	500	100	10
直径（毫米）	60	32	18
含纯金（盎司）	5	1	1/10
成色（%）	99.9	99.9	99.9
质量	精制	精制	普制
年号	1997	1997	1997
发行量（枚）	99	1600	48000
铸造单位	沈阳造币厂	上海造币厂	深圳国宝金币制造厂

Face Value (Yuan)	500	100	10
Diameter (mm)	60	32	18
Pure Gold Content (oz)	5	1	1/10
Fineness (%)	99.9	99.9	99.9
Quality	Proof	Proof	Bu.
Issuing Year	1997	1997	1997
Mintage (Pieces)	99	1600	48000
Minted by	Shenyang Mint	Shanghai Mint	Shenzhen Panda Gold Coin Mint

正　面

正　面

原　大 Full Size

面额（元）	2000	100
直径（毫米）	100	27
含纯金（公斤）	1	
含纯金（盎司）		0.458
成色（%）	99.9	91.6
质量	精制	精制
年号	1997	1997
发行量（枚）	15	2300
铸造单位	上海造币厂	沈阳造币厂

Face Value (Yuan)	2000	100
Diameter (mm)	100	27
Pure Gold Content(kg)	1	
Pure Gold Content(oz)		0.458
Fineness (%)	99.9	91.6
Quality	Proof	Proof
Issuing Year	1997	1997
Mintage (Pieces)	15	2300
Minted by	Shanghai Mint	Shenyang Mint

正　面

放　大

原　大 Full Size

面额（元）	100
直径（毫米）	32
含纯铂（盎司）	1
成色（%）	99.95
质量	精制
年号	1997
发行量（枚）	300
铸造单位	中国金币总公司

Face Value (Yuan)	100
Diameter (mm)	32
Pure Platinum Content (oz)	1
Fineness (%)	99.95
Quality	Proof
Issuing Year	1997
Mintage (Pieces)	300
Minted by	China Gold Coin Inc.

正 面 正 面

原 大 Full Size

面额（元）	100	5 0
直径（毫米）	80	70
含纯银（盎司）	12	5
成色（%）	99.9	99.9
质量	精制	精制
年号	1997	1997
发行量（枚）	500	1000
铸造单位	上海造币厂	沈阳造币厂

Face Value (Yuan)	100	50
Diameter (mm)	80	70
Pure Silver Content (oz)	12	5
Fineness (%)	99.9	99.9
Quality	Proof	Proof
Issuing Year	1997	1997
Mintage (Pieces)	500	1000
Minted by	Shanghai Mint	Shenyang Mint

共同正面

放　大

原　大 Full Size

面额（元）	10	10
直径（毫米）	40	32
含纯银（盎司）	1	1
成色（%）	99.9	99.9
质量	普制	精制
年号	1997	1997
发行量（枚）	50000	8000
铸造单位	上海造币厂	

Face Value (Yuan)	10	10
Diameter (mm)	40	32
Pure Silver Content (oz)	1	1
Fineness (%)	99.9	99.9
Quality	Bu.	Proof
Issuing Year	1997	1997
Mintage (Pieces)	50000	8000
Minted by	Shanghai Mint	

正 面

原 大 Full Size

放 大

面额（元）	10
直径（毫米）	36
含纯银（盎司）	0.6
成色（%）	90
质量	精制
年号	1997
发行量（枚）	6800
铸造单位	沈阳造币厂

Face Value (Yuan)	10
Diameter (mm)	36
Pure Silver Content (oz)	0.6
Fineness (%)	90
Quality	Proof
Issuing Year	1997
Mintage (Pieces)	6800
Minted by	Shenyang Mint

Series of Chinese Modern
Famous Paintings — Qi Baishi
Commemorative Coins

中國貴金屬紀念幣圖鑒

三、中国近代名画系列
——齐白石纪念币

一九九七年

为纪念齐白石先生逝世40周年，中国人民银行发行中国国画大师齐白石纪念币。该套纪念币由沈阳造币厂铸造，中国金币总公司总经销。

齐白石(1864～1957年)，中国近现代杰出的国画艺术大师、篆刻家、书法家和诗人。原名纯芝，字渭清，号兰亭；后更名璜，字滨生，号白石，别号借山吟馆主者、寄萍老人等。1957年9月，齐白石在北京病逝。

齐白石在绘画上不拘泥于前人技法，勇于探索，大胆革新，融汇了传统写意画和民间绘画的表现方法，主张作画“妙在似与不似之间，太似为媚俗，不似为欺世”，笔墨造型简练朴质，色彩鲜明热烈，格调清新，在艺术上达到了巧夺天工的卓越境界。

齐白石的画，题材非常广泛，其人物、山水、花卉画都有很高的艺术成就，尤精于画花鸟、草虫和鱼虾。他自谓一生是“为万虫写照，为百鸟传神”。他著名的画幅有《虾》、《松鼠葡萄》、《渔村夕照》、《老少年豆荚昆虫》、《延年益寿》、《钟馗》等。

中国国画大师齐白石纪念币共8个品种。其中1/2盎司精制金币(方型)和1盎司精制银币(方型)各1种，其背面图案均为齐白石所绘《松鼠葡萄》及面额；1盎司精制银币(方型)1种，其背面图案为齐白石所绘《虾》及面额；5盎司精制金币、银币各1种，其背面图案为齐白石所绘《大利》图及面额；12盎司精制银币1种，其背面图案为齐白石所绘《老少年豆荚昆虫》及面额；1公斤精制金币、银币各1种，其背面图案均为齐白石所绘《延年益寿》及面额。该套纪念币的正面图案均为国号、年号和齐白石肖像。

To mark the 40th anniversary of Mr. Qi Baishi's death, the People's Bank of China issued Qi Baishi commemorative coins minted and distributed by Shenyang Mint and China Gold Coin Inc. respectively.

Qi Baishi (1864 ~ 1957), a modern outstanding master of traditional Chinese painting, was named Chunzhi originally, with a style Weqing, assumed name lanting. Later he changed his name to Huang, style to Binsheng, assumed name Baishi and aliases as Host of the Jieshanyin House and Jiping Old Man etc. He died in Beijing in September 1957.

Qi Baishi was not limited to the techniques used by those earlier painters. Instead he explored and reformed bravely, combining the methods of traditional freehand brushwork painting and folk paintings. He holds that a good painting lies in the ambiguity between similarity and dissimilarity with simple and unadorned outline, bright color and fresh style, his works excels nature in artistic skills.

Qi Baishi's works range widely from figure paintings, landscape paintings to flower pieces with high artistic achievements. He was especially good at flower-and-bird, grass-and-insect, fish-and-shrimp paintings. He said himself to be painting all birds and insects all his life. His famous works include *Shrimp, Squirrel and Grape, Sunset of the Fishing village, The Child-like old and Pod and Insect, Prolong Life, Zhongkui* etc.

Qi Baishi Commemorative Coins include 8 kinds of coins: 1/2 oz. proof gold coin in square and 1 oz. proof silver coin in square, both having a common reverse depicting the picture of *Squirrel and Grape* by Qi Baishi and face values; 1 oz. proof silver coin in square with the reverse depicting the picture of *Shrimp* by Qi Baishi and face value; 5 oz. proof gold and silver coins each with the reverses depicting the picture of *Dali* (Unusually Lucky) by Qi Baishi and face value; one 12 oz. proof silver coin with the reverse depicting the picture of *Child-like Old and Pod and Insect* by Qi Baishi and face value; one 1 kg proof gold coin and one 1 kg proof silver coin with a common reverse depicting the picture of *Prolong Life* by Qi Baishi and face value .The obverses of this set all depict the picture of the title of PRC, issuing year and the statue of Qi Baishi.

正　面

原　大 Full Size

面额（元）	2000
直径（毫米）	100
含纯金（公斤）	1
成色（%）	99.9
质量	精制
年号	1997
发行量（枚）	25
铸造单位	沈阳造币厂

Face Value (Yuan)	2000
Diameter (mm)	100
Pure Gold Content (kg)	1
Fineness (%)	99.9
Quality	Proof
Issuing Year	1997
Mintage (Pieces)	25
Minted by	Shenyang Mint

正　面

正　面

原　大 Full Size

面额（元）	500	50
直径（毫米）	60	
规格（毫米）		19 × 29
含纯金（盎司）	5	1/2
成色（%）	99.9	99.9
质量	精制	精制
年号	1997	1997
发行量（枚）	99	5000
铸造单位		沈阳造币厂

Face Value (Yuan)	500	50
Diameter (mm)	60	
Size (mm)		19 × 29
Pure Gold Content (oz)	5	1/2
Fineness (%)	99.9	99.9
Quality	Proof	Proof
Issuing Year	1997	1997
Mintage (Pieces)	99	5000
Minted by		Shenyang Mint

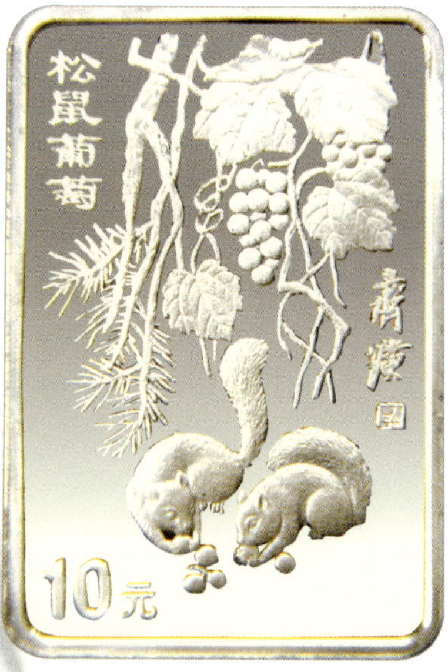

共同正面

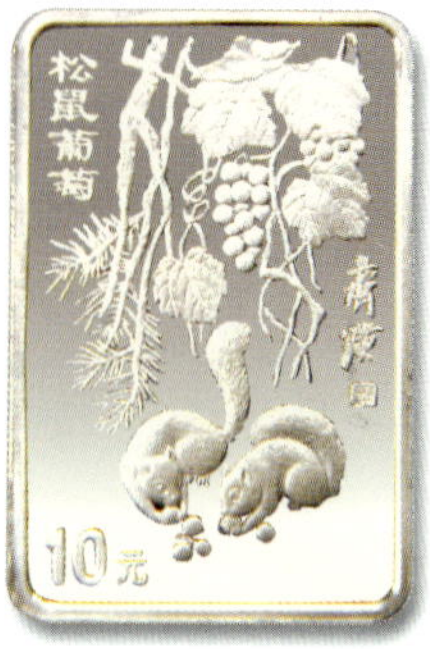

放　大

原　大 Full Size

面额（元）	10	10
规格（毫米）	27.5 × 42	27.5 × 42
含纯银（盎司）	1	1
成色（%）	99.9	99.9
质量	精制	精制
年号	1997	1997
发行量（枚）	11800	11800
铸造单位		沈阳造币厂

Face Value (Yuan)	10	10
Size (mm)	27.5 × 42	27.5 × 42
Pure Silver Content (oz)	1	1
Fineness (%)	99.9	99.9
Quality	Proof	Proof
Issuing Year	1997	1997
Mintage (Pieces)	11800	11800
Minted by		Shenyang Mint

正 面

原 大 Full Size

面额（元）	200
直径（毫米）	100
含纯银（公斤）	1
成色（%）	99.9
质量	精制
年号	1997
发行量（枚）	188
铸造单位	沈阳造币厂

Face Value (Yuan)	200
Diameter (mm)	100
Pure Silver Content (kg)	1
Fineness (%)	99.9
Quality	Proof
Issuing Year	1997
Mintage (Pieces)	188
Minted by	Shenyang Mint

正 面

原 大 Full Size

面额（元）	100
直径（毫米）	80
含纯银（盎司）	12
成色（％）	99.9
质量	精制
年号	1997
发行量（枚）	380
铸造单位	沈阳造币厂

Face Value (Yuan)	100
Diameter (mm)	80
Pure Silver Content (oz)	12
Fineness (%)	99.9
Quality	Proof
Issuing Year	1997
Mintage (Pieces)	380
Minted by	Shenyang Mint

正 面

原 大 Full Size

面额（元）	50	Face Value (Yuan)	50
直径（毫米）	70	Diameter (mm)	70
含纯银（盎司）	5	Pure Silver Content (oz)	5
成色（%）	99.9	Fineness (%)	99.9
质量	精制	Quality	Proof
年号	1997	Issuing Year	1997
发行量（枚）	999	Mintage (Pieces)	999
铸造单位	沈阳造币厂	Minted by	Shenyang Mint

1997 Issue of
Ma Zu Silver Coin

中國貴金屬紀念幣年鑒

四、1997年版妈祖银币

一九九七年

为了弘扬中华民族传统文化，中国人民银行发行1997年版妈祖银币。该币由上海造币厂铸造，中国金币总公司总经销。

妈祖是中国东南沿海著名的海上保护神。传说这位女神曾生活在人间，生于宋太祖建隆元年三月二十三，逝于宋太宗雍熙四年九月初九，这位姑娘生时“能言人休咎”，“能知人祸福”，通晓天文气象，擅长海上救护，精通医学，治病防疫，深受爱戴。在她死后，乡人就在湄洲岛上建了一个供养她的小庙以示感念。据说姑娘死后成为海神，继续保佑乡里，感应更为灵验，逐步成为东南沿海百姓共同的保护神。妈祖信仰也成了人们怀土思乡的重要寄托。

宋朝、元朝以来，妈祖屡受朝廷赐封，实际上妈祖在东南沿海的居民中一直受到真诚的供奉，已无需赐封来增添荣耀，只不过朝廷的赐封进一步扩大了妈祖信仰的区域而已。

1997年版妈祖银币为1盎司普制银币1种，正面图案为湄洲妈祖庙、国号、年号，背面图案为妈祖头像及面额。

To expand the influence of chinese traditional culture,the People's Bank of China issued 1997 Issue of Ma Zu Silver Coin,minted by Shanghai Mint and distributed by China Gold Coin Inc..

Ma Zu is a well-known protective goddess in the southeast littoral of China.In legend,she is said to have been living in our earthly world,and born on March 23 of the 1st year of Jianlong of Emperor Taizu of the Song Dynasty,and died on Sept 9 of the 4th year of Xiyong of Taizong of the same dynasty.In her lifetime,she could predict people's birth and death,weal and woe;expert at astronomy and weather,and was good at marine rescue,medicine,sickness-curing and epidemic prevention.Thus she was deeply loved by people.After her death,the villagers set up a small temple on Meizhou Island dedicated to her to express their gratitude.It is said that she became the sea goddess and went on protecting the land with sharper prognostication. Gradually Ma Zu has become the common protective goddess of the southeast people. The belief in Ma Zu has been an important soritual sustenance for people's homesickness.

Glories had been bestowed on Ma Zu by the royal courts of both Song and Yuan Dynasty .In fact she did not need those honors at all because she has been sincerely worshiped by people off the southeast sea coast.The bestowals only helped to enlarge the areas where people worship her.

1997 Issue of Ma Zu Silver Coin is one 1 oz. silver bu.coin,with the obverse depicting the picture of the Ma Zu Temple in Meizhou,title of PRC and the issuing year,and with the reverse depicting the picture of the statue of Ma Zu and face value.

正　面

原　大 Full Size

放　大

面额（元）	10
直径（毫米）	40
含纯银（盎司）	1
成色（%）	99.9
质量	普制
年号	1997
发行量（枚）	50000
铸造单位	上海造币厂

Face Value (Yuan)	10
Diameter (mm)	40
Pure Silver Content (oz)	1
Fineness (%)	99.9
Quality	Bu.
Issuing Year	1997
Mintage (Pieces)	50000
Minted by	Shanghai Mint

1997 Issue of the
Avalokitesvara Buddha
Gold and Silver Coin
Series

中國貴金屬紀念幣圖鑒

五、1997年版观世音菩萨金银币

一九九七年

为使世界了解中国文化传统，中国人民银行发行1997年版观世音菩萨金银币。该套币由上海造币厂铸造，中国金币总公司总经销。

观世音是梵文Avalokites' Vara的意译，据说其可以“观察”世界上的一切声音，所以名为“观世音”菩萨。唐代避李世民之讳，改称为观音。据佛经所载，观世音为了教化不同层次、不同环境的众生，可以化现出三十二种化身及观音本相共三十三身。后来佛教根据观音三十三身的说法，绘制了三十三种观音的画像，即“三十三观音”。

浙江省境内的普陀山是中国四大佛教名山之一。据说五代时和尚慧锷建“不肯去”观音院，开创佛寺之始。从此，普陀山成为供奉观音的道场。

该套金银币共有6个品种。其中1/10盎司、1/20盎司金币各1种，1盎司普制银币1种，1/2盎司精制银币2种(左手托瓶观音和右手托瓶观音各1种)，其背面图案为半身玉瓶观音像及面额；另有3.3两精制银币1种，其背面图案为送子观音像及面额。这套金银币的正面图案均为国号、年号、普陀山。

To inform the world of Chinese traditional culture, the People's Bank of China issued 1997 Issue of the Avalokitesvara Buddha Gold and Silver Coins minted and distributed by Shanghai Mint and China Gold Coin Inc. respectively.

Guanshiyin is a Chinese transliteration of the Sanskrit word Avalokitesvara. It is said that He could 'observe' all of the sound in the world, and so He is called 'observe the sound in the world' Buddha (Chinese *Guanshiyin*). In the Tang Dynasty He was renamed 'observe the sound' (Chinese *Guanyin*) to avoid the taboo on the personal name of Emperor Li Shimin. According to the Buddhist Scripture, Avalokitesvara could appear as 32 kinds of nirmanakaya (metamorphosic body) and His true body totaling 33 bodies in order to moralize all living creatures of various levels and circumstances. Subsequently Buddhism had drawn 33 kinds of portraits of Avalokitesvara according to this, called '33 Avalokitesvara'.

The Putuo Mount situated in Zhejiang province is one of the Chinese Four Famous Buddhist Mounts. It is said that a monk named Hui-e built an Avalokitesvara temple named 'Not Willing to Go' in the Five Dynasties time, which marked the beginning of temple construction on the Putuo Mount. Since then the Putuo Mount has become the rite of making offerings to Avalokitesvara.

1997 issue of the Avalokitesvara gold and silver coins includes 6 kinds: 1/10 oz. and 1/20 oz. gold coins, 1 oz. bu. silver coin, two kinds of 1/2 oz. proof silver coins (Holding-bowl with left hand Avalokitesvara and holding-bowl with Right Hand Avalokitesvara), with a common reverse depicting the picture of the bust of Jade Flask Avalokitesvara and face value. There's one with 3.3 liang (165g) proof silver coin with the reverse depicting the picture of the Statue of Birth Giving Avalokitesvara and face value. The obverses of this set all depict the picture of the title of PRC, issuing year and the Putuo Mount.

放　大

共同正面

原　大 Full Size

面额（元）	10	5
直径（毫米）	18	14
含纯金（盎司）	1/10	1/20
成色（%）	99.9	99.9
质量	普制	普制
年号	1997	1997
发行量（枚）	10000	35000
铸造单位	上海造币厂	

Face Value (Yuan)	10	5
Diameter (mm)	18	14
Pure Gold Content (oz)	1/10	1/20
Fineness (%)	99.9	99.9
Quality	Bu.	Bu.
Issuing Year	1997	1997
Mintage (Pieces)	10000	35000
Minted by	Shanghai Mint	

共同正面

原 大 Full Size

面额（元）	50	10	5	5
直径（毫米）	60	40	33	33
含纯银（盎司）		1	1/2	1/2
含纯银（两）	3.3			
成色（%）	99.9	99.9	99.9	99.9
质量	精制	普制	精制	精制
年号	1997	1997	1997	1997
发行量（枚）	5000	30000	10000	10000
铸造单位	上海造币厂			

Face Value (Yuan)	50	10	5	5
Diameter (mm)	60	40	33	33
Pure Silver Content (oz)		1	1/2	1/2
Pure Silver Content (Liang)	3.3			
Fineness (%)	99.9	99.9	99.9	99.9
Quality	Proof	Bu.	Proof	Proof
Issuing Year	1997	1997	1997	1997
Mintage (Pieces)	5000	30000	10000	10000
Minted by	Shanghai Mint			

1997 Issue of Unicorn
Gold and Silver Coin Series

中國貴金屬紀念幣圖鑑

六、1997年版麒麟金银币

一九九七年

麒麟是人们传统中的一种罕见的神灵吉祥之物，古代以麟出现为祥瑞，因此又称麟为“祥麟”。为了弘扬中国传统文化，中国人民银行发行1997年版麒麟金银币，该套币分别由深圳国宝金币制造厂、中国金币总公司铸造，中国金币总公司总经销。

古代传说麟是龙子，即龙与母牛交配而产，麒麟的形态是“麇身、牛尾、狼蹄、一角”。大凡遇麟出现，是被当作大瑞现象报告给官府的，朝廷还要举行仪式或以某种形式来承应天赐祥瑞的，在中国最早的诗歌总集《诗经》中有《麟之趾》一诗，用麟的形象来赞美宽厚仁爱的文王，可见麟不仅神灵之极，而且仁厚之至。这种对麟的赞美在我们今天的语言中还可以看出痕迹，如“凤毛麟角”、“麒麟儿”。

1997年版麒麟金银币共发行5个品种，包括1/10盎司精制金币1种，普制银币2种（1盎司、20克各1种），1盎司精制银币1种，1盎司精制铂币1种。正面图案均为国号、年号、麒麟，背面图案均为西方独角兽及面额。

Unicorn is a kind of unusually magic and auspicious animal in Chinese tradition. In the ancient time, people took the appearance of unicorn as a kind of auspicious sign, so they also called unicorn 'auspicious unicorn'. To enhance Chinese traditional culture, the People's Bank of China issued the 1997 issue of unicorn gold and silver coins, minted by Shenzhen Panda Gold Coin Mint and China Gold Coin Inc. respectively, distributed by the latter.

In the ancient legend, unicorn was the son of dragon and cow. Its shape was 'the body of an elk, the tail of an ox, the hoofs of a wolf and a single horn'. Once the unicorn appeared it would be taken as a great auspicious sign to be reported to the government. The royal court would perform a ceremony or other forms to thank the heaven bestowing the auspicious sign. *Book of Poetry*, the earliest anthology of verse of China, has a verse titled *The Good Unicorn*, which praises the clement and kindhearted King Wen as the image of unicorn, thus shows the unicorn is not only very magic but also very clement and kindhearted. This kind of praise of the unicorn can still be traced to nowadays language, such as 'precious and rare as phoenix feathers and unicorn horns' and 'the son of unicorn' etc.

1997 issue of unicorn gold and silver coins include 5 kinds of coins: one kind of 1/10oz.proof gold coin, two kinds of bu. silver coins (1 oz. and 20g), one kind of 1 oz .proof silver coin, one kind of 1 oz.proof platinum coin. The obverses all depict the picture of the title of PRC, issuing year and unicorn, and the reverses all depict the picture of western unicorn and face value.

放 大

正 面

原 大 Full Size

面额（元）	10
直径（毫米）	18
含纯金（盎司）	1/10
成色（%）	99.9
质量	精制
年号	1997
发行量（枚）	5000
铸造单位	深圳国宝金币制造厂

Face Value (Yuan)	10
Diameter (mm)	18
Pure Gold Content (oz)	1/10
Fineness (%)	99.9
Quality	Proof
Issuing Year	1997
Mintage (Pieces)	5000
Minted by	Shenzhen Panda Gold Coin Mint

共同正面

放　大

原　大 Full Size

面额（元）	10	10
直径（毫米）	40	40
含纯银（盎司）	1	1
成色（%）	99.9	99.9
质量	精制	普制
年号	1997	1997
发行量（枚）	8000	
铸造单位	深圳国宝金币制造厂	

Face Value (Yuan)	10	10
Diameter (mm)	40	40
Pure Silver Content (oz)	1	1
Fineness (%)	99.9	99.9
Quality	Proof	Bu.
Issuing Year	1997	1997
Mintage (Pieces)	8000	
Minted by	Shenzhen Panda Gold Coin Mint	

放　大

正　面

原　大 Full Size

面额（元）	5
直径（毫米）	36
含纯银（克）	20
成色（%）	99.9
质量	普制
年号	1997
铸造单位	深圳国宝金币制造厂

Face Value (Yuan)	5
Diameter (mm)	36
Pure Silver Content (g)	20
Fineness (%)	99.9
Quality	Bu.
Issuing Year	1997
Minted by	Shenzhen Panda Gold Coin Mint

面额（元）	100	Face Value (Yuan)	100
直径（毫米）	32	Diameter (mm)	32
含纯铂（盎司）	1	Pure Platinum Content (oz)	1
成色（%）	99.9	Fineness (%)	99.9
质量	精制	Quality	Proof
年号	1997	Issuing Year	1997
发行量（枚）	500	Mintage (Pieces)	500
铸造单位	中国金币总公司	Minted by	China Gold Coin Inc.

World Wild Animals
Foundation
Commemorative Coin
(Panda Silver Coin)

中國貴金屬紀念幣考鑒

七、世界野生动物基金会纪念币（熊猫银币）

一九九七年

为宣传世界野生动物基金会为保护世界范围内野生生物所作出的杰出贡献，中国人民银行于1997年发行世界野生动物基金会纪念币(熊猫银币)。该币由上海造币厂铸造，中国金币总公司总经销。

世界野生动物基金会成立于1961年，是为保护世界自然环境及生物而建立的资金援助机构，总部设在瑞士，在许多国家设有基金会的本国委员会。1988年后更名为“世界自然保护基金会”。该机构以资金援助的方式推进各国通过开展宣传活动和教育事业以及必要的救助和保护活动，达到保护自然特别是自然界生存的野生生物的目的。中国于1980年3月加入该机构，接受其在自然保护事业各方面的资金和人才援助。

世界野生动物基金会纪念币(熊猫银币)为15克精制银币1种，其正面图案为国徽、国号及年号，背面图案为熊猫食竹图、野生动物基金会WWF标志及面额。

To publicize the outstanding contributions made by the World Wild Animals Foundation in protecting wild animals on a worldwide scale, the People's Bank of China issued the World Wild Animals Foundation Silver Coin (Panda Silver Coin) minted by Shanghai Mint and distributed by China Gold Coin Inc..

World Wild Animals Foundation was established in 1961 with its headquarter in Switzerland and local committees in many countries. It's a fund-aid organization with the aim of protecting world's natural environment and wild lives. It changed its name to World Nature-protecting Foundation in 1988. It aims at protecting nature, especially the wild lives in existence at present by means of fund aid to promote every nation's propaganda, education cause and necessary rescue and protective activities. China joined in the organization in 1980, accepting its aid in fund and qualified personnel in every aspects of nature protecting cause.

World Wild Animals Foundation commemorative Coin (panda silver coin) is one proof silver coin with a gross weight of 15 grams. The obverse depicts the picture of the national emblem, title of PRC and the issuing year while the reverse depicts the picture of panda eating bamboo, logo of WWF and face value.

正　面

原　大 Full Size

放　大

面额（元）	3
直径（毫米）	30
含纯银（盎司）	0.434
成色（%）	90
质量	精制
年号	1997
发行量（枚）	75000
铸造单位	上海造币厂

Face Value (Yuan)	3
Diameter (mm)	30
Pure Silver Content (oz)	0.434
Fineness (%)	90
Quality	Proof
Issuing Year	1997
Mintage (Pieces)	75000
Minted by	Shanghai Mint

Fifth Set in the Series
of Chinese
Endangered Wild Animals
Gold and Silver Coins

中國貴金屬紀念幣圖鑒

八、中国珍稀野生动物金银币
（第5组）

一九九七年

为了支持和推动拯救、保护濒危珍稀野生动物工作，宣传保护野生动物对人类、自然界生态平衡的意义，中国人民银行于1988年开始发行中国珍稀野生动物金银币，1997年发行了中国珍稀野生动物金银币第5组。该组金银币由沈阳造币厂铸造，中国金币总公司总经销。这组金银币以中华白海豚和白天鹅为题材。

中华白海豚，又名白鳍豚、白暨豚，简称白暨或白旗。小型齿鲸类，淡水豚科。仅产于中国洞庭湖和长江中下游地区，为特有的水生哺乳动物，现存数量仅百头左右。中华白海豚有“长江里的大熊猫”之称，属国家一级保护动物。

白天鹅，古代曾有鹄、白雁等名称。雁形目，鸭科，世界范围内均有分布。总称下有五个不同的种，中国境内有三种：大天鹅、小天鹅、疣鼻天鹅，国家二级保护鸟。天鹅是优雅、高贵、善良、圣洁的象征，是珍贵飞禽。中国新疆的巴音布鲁克“天鹅湖”是最著名的天鹅繁殖基地，江西的鄱阳湖则是最重要的天鹅越冬中心。

此组币共4个品种，其中1/2盎司精制金币1种，1盎司精制银币2种，5盎司精制金币1种。正面图案均为国徽、年号、国号。背面图案：1/2盎司、5盎司金币为母子中华白海豚图、香港远景及面额；2种1盎司银币，一为中华白海豚嬉戏图及面额，一为白天鹅及面额。

To support and promote the work of rescuing and protecting endangered wild animals as well as to propagate the importance of protecting wild animals to the ecological balance of human and nature, the People's Bank of China has been issuing the China Endangered Wild Animals Gold and Silver Coins since 1998. In 1997, the 5th set of China Endangered Wild Animals Gold and Silver Coins were issued, minted by Shenyang Mint and distributed by China Gold Coin Inc.. This set of gold and silver coins takes the Chinese white dolphin and white swan as its subject matter.

Chinese white dolphin also called Baiqi dolphin or Baiji dolphin is abbreviated as Baiji or Baiqi. It belongs to the small teeth whale category and fresh water dolphin family .It only grows in the Dongting Lake and the middle and lower reaches of the Yangtse River. It is a unique aquatic mammal with a limited number of 100 or so. Chinese white dolphin is known as Giant Panda in the Yangtse River and recognized as the first-grade protected animal.

White swan was called Swan (Chinese *hu*) and White Wild Goose (Chinese *baiyan*) etc. It belongs to wild goose order and duck family. In general, it has five species spreading all over the world. In China, there are three species: giant swan, small swan and wart-nosed swan, all being listed as the national second-grade protected birds. Swan, a rare bird, is the symbol of elegance, nobleness, kindness and purity. The Swan Lake in Bayinbuluke of Xinjiang Province of China is the most famous progenitive base for swan while the Boyang Lake of Jiangxi province is the most important overwintering center.

This set of coins contains 4 kinds: one 1/2 oz. proof gold coin ,two kinds of 1 oz. proof silver coins and one 5 oz. proof gold coin, all having a common obverse depicting the picture of the national emblem, issuing year and the title of PRC. The reverses of the 1/2 oz. and 5 oz. gold coins depict the picture of mother dolphin and her baby, Hong Kong's distant view and face value. One of the 1 oz. silver coins has a reverse depicting the picture of playing Chinese White dolphin and face value, and that of the other depicting the picture of white swan and face value.

共同正面

原　大 Full Size

面额（元）	500	50
直径（毫米）	60	27
含纯金（盎司）	5	1/2
成色（%）	99.9	99.9
质量	精制	精制
年号	1997	1997
发行量（枚）	188	30000
铸造单位	沈阳造币厂	

Face Value (Yuan)	500	50
Diameter (mm)	60	27
Pure Gold Content (oz)	5	1/2
Fineness (%)	99.9	99.9
Quality	Proof	Proof
Issuing Year	1997	1997
Mintage (Pieces)	188	30000
Minted by	Shenyang Mint	

共同正面

原 大 Full Size

面额（元）	10	10
直径（毫米）	40	40
含纯银（盎司）	1	1
成色（%）	99.9	99.9
质量	精制	精制
年号	1997	1997
发行量（枚）	68000	68000
铸造单位	沈阳造币厂	

Face Value (Yuan)	10	10
Diameter (mm)	40	40
Pure Silver Content (oz)	1	1
Fineness (%)	99.9	99.9
Quality	Proof	Proof
Issuing Year	1997	1997
Mintage (Pieces)	68000	68000
Minted by	Shenyang Mint	

The Commemorative Coins
of the 70th Anniversary
of the Founding
of the People's Liberation Army

中國貴金屬紀念幣圖鑒

九、中国人民解放军建军
70周年纪念币

一九九七年

为纪念中国人民解放军建军70周年，中国人民银行发行中国人民解放军建军70周年纪念币。该套纪念币由上海造币厂铸造，中国金币总公司总经销。

1927年8月1日，中国共产党发动和领导了南昌起义，打响了武装反抗国民党反动派的第一枪，这个伟大事件标志着中国共产党开始创建自己的革命军队，中国人民解放军从此诞生。光辉的8月1日，成为人民军队建军的纪念日。

中国人民解放军建军70周年纪念币是中华人民共和国成立以来首次发行的以建军为题材的纪念币。此套纪念币共3个品种，其中1/2盎司精制金币1种，1盎司精制银币2种。金币、银币正面图案均为八一军徽、长城、年号、国号及“中国人民解放军建军70周年”字样。1/2盎司精制金币背面图案为毛泽东在井冈山时半身像及面额。2种银币背面图案分别是：一种为南昌起义时的周恩来和其他人物群像及面额；一种为陆海空三军战士像及面额。

To mark the 7oth anniversary of the founding of the People's Liberation Army of China, the People's Bank of China issued the commemorative coins, minted by Shanghai Mint and distributed by China Gold Coin Inc..

On 1st August 1927, the Communist Party of China launched and led Na Chang Uprising firing the first shot against the Kuomintang reactionaries. This event marked the beginning of CCP's establishment of its own revolutionary forces. The people's Liberation Army was founded. The glorious date, August 1, became the commemorative day of the founding of PLA.

The 70th anniversary of the funding of PLA commemorative coin is the first one issued with the theme of the funding of PLA. This set of coins includes 3 kinds: one 1/2 oz. proof gold coin, two kinds of 1 oz. proof silver coins. Both of the gold and silver coins have an obverse depicting the picture of the army emblem, Great Wall, issuing year, title of PRC and the characters '70th Anniversary of the Founding of PLA'. The reverse of the 1/2 oz. proof gold coin depicts the picture of the bust of Mao Zedong on Jinggang Mount and face value. The reverse of one silver coin depicts the picture of the group picture of Zhou Enlai and other figures and face value, and that of the other depicts the picture of the ground-force, naval and air-forced soldiers and face value.

正　面

原　大 Full Size

放　大

面额（元）	50
直径（毫米）	27
含纯金（盎司）	1/2
成色（%）	99.9
质量	精制
年号	1997
发行量（枚）	12000
铸造单位	上海造币厂

Face Value (Yuan)	50
Diameter (mm)	27
Pure Gold Content (oz)	1/2
Fineness (%)	99.9
Quality	Proof
Issuing Year	1997
Mintage (Pieces)	12000
Minted by	Shanghai Mint

共同正面

放　大

原　大 Full Size

面额（元）	10	10
直径（毫米）	40	40
含纯银（盎司）	1	1
成色（%）	99.9	99.9
质量	精制	精制
年号	1997	1997
发行量（枚）	30000	30000
铸造单位	上海造币厂	

Face Value (Yuan)	10	10
Diameter (mm)	40	40
Pure Silver Content (oz)	1	1
Fineness (%)	99.9	99.9
Quality	Proof	Proof
Issuing Year	1997	1997
Mintage (Pieces)	30000	30000
Minted by	Shanghai Mint	

1997 Issue of Chinese
Tourist Year
Commemorative Coin

中國貴金屬紀念幣年鑑

十、1997年中国旅游年纪念币

一九九七年

为纪念“’97中国旅游年”活动，中国人民银行发行1997年中国旅游年纪念币。该币由沈阳造币厂铸造，中国金币总公司总经销。

“’97中国旅游年”活动是国家旅游局和国家民航总局继“’92友好观光年”后又一次联合主办的大型旅游活动，旨在向国际市场进一步展示中国美丽的山水风光、多样的文物古迹、奇特的民俗风情和改革开放的新形象。

旅游年的主题口号是：十二亿人喜迎’97中国旅游年；游中国——全新的感受。活动标志由马踏飞燕、长城和“’97中国旅游年”字样组成。吉祥物为中国国宝大熊猫。

1997年中国旅游年纪念币为1盎司普制熊猫加字银币1种，正面图案为国号、年号、北京天坛祈年殿及“’97中国旅游年”字样，背面图案为大熊猫、松树及面额。

To mark the movement of 1997 Chinese Tourist Year, the People's Bank of China issued the 1997 issue of Chinese Tourist Year commemorative coin, minted by Shenyang Mint and distributed by China Gold Coin Inc..

The 1997 Chinese Tourist Year was another large-scale tourist movement succeeding the 1992 Friendship Tourist Year organized by the joint efforts of National Tourist Bureau and National Civil Aviation Bureau. Its purpose was to further display the picturesque mountain-and-water sceneries of China, various cultural relics and sites, special customs and new look of opening up and reform.

The theme slogan of the tourist year is: Joyously Greeting the 1997 Chinese Tourist Year by 1.2 billion people; and Touring in China—a brand-new experience. The symbol of the movement consists of the Bronze Galloping Horse with a hoof on a Flying Bird, the Great Wall, and Chinese characters ‘’97 Chinese Tourist Year’. The mascot is the Chinese national treasure, giant panda.

The 1997 issue of Chinese Tourist Year is one 1 oz. bu. silver panda coin plus words. The obverse depicts the picture of the title of PRC, issuing year, the Hall of prayer for Good Harvests of the Temple of Heaven in Beijing and Chinese characters ‘’97 Chinese Tourist Year’, and the reverse depicts the picture of giant panda, pine tree and face value.

正 面

原 大 Full Size

放 大

面额（元）	10	Face Value (Yuan)	10
直径（毫米）	40	Diameter (mm)	40
含纯银（盎司）	1	Pure Silver Content (oz)	1
成色（%）	99.9	Fineness (%)	99.9
质量	普制	Quality	Bu.
年号	1997	Issuing Year	1997
发行量（枚）	50000	Mintage (Pieces)	50000
铸造单位	沈阳造币厂	Minted by	Shenyang Mint

The Founding of
Chongqing Municipality
Commemorative Coin

中國貴金屬紀念幣圖鑒

十一、重庆直辖市成立纪念币

一九九七年

为纪念重庆直辖市的成立，中国人民银行发行重庆直辖市成立纪念币。该币由上海造币厂铸造，中国金币总公司总经销。

重庆市是中国西南地区和长江上游最大的经济中心城市。1997年3月14日八届全国人大五次会议批准设立重庆直辖市，成为继北京、天津、上海之后的中国第四个直辖市。新设立的重庆直辖市在原重庆市行政区划的基础上新增四川省的万县市、涪陵市和黔江地区，主要分布在长江沿线，基本处于云贵川藏的腹地，总面积8.24万平方公里，总人口3002万，人口数量居各直辖市之首。

重庆，简称"渝"，作为巴渝文化的发祥地，有文字记载的历史已有3000多年。此次建制直辖市，不仅志在振兴发展西部，带动中国的整体起飞，也为重庆这座历史古城带来了新的生机和蓬勃兴旺的强大动力。

该套纪念币为1盎司普制银币1种，正面图案为国号、年号、北京天坛祈年殿及"重庆直辖市成立纪念"字样，背面图案为大熊猫、松树及面额。

To mark the founding of Chongqing Municipality, the People's Bank of China issued the commemorative coin of the founding of Chongqing Municipality, minted by Shanghai Mint and distributed by China Gold Coin Inc..

Chongqing City is the largest economic center in the southwest of China and the upper reaches of the Yangtse River. On March 14,1997, the 5th conference of the 8th session of People's Congress authorized to establish Changqing Municipality, the fourth one in China following Beijing, Tianjin and Shanghai municipalities. On the basis of the original Chongqing city, the newly founded municipality extends into Wanxian, Fuling and Qianjiang area. It mainly distributes along the Yangtse River and situates in the hinterland of Yunnan,Guizhou, Sichuan and Tibet. It has a total area of 82400 square kilometers, and a population of 30020000, which ranks the first in the four municipalities.

Chongqing, called Yu for short, is the birthplace of the Bayu Culture. It has a 3000-year history of written records. Founding Chongqing Municipality aims at rejuvenating the western area, driving the comprehensive development of China as well as giving impetus and vitality to the historical city.

The commemorative coin of the founding of Chongqing Municipality is one 1 oz. bu. silver coin. The obverse depicts the picture of the title of PRC, issuing year, the Hall of Prayer for Good Harvests of the Temple of Heaven and the Chinese characters 'The Founding of Chongqing Municipality Souvenir', and the reverse depicts the picture of giant panda, pine tree and face value.

正 面

放 大

原 大 Full Size

面额（元）	10
直径（毫米）	40
含纯银（盎司）	1
成色（%）	99.9
质量	普制
年号	1997
发行量（枚）	50000
铸造单位	上海造币厂

Face Value (Yuan)	10
Diameter (mm)	40
Pure Silver Content (oz)	1
Fineness (%)	99.9
Quality	Bu.
Issuing Year	1997
Mintage (Pieces)	50000
Minted by	Shanghai Mint

Third Set in the Series
of the Return
of Hong Kong to China
Commemorative Coins

中國貴金屬紀念幣彙鑒

十二、香港回归祖国纪念币
（第3组）

一九九七年

1997年7月1日，中英两国政府在香港会展中心举行了交接仪式，香港终于结束了长达一个半世纪的殖民统治，回到了祖国的怀抱。为纪念香港回归祖国这一重大历史事件，中国人民银行发行香港回归祖国金银纪念币1套，共3组，第1组、第2组和第3组分别于1995年12月、1996年7月和1997年7月发行。香港回归祖国纪念币(第3组)，分别由上海造币厂、深圳国宝金币制造厂铸造，中国金币总公司总经销。

香港，包括香港岛、九龙、新界本土及离岛(135个岛屿)四部分，地处珠江三角洲南部，珠江出海口东侧，陆地面积1092平方公里，人口642万多人，是世界上人口最密集的地方之一。

香港历来是中国神圣领土的一部分。英国侵略者从19世纪40年代到19世纪90年代末不断扩大对华掠夺，通过一系列不平等条约占领了香港。1984年12月，中英两国政府签署了关于香港问题的联合声明，中国将在1997年收回香港，对香港恢复行使主权。

香港回归祖国纪念币(第3组)共4个品种。其中5盎司精制金币1种，其背面图案为邓小平肖像、香港远景、纪念文字及面额;1/2盎司精制金币、1盎司精制银币、1盎司普制银币各1种，其背面图案为香港特别行政区区旗、会展中心、香港远景、纪念文字及面额。此组纪念币的正面图案均为天安门、华表、牡丹花图案。

On July 1st, 1997, Chinese and British governments held the hand-over ceremony at Hong Kong Exhibition Center, which marked the end of its being colonized for nearly one and a half centuries and the return to the motherland. To mark the great historical event of Hong Kong's Return to China, the People's Bank of China issued a series of gold and silver commemorative coins of the return of Hong Kong to China including three sets, the first set, second and third sets were issued in December, 1995, July, 1996, and July, 1997 respectively. The third set was minted by Shanghai Mint and Shengzhen Panda Gold Coin Mint respectively, and was distributed by China Gold Coin Inc..

Hong Kong consists of four parts: Hong Kong Island, Kowloon, New Territories and Lee Island (135 islands).It is located in the south of the Pearl River Delta, to the east of the Pearl River's Mouth to the sea, with the land area of 1092 square kilometers, and the population of more than 6420000. It is one of the most densely populated areas in the world.

Hong Kong has been a part of Chinese sacred territory from time immemorial. British invaders continuously strengthened their invasion to China from the 1840's to the 1890's, and occupied Hong Kong through a series of unequal treaties. In December 1984, Chinese and British governments signed the Joint Declaration On the Question of Hong Kong stipulating that the Chinese government would restore Hong Kong and resume the exercise of sovereignty over Hong Kong in 1997.

The return of Hong Kong to China commemorative coins (3rd set) contain four kinds: one 5 oz. proof gold coin with the reverse depicting the picture of the portrait Deng Xiaoping, distant view of Hong Kong, commemorative characters and face value; one 1/2 oz. proof gold coin, one 1 oz. proof silver coin and one 1 oz. bu. silver coin with the common reverse depicting the picture of the Regional Flag of Hong Kong Special Administration Region, Exhibition Center, distant view of Hong Kong, commemorative characters and face value. The common obverse of this set depicts the picture of the Gate of Heavenly Peace, cloud pillar and peony flower.

正　面

正　面

原　大　Full Size

面额（元）	500	50
直径（毫米）	60	27
含纯金（盎司）	5	1/2
成色（%）	99.99	99.9
质量	精制	精制
年号	1997	1997
发行量（枚）	228	11800
铸造单位	上海造币厂	

Face Value (Yuan)	500	50
Diameter (mm)	60	27
Pure Gold Content (oz)	5	1/2
Fineness (%)	99.99	99.9
Quality	Proof	Proof
Issuing Year	1997	1997
Mintage (Pieces)	228	11800
Minted by	Shanghai Mint	

共同正面

放　大

原　大 Full Size

面额（元）	10	10
直径（毫米）	40	40
含纯银（盎司）	1	1
成色（%）	99.9	99.9
质量	精制	普制
年号	1997	1997
发行量（枚）	88000	800000
铸造单位	上海造币厂	上海造币厂 深圳国宝金币制造厂

Face Value (Yuan)	10	10
Diameter (mm)	40	40
Pure Silver Content (oz)	1	1
Fineness (%)	99.9	99.9
Quality	Proof	Bu.
Issuing Year	1997	1997
Mintage (Pieces)	88000	800000
Minted by	Shanghai Mint	Shanghai Mint Shenzhen Panda Gold Coin Mint

First Set in the Series
of the Return
of Macao to China
Commemorative Coins

中國貴金屬紀念幣圖鑒

十三、澳门回归祖国纪念币（第1组）

一九九七年

根据中葡两国政府于1987年签署的联合声明，中国政府将于1999年12月20日对澳门恢复行使主权，澳门将成为中国特别行政区。为纪念澳门回归祖国这一重大历史事件，中国人民银行决定在全球限量发行澳门回归祖国金银纪念币1套，共3组。第1组于1997年12月发行。澳门回归祖国纪念币第1组由沈阳造币厂铸造，中国金币总公司总经销。

澳门位于中国大陆东南沿海、珠江口西岸，与香港、广州鼎足分立于珠江三角洲外缘。澳门地区由澳门半岛、凼仔岛和路环岛三部分组成。

澳门自古就是中国领土。澳门在公元前3世纪，即秦始皇第一次统一中国时期，已正式纳入中国版图。1535年葡萄牙人贿赂广东地方官取得了在澳门码头停靠船舶进行贸易的权利，1557年开始在澳门长期居住。1840年鸦片战争后，葡萄牙殖民主义者又强占了凼仔岛和路环岛。1887年葡萄牙又强迫清政府先后签订了《中葡会议草约》和《中葡北京条约》，从此，葡萄牙一直霸占澳门。

中华人民共和国成立之后，中国政府多次发表声明：澳门历来是中国领土，澳门问题原属历史遗留问题。经多次谈判，中葡两国政府于1987年签署联合声明，中国政府将于1999年12月20日对澳门恢复行使主权。

澳门回归祖国纪念币(第1组)共4个品种，其中1/2盎司、5盎司精制金币各1种，1盎司、5盎司精制银币各1种。其正面图案均为国号、天安门、牡丹花，背面图案均为邓小平半身像、澳门海景、中英葡文“一国两制”字样及面额。

The Joint Declaration of the Government of PRC and the Government of Republic of Portugal signed in 1987 proclaims that Chinese government will resume exercise of sovereignty over Macao with the effect from 20 December 1999. Macao will become a special administrative region of China. To mark this significant historical event, the People's Bank of China decided to issue a series of commemorative coins in a limited number all over the world. This series includes 3 sets with the first, second and the third one issued in December 1997,1998 and 1999 respectively. The first set was minted by Shenyang Mint and distributed by China Gold Coin Inc..

Macao is located along the southeast seacoast of the Mainland and the two sides of the Pearl River, forming a trilogy with Hong Kong and Guangzhou on the outer brink of the Pearl River Delta. Macao comprises the Macao peninsula, Taipa Island and Coloane Island.

Macao has been Chinese territory from time immemorial. In the 3rd century B.C. Macao was included in Chinese territory by Emperor Qinshihuang of Qin Dynasty, who united China for the first time in Chinese history. In 1535, the Portuguese, by offering bribes to the local officials in Guangzhou acquired facilities of port calls at Macao dock and the right to conduct trade there. In 1557 they began to settle in Macao. After the Opium War in 1840,Portugal colonists forcibly occupied the Taipa and Coloane Islands.In 1887,they compelled the Qing government to sign on the Draft Treaty of *the Sino-Portugal Meeting* and the *Treaty of Peking of China and Portugal*. Since then Portuguese have been occupying Macao till now.

After the founding of PRC, the government has on many occasions expounded its position on the question of Macao, that is, Macao has been part of Chinese territory and the question of Macao is left over from history. The government of China and that of Portugal signed a joint declaration in 1987, after several rounds of negotiations, which stipulates that Chinese government will resume the exercise of sovereignty over Macao with effect from 20 December 1999.

The first set in the series of the return of Macao to China commemorative coins contains 4 kinds: 1/2 oz. proof gold coin, 5 oz. proof gold coin, 1 oz. proof silver coin, and 5 oz. proof silver coin. The coins share a common obverse depicting the picture of the title of PRC, Gate of Heavenly Peace and peony flower. The reverses all depict the picture of the bust of Deng Xiaoping, Macao's sea-view, 'one country, two systems' in both Chinese and Portuguese and face value.

共同正面

原 大 Full Size

面额（元）	500	50
直径（毫米）	60	27
含纯金（盎司）	5	1/2
成色（%）	99.99	99.9
质量	精制	精制
年号	1997	1997
发行量（枚）	228	11800
铸造单位		沈阳造币厂

Face Value (Yuan)	500	50
Diameter (mm)	60	27
Pure Gold Content (oz)	5	1/2
Fineness (%)	99.99	99.9
Quality	Proof	Proof
Issuing Year	1997	1997
Mintage (Pieces)	228	11800
Minted by		Shenyang Mint

共同正面

原 大 Full Size

面额（元）	50	10
直径（毫米）	70	40
含纯银（盎司）	5	1
成色（%）	99.9	99.9
质量	精制	精制
年号	1997	1997
发行量（枚）	5000	88000
铸造单位	沈阳造币厂	

Face Value (Yuan)	50	10
Diameter (mm)	70	40
Pure Silver Content (oz)	5	1
Fineness (%)	99.9	99.9
Quality	Proof	Proof
Issuing Year	1997	1997
Mintage (Pieces)	5000	88000
Minted by	Shenyang Mint	

Sino-Thailand Friendship
Commemorative Coins

中國貴金屬紀念幣圖鑒

十四、中—泰友谊纪念币

一九九七年

为进一步推动中泰两国的友好合作关系，增强两国政府和人民间的传统友谊，中国人民银行发行中泰友谊纪念币。该套纪念币由深圳国宝金币制造厂铸造，中国金币总公司总经销。

中国和泰国是有着传统友谊的近邻。自1975年建交以来，在中泰两国政府和人民的共同努力下，两国在政治、经济、文化、科学各方面的友好合作关系得到了全面迅速的发展。

近年来，中泰两国贸易额不断增长，双方投资不断增加，金融业、基础设施建设等方面的合作也在不断加强。尽管国际风云变幻，但中泰两国间的信任、理解、真诚合作始终如一。中泰友谊是不同制度国家间和睦相处的典范。

此套纪念币共2个品种，其中1盎司、1公斤精制银币各1种。正面图案均为国号、年号、中国故宫及泰国王宫，背面图案均为中国乐山大佛、泰国玉佛、纪念文字及面额。

In order to push forward the friendship and the cooperation between China and Thailand as well as to strengthen the traditional friendship between the two counties, the People's Bank of China issued the Sino-Thailand friendship commemorative coins, which were minted by Shenzhen Panda Gold Coin Mint,and distributed by China Gold Coin Inc..

China and Thailand are close neighbors with traditional friendship. Since the establishment of diplomatic relationship in 1975, with the joint efforts of the people and governments in both countries, the cooperative relationship in the fields of politics, economy, culture and science has made all-round and quick development.

In recent years, the total volumes of trade and the investment have been increasing steadily, and the cooperation in finance and constructions of infrastructure has also been strengthened. Though in a changeable international situation, the trust, understanding and sincere cooperation between the two countries have been as consistent as ever before. The Sino-Thailand friendship sets a good example for harmony between countries with different systems.

This set contains two kinds: 1 oz. proof silver coin and 1 kg proof silver coin. They have a common obverse depicting the picture of the title of PRC, issuing year, Chinese Imperial Palace and Thailand's Palace, and a common reverse depicting the picture of the Statue of Leshan Buddha of China, Jade Buddha of Thailand, commemorative words and face value.

正 面

原 大 Full Size

面额（元）	200
直径（毫米）	100
含纯银（公斤）	1
成色（%）	99.9
质量	精制
年号	1997
发行量（枚）	680
铸造单位	深圳国宝金币制造厂

Face Value (Yuan)	200
Diameter (mm)	100
Pure Silver Content (kg)	1
Fineness (%)	99.9
Quality	Proof
Issuing Year	1997
Mintage (Pieces)	680
Minted by	Shenzhen Panda Gold Coin Mint

正　面

原　大 Full Size

放　大

面额（元）	10
直径（毫米）	40
含纯银（盎司）	1
成色（%）	99.9
质量	精制
年号	1997
发行量（枚）	45000
铸造单位	深圳国宝金币制造厂

Face Value (Yuan)	10
Diameter (mm)	40
Pure Silver Content (oz)	1
Fineness (%)	99.9
Quality	Proof
Issuing Year	1997
Mintage (Pieces)	45000
Minted by	Shenzhen Panda Gold Coin Mint

First Set in the Series of the Chinese Minority Nationalities' Culture Silver Coins

中國貴金屬紀念幣圖鑒

十五、中国少数民族文化银币（第1组）

一九九七年

中华文化是由汉族与各少数民族共同创造积累的，丰富多采的少数民族文化使得中华文化更加灿烂夺目。为弘扬中国少数民族文化，中国人民银行发行中国少数民族文化银币第1组，该组银币由上海造币厂铸造，中国金币总公司总经销。

这组银币，以四位少数民族英雄格萨尔王、奢香夫人、冼夫人和嘎达梅林为表现题材。格萨尔王(公元11世纪)是藏族史诗《格萨尔王》中记载的英雄，传说格萨尔王是天神的儿子，为拯救人间的灾难，下界投生。奢香夫人(公元1358~1396年)是元末明初西南彝族“默部”首领霭翠的夫人，丈夫去世后出任土司首领，主动与明朝修好，为促进民族团结、国家统一作出了杰出的贡献。冼夫人(公元513~602年)是一名黎族女性英雄，与高凉太守冯宝成亲，二人共同治理地方，在冼夫人“人人平等，一视同仁”的处事原则下，少数民族聚居的岭南地区秩序井然。嘎达梅林是一名蒙古族英雄(公元1892~1931年)，为了维护内蒙古游牧民族的利益，率众起义，在战斗中壮烈牺牲。这些少数民族英雄为中华民族的统一和各民族的团结作出了杰出的贡献。

中国少数民族文化银币(第1组)共4个品种，均为1盎司精制银币，其正面图案均为国号、年号、北京民族文化宫，背面图案分别为格萨尔王、奢香夫人、冼夫人、嘎达梅林四位少数民族英雄形象及面额。

Chinese culture is created and accumulated by the joint efforts of the Han nationality and the minority nationalities. The rich and colorful minority culture makes a brilliant part of Chinese culture. To enhance Chinese minority culture, the People's Bank of China issued the first set of Chinese minority culture silver coins, minted by Shanghai Mint and distributed by China Gold Coin Inc..

This set of silver coins depicts four minority heroes: King Gesaer, Madam Shexiang, Madam Xian and Gadameilin. King Gesaer (11th century A.D.) was a hero recorded in the Tibet epic *king Gesaer*. In the legend king Gesaer was the son of the God, and was delivered to the earthly world to save people from sins. Madam Shexiang (1358 ~ 1396 A.D., late Yuan — early Ming Dynasty), was the wife of Aicui, the chief of 'Mo', which was among the southwest Yi Nationality. After her husband died, Madam Shexiang succeeded as the leader and began to foster cordial relations with Ming Dynasty. She made great contributions to the integration of nationalities and the unity of the country. Madam Xian (513 ~ 602 A.D.) was a heroine of the Li Nationality, who married Feng Bao-cheng, governor of Gaoliang. Under her principle of 'Everybody be treated equally', the couple governed the Minority inhabiting region together, Lingnan region was brought into good order. Gadameilin (1892 ~ 1931A.D.) was a Mongolia hero. In order to defend the nomadic people's benefits, he initiated an uprising and died heroically in the fighting. These minority heroes and heroines made outstanding contributions to the integrity to nationalities and the unity of the country.

Chinese Minority Nationalities' Culture silver coins (the 1st set) include 4 kinds, all of which are 1 oz. proof silver coins. The common obverse depicts the picture of the title of PRC, issuing year and Beijing Nationalities Culture Palace. The reverses depict the pictures of the four heroes' and heroines' images respectively and face value.

共同正面

原 大 Full Size

面额（元）	10	10
直径（毫米）	40	40
含纯银（盎司）	1	1
成色（%）	99.9	99.9
质量	精制	精制
年号	1997	1997
发行量（枚）	28000	28000
铸造单位	上海造币厂	

Face Value (Yuan)	10	10
Diameter (mm)	40	40
Pure Silver Content (oz)	1	1
Fineness (%)	99.9	99.9
Quality	Proof	Proof
Issuing Year	1997	1997
Mintage (Pieces)	28000	28000
Minted by	Shanghai Mint	

原　大 Full Size

面额（元）	10	10
直径（毫米）	40	40
含纯银（盎司）	1	1
成色（%）	99.9	99.9
质量	精制	精制
年号	1997	1997
发行量（枚）	28000	28000
铸造单位	上海造币厂	

Face Value (Yuan)	10	10
Diameter (mm)	40	40
Pure Silver Content (oz)	1	1
Fineness (%)	99.9	99.9
Quality	Proof	Proof
Issuing Year	1997	1997
Mintage (Pieces)	28000	28000
Minted by	Shanghai Mint	

Chinese Traditional
Auspicious Picture
— *Auspicious Happiness*
in Superabundance
Gold and Silver Coins

中國貴金屬紀念幣圖鑒

十六、中国传统吉祥图
——《吉庆有余》金银币

一九九七年

为了弘扬中国传统文化，中国人民银行发行中国传统吉祥图——《吉庆有余》金银币。该套金银币分别由沈阳造币厂、中国金币总公司铸造，中国金币总公司总经销。

这套金银币的图案取材于中国民间传统吉祥图案——《吉庆有余》图，画面上一个喜气洋洋的童子怀抱一条大鱼，坐在莲叶上，旁边盛开的莲花环绕。鱼者，"余"也，"莲"者，连也。童子抱鱼，即为"吉庆有余"之意，再配上莲花，表示连年有余。吉庆有余是中国民间传统的吉祥图，是勤劳淳朴的人们在新年来临之际对下一年的良好祝愿，表现了人民对富足美好生活的向往。

《吉庆有余》金银币共有10个品种，其中1/2盎司、1盎司普制银币各1种，1盎司、2盎司加厚普制银币各1种，5盎司精制银币1种，1/10盎司、1/20盎司普制金币各1种，1盎司、1/2盎司精制彩色银币各1种，1/10盎司精制彩色金币1种。此次发行的《吉庆有余》彩色金币是中国人民银行首次发行的彩色金币。其正面图案为国号、年号、华表、牡丹花，背面图案为中国民间传统吉祥图案"吉庆有余"及面额。

To popularize Chinese traditional culture, the People's Bank of China issued the Chinese traditional auspicious picture-*Auspicious Happiness in Superabundance* gold and silver coins, minted by Shenyang Mint and China Gold Coin Inc. respectively, distributed by the latter.

This set of gold and silver coins depicts the Chinese traditional auspicious picture–*Auspicious Happiness in Superabundance*, in which a happy little boy embraces a big fish, sitting on a lotus leaf, surrounded by blooming lotus flowers. In Chinese language 'fish' stands for 'superabundance', and 'lotus' stands for 'continuous', therefore this picture implies the meaning of 'having overflowing auspiciousness continuously in each year'. The *Auspicious Happiness in Superabundance* is a typical traditional Chinese auspicious picture, which indicates the working people's best wishes for a new year and longing for happy and wealthy life.

This set includes 10 kinds of coins: 2 kinds of bu. silver coins (one 1/2 oz., one 1 oz.), 2 kinds of thickened bu. silver coins (one 1 oz., one 2 oz.), 1 kind of proof silver coin (5 oz.), two kinds of bu. gold coins (one 1/10 oz., one 1/20 oz.), 2 kinds of colorful proof silver coins (one 1 oz., one 1/2 oz.), and one 1/10 oz. colorful proof gold coin. The colorful gold one was the first issue of colorful gold coin issued by the People's Bank of China. The common obverse depicts the picture of the title of PRC, issuing year, cloud pillar and peony flowers. The common reverse depicts the picture of the traditional Chinese auspicious picture–*Auspicious Happiness in Superabundance* and face value.

共同正面

原　大 Full Size

放　大

面额（元）	10	5
直径（毫米）	18	14
含纯金（盎司）	1/10	1/20
成色（%）	99.9	99.9
质量	普制	普制
年号	1997	1997
发行量（枚）	100000	100000
铸造单位	沈阳造币厂	

Face Value (Yuan)	10	5
Diameter (mm)	18	14
Pure Gold Content (oz)	1/10	1/20
Fineness (%)	99.9	99.9
Quality	Bu.	Bu.
Issuing Year	1997	1997
Mintage (Pieces)	100000	100000
Minted by	Shenyang Mint	

共同正面

原 大 Full Size

面额（元）	100	50
直径（毫米）	80	70
含纯银（盎司）	12	5
成色（%）	99.9	99.9
质量	精制	精制
年号	1997	1997
发行量（枚）	2000	3800
铸造单位	沈阳造币厂	

Face Value (Yuan)	100	50
Diameter (mm)	80	70
Pure Silver Content (oz)	12	5
Fineness (%)	99.9	99.9
Quality	Proof	Proof
Issuing Year	1997	1997
Mintage (Pieces)	2000	3800
Minted by	Shenyang Mint	

共同正面

放　大

原　大 Full Size

面额（元）	10	5
直径（毫米）	40	33
含纯银（盎司）	1	1/2
成色（%）	99.9	99.9
质量	普制	普制
年号	1997	1997
发行量（枚）	80000	80000
铸造单位	沈阳造币厂	

Face Value (Yuan)	10	5
Diameter (mm)	40	33
Pure Silver Content (oz)	1	1/2
Fineness (%)	99.9	99.9
Quality	Bu.	Bu.
Issuing Year	1997	1997
Mintage (Pieces)	80000	80000
Minted by	Shenyang Mint	

正　面

原　大 Full Size

放　大

面额（元）	10	Face Value (Yuan)	10
直径（毫米）	18	Diameter (mm)	18
含纯金（盎司）	1/10	Pure Gold Content (oz)	1/10
成色（%）	99.99	Fineness (%)	99.99
质量	精制	Quality	Proof
年号	1997	Issuing Year	1997
发行量（枚）	20000	Mintage (Pieces)	20000
铸造单位	中国金币总公司	Minted by	China Gold Coin Inc.

共同正面

原　大 Full Size

面额（元）	10	5
直径（毫米）	40	36
含纯银（盎司）	1	1/2
成色（%）	99.9	99.9
质量	精制	精制
年号	1997	1997
发行量（枚）	100000	100000
铸造单位	中国金币总公司	

Face Value (Yuan)	10	5
Diameter (mm)	40	36
Pure Silver Content (oz)	1	1/2
Fineness (%)	99.9	99.9
Quality	Proof	Proof
Issuing Year	1997	1997
Mintage (Pieces)	100000	100000
Minted by	China Gold Coin Inc.	

1997 Issue
of the Spring-hugging
Gold and Silver Coins

中國貴金屬紀念幣彙鑒

十七、1997年版迎春金银币

一九九七年

为了弘扬传统文化，中国人民银行发行1997年版迎春金银币。该套金银币由上海造币厂铸造，中国金币总公司总经销。

这套币以中国民间传统的迎春习俗为题材，以传统的迎春图“闹春”为背面图案，画面上三个小孩在放爆竹。放爆竹是中国传统的过年风俗，点燃的爆竹以隆隆巨响传递着春的脚步，响声轰走了旧年的陈腐气息，带来了新年的欢腾和喜庆。画面上还有盛开的腊梅和飞翔的喜鹊，这也是传统的吉祥物，腊梅代表旺盛的生命力，喜鹊传递喜讯，都表现了人们对新春的美好祝愿。

1997年版迎春金银币共6个品种，包括1/4盎司、1/10盎司普制金币各1种，5盎司精制金币1种，1盎司普制银币1种，1盎司、5盎司精制银币各1种。正面图案为国号、年号、宫灯及装饰线，背面图案为迎春图“闹春”及面额。

To popularize traditional Chinese culture, the People's Bank of China issued the 1997 issue of the Spring-hugging gold and silver coins, minted by Shanghai Mint and distributed by China Gold Coin Inc..

This set of coins takes the Chinese tradition of celebrating the Spring Festival as the theme, with the reverses depicting the traditional 'Spring -hugging' picture. In the picture there are three children lighting up firecrackers, which is a tradition to celebrate the Spring Festival in China. The thunderous booming of crackers passes the steps of the coming spring, drives off the staleness of the last year, and brings joy and happiness of a new year. In the picture there are also blooming calyx canthus and flying magpies, which are also traditional mascots. Calyx canthus stands for exuberant vitality and magpies deliver good news. The whole picture conveys people's best wishes for the new year.

The 1997 issue of the Spring-hugging gold and silver coins includes 6 kinds: 2 kinds of bu. gold coins (one 1/4 oz., one 1/10 oz.), one 5 oz. proof gold coin, one 1 oz. bu. silver coin, and 2 kinds of proof silver coins (one 1 oz., one 5 oz.). The common obverse depicts the picture of the title of PRC, issuing year, palace lantern and the decorating line. The common reverse depicts the picture of the traditional 'spring-hugging' picture and face value.

共同正面

原　大 Full Size

面额（元）	500	25	10
直径（毫米）	60	22	18
含纯金（盎司）	5	1/4	1/10
成色（％）	99.9	99.9	99.9
质量	精制	普制	普制
年号	1997	1997	1997
发行量（枚）	188	10000	60000
铸造单位	上海造币厂		

Face Value (Yuan)	500	25	10
Diameter (mm)	60	22	18
Pure Gold Content (oz)	5	1/4	1/10
Fineness (%)	99.9	99.9	99.9
Quality	Proof	Bu.	Bu.
Issuing Year	1997	1997	1997
Mintage (Pieces)	188	10000	60000
Minted by	Shanghai Mint		

共同正面

原　大 Full Size

面额（元）	50	10	10
直径（毫米）	70	40	40
含纯银（盎司）	5	1	1
成色（%）	99.9	99.9	99.9
质量	精制	精制	普制
年号	1997	1997	1997
发行量（枚）	1500	60000	60000
铸造单位	上海造币厂		

Face Value (Yuan)	50	10	10
Diameter (mm)	70	40	40
Pure Silver Content (oz)	5	1	1
Fineness (%)	99.9	99.9	99.9
Quality	Proof	Proof	Bu.
Issuing Year	1997	1997	1997
Mintage (Pieces)	1500	60000	60000
Minted by	Shanghai Mint		

Second set in the Series
of Chinese Traditional Culture
— Chinese
5000-Year-Long Culture
Gold and Silver Coins

中國貴金屬紀念幣圖鑑

十八、中国传统文化系列——中华五千年文化金银币(第2组)

一九九七年

为弘扬中国传统文化，中国人民银行自1995年开始发行中国传统文化——中华五千年文化金银币，1997年发行中华五千年文化金银币第2组。该组金银币由沈阳造币厂铸造，中国金币总公司总经销。

中华五千年文化金银币以在中国五千年文化发展史上有重大影响的人物、艺术形式和名胜古迹为题材。中华五千年文化金银币第2组选取了庄子、成吉思汗、京剧艺术、杂技、北京故宫保和殿为表现题材。

庄子，姓庄名周，战国时期的宋国蒙城人。庄子是道家学派的代表人物，中国文化史上具有重大影响的思想家。庄子是一个潇洒明智、深刻达观的人，他的思想和处世态度几千年来一直有着不衰的魅力。

成吉思汗是中华民族的一员——蒙古民族世代供奉的神，是历史上最伟大的军事家之一。成吉思汗出生于1162年，其父给他起名铁木真。他青少年时期生活艰难。铁木真当上部落首领后，统一了各部落。与此同时，他又开始西征，西征给中亚、西亚以及欧洲一些国家和人民带来了巨大的灾难，西征客观上也起了沟通中西交通和促进中外文化交流的作用。

京剧是全国性的主要剧种之一，京剧艺术是中国戏曲中最有影响的艺术形式之一，深受人们的喜爱。清中叶以来，以西皮、二黄为主要腔调的徽调、汉调相继进入北京，徽汉合流演变为北京皮黄戏，即京剧。京剧一些很有影响的曲目的题材选自明代长篇小说《西游记》，且多以《西游记》中的孙悟空为主人公，孙悟空也因此成为京剧艺术中的典型形象。

杂技在中国有着悠久的历史。早在两千多年前的春秋战国时期中国就有杂技的萌芽形式出现，如秦朝的“角觝”，到了汉代，杂技已初步形成。杂技来源于民间，其共同特点是以健美有力的形体动作和灵巧迅速的手法表演各种难度很高的技艺，表现劳动人民的智慧、勇敢、乐观和坚强毅力。杂技一般包括蹬技、手技、顶技、踩技、口技，通常把戏法、魔术、马戏、驯兽包括在内。

北京故宫保和殿是中国明清时期举行科举考试中最高级别考试的考场，这种考试名为“殿试”，就是皇帝亲自出题考试选拔人才。其实皇帝并不亲临考场，只是虚设御座，由大臣宣读考题。被“殿试”录取的称为“进士”，前三名为状元、榜眼、探花。

中华文化五千年金银币(第2组)共10个品种，其中1/10盎司精制金币5种，20克精制银币5种，其正面图案均为国号、年号、中国长城，背面图案分别为庄子、成吉思汗、京剧艺术(孙悟空)、古代杂技、北京故宫保和殿及面额。

To enhance Chinese traditional culture, the People's Bank of China issued the first set of in the series of Chinese traditional culture-Chinese 5000-year-long culture gold and silver coins in 1995. The second set was issued in 1997, minted by Shenyang Mint, distributed by China Gold Coin Inc..

The Chinese 5000-year-long culture gold and silver coins take the most influential figures, art forms and places of historic interest as the themes. The 2nd set describes Zhuangzi, Genghis Khan, Beijing Opera, acrobatics and Baohe Hall of the Imperial Palace.

Zhuangzi, whose real name was Zhuang Zhou, was born in the Meng city of Song Kingdom of the Warring States period. He was the most important representative of the Taoist school, and a significant thinker of much influence in the history of Chinese culture. Zhuangzi was wise and degage as well as profound and philosophical. His thoughts and philosophy of life have been appealing for several thousand years.

Genghis Khan was one of the most outstanding strategists in the Chinese history, piously worshiped by the Mongolian people, a deity from generation to generation. He was born in 1162 and was given the name Tamburlaline by his father. He lived a hard life during his early years. After he became the tribe leader, he united the other tribes of Mongol. Meanwhile he started the Western Expedition, which had brought calamities to Central Asia, West Asia and some European countries, but also had objectively linked up the communication between China and the West and promoted the cultural exchange between the two sides.

Peking Opera is one of the major national operas in China, which is of much influence and very popular among Chinese people. Since the middle Qing Dynasty, two kinds of local operas -Hui and Han had entered into Beijing and they combined together and developed into a new kind of opera — Peking Opera. Some famous stories performed in Peking Opera are from a novel of Ming Dynasty — *Record of a Journey to the West*, and mainly depict the leading character Sun Wu-Kong, who therefore has become a typical figure in Peking Opera.

Acrobatics has a long history in China that can be traced back to two thousand years ago during the Spring and Autumn Period and the Warring States Period. The embryonic form of acrobatics —'Jiaodi', sprouted in the Qin Dynasty and developed into acrobatics from Han Dynasty. Acrobatics originated from common people, it has the common feature of performing all kinds of difficult exercises showing the acrobats' muscular actions and quick and agile movements which convey the working people's wisdom, braveness, adamancy and optimistic attitudes towards life. Acrobatics usually includes jiggling with feet, jigging with head and vocal mimicry, and sometimes count in conjuring, magic conjuring, circus and animal taming.

The Baohe Hall of the Imperial Palace is the examination hall where the highest imperial examination was held in Ming and Qing Dynasties. The highest imperial examination is called 'Dianshi' (final imperial examination). The examination paper is set by the emperor to select excellent talents. Actually the emperor was not in the examination hall himself, and there was only his bed of state. The Minister read out the paper and acted as the invigilator. Those who passed the exam were called 'jin shi', and the top three were called 'zhuang yuan', 'bang yan' and 'tan hua' respectively.

The Chinese 5000-year-long culture gold and silver coins (the 2nd set) include 10 kinds of coins: five kinds of 1/10 oz. proof gold coins and five kinds of 20g silver coins, with the common obverse depicting the picture of the title of PRC, issuing year and the Great Wall, and with the reverses depicting the pictures of Zhangzi, Genghis Khan, Beijing Opera (Sun Wu-kong), ancient acrobatics, Baohe Hall of the Imperial Palace respectively and face value.

放 大

共同正面

原 大 Full Size

面额（元）	10	10	10	10	10
直径（毫米）	18	18	18	18	18
含纯金（盎司）	1/10	1/10	1/10	1/10	1/10
成色（%）	99.9	99.9	99.9	99.9	99.9
质量	精制	精制	精制	精制	精制
年号	1997	1997	1997	1997	1997
发行量（枚）	16000	16000	16000	16000	16000
铸造单位	沈阳造币厂				

Face Value (Yuan)	10	10	10	10	10
Diameter (mm)	18	18	18	18	18
Pure Gold Content (oz)	1/10	1/10	1/10	1/10	1/10
Fineness (%)	99.9	99.9	99.9	99.9	99.9
Quality	Proof	Proof	Proof	Proof	Proof
Issuing Year	1997	1997	1997	1997	1997
Mintage (Pieces)	16000	16000	16000	16000	16000
Minted by	Shenyang Mint				

共同正面

原 大 Full Size

面额（元）	5	5	5	5	5
直径（毫米）	36	36	36	36	36
含纯银（克）	20	20	20	20	20
成色（%）	90	90	90	90	90
质量	精制	精制	精制	精制	精制
年号	1997	1997	1997	1997	1997
发行量（枚）	35000	35000	35000	35000	35000
铸造单位	沈阳造币厂				

Face Value (Yuan)	5	5	5	5	5
Diameter (mm)	36	36	36	36	36
Pure Silver Content (g)	20	20	20	20	20
Fineness (%)	90	90	90	90	90
Quality	Proof	Proof	Proof	Proof	Proof
Issuing Year	1997	1997	1997	1997	1997
Mintage (Pieces)	35000	35000	35000	35000	35000
Minted by	Shenyang Mint				

Second Set in the Series
of Chinese Traditional Culture
— The Yellow River Culture
Gold and Silver Coins

中國貴金屬紀念幣券鑒

十九、中国传统文化系列——黄河文化金银币（第2组）

一九九七年

滔滔黄河，亘古绵延。它不仅孕育了代代不已的中华民族，也塑造出了辉煌壮观的黄河文化，成为中华文明的发源地。为了弘扬传统文化，中国人民银行自1995年开始发行中国传统文化系列——黄河文化金银币，1997年发行了黄河文化金银币第2组。该组金银币由上海造币厂铸造，中国金币总公司总经销。

黄河文化金银币(第2组)以后羿射日、嫦娥奔月等神话传说，书法艺术，钱币铸造技术，青铜铸艺，陶瓷工艺等为题材，展现了黄河文化的杰出成就。

传说羿是中国弓箭的发明者，他射技高超，百发百中。据《山海经》记载，有一次，十个太阳一齐出现，晒焦了庄稼，天帝尧就令羿仰天射击十个太阳，羿射中了九个太阳，因此天上只留下一个太阳，给人们带来光明和温暖。

嫦娥奔月是中国古代最优美的传说之一。传说嫦娥是羿的妻子。羿向西王母求来不死之药，还没来得及吃，嫦娥就把它偷了出来，私下吃掉了，成为神仙，飞奔到月亮上，做了月神。这个传说充分地表现了古代人民奇异的幻想能力和延年益寿的美好愿望。

中国书法是以汉字为表现对象的线条造型艺术，也就是汉文字的美化。中国的书法艺术源远流长，远在先秦时代的文字中，就孕育着书法美的萌芽。魏晋以后，名家辈出，如钟繇、王羲之、颜真卿、柳公权等。书法艺术蕴藏着中华民族的气节和品质，它以其独特的艺术魅力，不仅获得东方人的喜爱，而且得到了西方艺术家的欣赏。

“钱”字在古代与“泉”音相同，所以两者常常谐音使用。中国的铸币历史源远流长。早在商朝末年，中国已经开始用铜铸币了，最早的铸币是一种形状像农具的布钱。到了春秋战国时代，由于当时还没有形成统一的中央集权的国家，各个地区便铸造了各自的货币。秦始皇平定了东方六国，统一了货币制度。古人认为，天圆地方，因此秦始皇将钱铸成方孔圆钱，以后历代直至清末，都沿用秦制铸币。

商代开始，中国已有了精美的青铜艺术。这种青铜器艺术，由于奴隶们手艺的分工，在冶炼、熔铸、造型等各方面，都达到了很高成就。器物上的镂刻，精细而富丽，有的在花纹中还嵌以绿松宝石，大部分在回纹中间饰以饕餮，工艺之复杂和精美，令人惊叹。现在出土的司母戊大方鼎，更是证明了当时青铜铸艺的发达。

陶瓷艺术是造型艺术之一。陶瓷系由粘土、长石、石英等为主的混合物，经成型、干燥、烧制而成的制品总称。陶瓷艺术即陶瓷日用品、陈设品的烧制工艺及其造型、釉色和装饰所呈现的艺术特点。中国唐代陶瓷的制作艺术已达到高度成熟水平。宋代制瓷业蓬勃发展，名窑涌现。明清时代陶瓷从制坯、装饰、施釉到烧成，技术上都超过了前代。中国陶瓷业至今兴盛不衰，宜兴的紫砂壶、石湾的陶塑等均闻名于世。

黄河文化金银币(第2组)共7个品种，其中1/2盎司、5盎司精制金币各1种，27克精制银币4种，5盎司精制银币1种。其正面图案均为国号、年号、汉砖团龙图，背面图案分别为后羿射日图、嫦娥奔月图、古代汉字书法、古代铸币图、古代青铜铸艺图、古代陶瓷艺匠图及面额。

The Yellow River has been running from time immemorial. It has fostered generations and generations of Chinese people, as well as the splendid Yellow River culture. It is ranked the cradle of Chinese civilization. To enhance traditional culture, the People's Bank of China issued the Chinese traditional culture series-the Yellow River culture gold and silver coins in 1995. In 1997, the second set of this series was issued, which was minted by Shanghai Mint and distributed by China Gold Coin Inc..

The Yellow River Culture gold and silver coins (the 2nd set) draw materials from the mythical legends about Houyi shooting the suns and the goddess Chang'e flying to the moon, calligraphy, coin casting technology, bronze casting arts, ceramic technology, which show the outstanding achievements of the Yellow River culture.

It was said that Yi, the inventor of Chinese bow and arrow, was good at shooting and the shots hit every time. There is a story about him in *Shanhai Jing*-a legendary collection of China: once upon a time, ten suns rose together and scorched the crops. Yi was ordered by God Yao to shoot at the ten suns, and he shot down nine of them. So only one sun was left in the sky, which brings brightness and warmness to human beings.

The Goddess Chang'e flying to the moon is one of the most beautiful stories in ancient China. It was said that the Goddess Chang'e was Yi's wife. Before Yi taking the elixir of life, which he got from the Queen Mother of the West (His Wang Mu), Chang'e stole and took it, later she flew to the moon and became the Goddess in the Moon. The legend fully showed the ancient people's rich imagination and their wish of being immortal.

Chinese calligraphy is a plastic art of lines with Chinese characters as its object of expression, namely, the Chinese character beautifying. Chinese calligraphy has a long and brilliant history. The Chinese character in the Pre-Qin Dynasty period has already carried with itself the seeds of calligraphy's beauty. After Wei and Jin Dynasty, important calligraphers appeared one after another, such as Zhong You, Wang Xizhi,Yan Zhenqing and Liu Gongquan. The calligraphy containing the integrity and quality of Chinese people, wins both the favors of the Oriental and the appreciation of western artists because of its unique artistic charm.

The Chinese character 钱(*qian*, money) has the same pronunciation as 泉(*quan*, fount), so the two words usually were used nomophonicly. China's history of coin casting can be dated back as early as the later phase of Shang dynasty, when China had already begun to use bronze casting coin. The earliest cast coin was Spade Coin similar to farm tools in shape, till the Spring and Autumn period, different regions cast their own coins respectively because there had not had a centralized power and unified nation. Emperor Qinshihuang united the other six kingdoms and then unified the currency. The ancient people thought that the sky was round and the ground was square, so Emperor Qinshihuang minted the Circular Coin with a Square hole in the center. From then on all the dynasties continued to use this kind of coin until the end of Qing Dynasty.

China had already had exquisite bronze arts ever since the Shang Dynasty. This sort of bronze arts had made very great achievements in the aspects of smelting, casting and modeling, due to the division of labor among the slaves. The enchasing on the utensils is elaborate. Some of them are inlayed with turquoises in the designs. *Taotie* (a mythical ferocious animal) is the main subject decorated among the frets on most utensils. One can't help being amazed at the complexity and fineness of them. The unearthed *Si Muwu Fangding* further proves the sophistications of bronze casting arts.

Ceramic art is one of the plastic arts. Ceramic is a general term of the products made of the mixture of clay, feldspar and quartz after a process of shaping, drying and baking. Ceramic art refers to the baking techniques of the daily-used utensils and furnishings, and the characteristics expressed by the shapes, glaze colors and decorations. The ceramic craftsmanship reached a high level of watching in the Tang Dynasty, prospered with many famous chinaware kilns in the Song Dynasty, and became more developed in the Ming and Qing Dynasties, when the technologies of body blank, decoration, glazing and baking exceeded the past. Chinese ceramic industry has been flourishing till nowadays. The purple-sand pot of Yinxing and the pottery sculpture of Shiwan etc. enjoy great popularity all over the world.

The Yellow River culture gold and silver coins (the second set) have 7 kinds: one kind of 1/2 oz. proof gold coin; one kind of 5 oz. proof gold coin, four kinds of 27g proof silver coins, one kind of 5 oz. proof silver coin. The common obverse depicts the picture of the title of PRC, issuing year and the picture of Clustering Dragon on brick of the Han Dynasty. The reverses depict the pictures of Houyi shooting at the suns, Goddess Chang'e flying to the moon, calligraphy of ancient character, ancient coin casting, ancient casting process of bronze, ancient ceramist and face value respectively.

共同正面

原 大 Full Size

面额（元）	500	50
直径（毫米）	60	27
含纯金（盎司）	5	1/2
成色（%）	99.9	99.9
质量	精制	精制
年号	1997	1997
发行量（枚）	128	3000
铸造单位	上海造币厂	

Face Value (Yuan)	500	50
Diameter (mm)	60	27
Pure Gold Content (oz)	5	1/2
Fineness (%)	99.9	99.9
Quality	Proof	Proof
Issuing Year	1997	1997
Mintage (Pieces)	128	3000
Minted by	Shanghai Mint	

正　面

原　大　Full Size

面额（元）	50	Face Value (Yuan)	50
直径（毫米）	70	Diameter (mm)	70
含纯银（盎司）	5	Pure Silver Content (oz)	5
成色（%）	99.9	Fineness (%)	99.9
质量	精制	Quality	Proof
年号	1997	Issuing Year	1997
发行量（枚）	1000	Mintage (Pieces)	1000
铸造单位	上海造币厂	Minted by	Shanghai Mint

共同正面

原 大 Full Size

面额（元）	10	10	10	10
直径（毫米）	38.6	38.6	38.6	38.6
含纯银（克）	27	27	27	27
成色（%）	92.5	92.5	92.5	92.5
质量	精制	精制	精制	精制
年号	1997	1997	1997	1997
发行量（枚）	10000	10000	10000	10000
铸造单位	上海造币厂			

Face Value (Yuan)	10	10	10	10
Diameter (mm)	38.6	38.6	38.6	38.6
Pure Silver Content (g)	27	27	27	27
Fineness (%)	92.5	92.5	92.5	92.5
Quality	Proof	Proof	Proof	Proof
Issuing Year	1997	1997	1997	1997
Mintage (Pieces)	10000	10000	10000	10000
Minted by	Shanghai Mint			

Third Set in the Series of
The Romance of the Three Kingdoms
Gold and Silver Coins

中國貴金屬紀念幣彙鑒

二十、中国古典文学名著《三国演义》金银币(第3组)

一九九七年

《三国演义》是元明之际罗贯中编著的一部长篇历史小说，是中国四大古典文学名著之一。为弘扬中国古代文化，中国人民银行自1995年开始发行《三国演义》金银币，1997年发行了《三国演义》金银币第3组。该组金银币由上海造币厂铸造，中国金币总公司总经销。

《三国演义》金银币选取《三国演义》中的典型人物形象和有重要影响的事件、战役为题材。《三国演义》金银币第3组选取的人物是孙策、孙权、周瑜、鲁肃，还选取了孙刘联姻这一重要事件和赤壁之战这一重要战役。

孙策，字伯符，孙坚长子。他率兵先后打败刘繇、严白虎、王朗等，占据吴、会稽、庐江、豫章等六郡，建立孙氏政权，人称“小霸王”。建安五年，被人行刺而死，年仅26岁。

孙权是孙策之弟，他也是吴国的建立者。孙权开朗大度，善于决断，又喜结交侠士，很有才能。他占据江东，和曹、刘三分天下，是一个重要的政治人物。

周瑜是东吴名将，聪明英气，风流倜傥，他指挥了著名的赤壁之战，颇显才华。后被诸葛亮三气而死，年仅36岁。《三国演义》中的情节实际是虚构的，周瑜是病死的，他是历史上杰出的青年将领。

鲁肃也是东吴名将，周瑜临死前推荐鲁肃接替自己的位置。《三国演义》里把他写成一个没有能力的忠厚长者，实与历史不符。历史上的鲁肃，是一个很有谋略、很有作为的人物。

孙刘联姻是《三国演义》第54～55回的内容。周瑜本想借招亲之名，骗刘备到南徐，逼其交出荆州。诸葛亮出了一条锦囊计应对，使东吴赔了夫人又折兵。

赤壁之战是决定三国鼎立局面的重要战役。公元108年，曹操以20万兵力攻孙权，孙刘联军只有5万，但他们利用曹军远来疲惫、骄傲轻敌、不习水战等弱点，采用火攻，大败曹军。这也是一次以弱胜强的著名战役，三国鼎立局面由此形成。

《三国演义》金银币(第3组)共7个品种，其中27克精制银币4种，5盎司精制银币1种，1/2盎司、5盎司精制金币各1种。其正面图案均为作者罗贯中肖像、国号、年号，背面图案分别为周瑜、鲁肃、孙权、孙策、孙刘联姻图、赤壁之战图及面额。

The Romance of Three Kingdoms, one of the Four Great Chinese Classical Works, is a long historical novel written by Luo Guanzhong, who lived in the period of late Yuan to early Ming Dynasties. In order to popularize Chinese ancient culture, the People's Bank of China has been issuing *The Romance of Three kingdoms* gold and silver coins since 1995, and in 1997 issued the third set, which was minted by Shanghai Mint and distributed by China Gold Coin Inc..

The Romance of Three Kingdoms gold and silver coins choose the influential events and wars, as well as typical figures in the novel as the themes. This set choose such figures as Sun Ce, Sun Quan, Zhou Yu, Lu Su and the important event-the intermarriage between Sun and Liu, and the crucial warfare–Chibi Warfare.

Sun Ce, given name Bofu, the heir of Sun Jian, after defeating Liu You, Yan Baihu and Wang Lang in succession, occupied six prefectures such as Wu, Kuaiji, Lujiang and Yuzhang, and set up his own regime. He has been given a nickname 'Junior Overlord'. In the fifth year of Jian'an period, he was assassinated, when he was only 26 years old.

Sun Quan, the younger brother of Sun Ce, was also one of the founders of Kingdom Wu. He was broad-minded and decisive. He was also fond of making acquaintance with knight-errant. In a word he was a competent man. Occupying the eastern area of the Yangtse River, he shared China with Cao Cao and Liu Bei. He was an important politician in Chinese history.

Zhou Yu, who conducted the famous Chibi Warfare, was a well-known general of kingdom Wu. He was intelligent and handsome. Later he was enraged to death by Zhu Geliang at the age of 36 (Zhu Geliang, the intelligent chancellor of kingdom Shu). The plot of *The Romance of Three kingdoms* is fictive. In fact, he died in illness. He was an outstanding young general in Chinese history.

Zhou Yu recommended Lu Su to take over his own position when Zhou was dying, who was also a well-known general of Kingdom Wu. Lusu was depicted as a meek elder statesman without capability in the novel, which didn't agree with the fact. In the history, Lusu was a figure of strategies and accomplishments.

The intermarriage between Sun and Liu is the contents of the 54th and 55th chapters. Zhou Yu had planed to deceive Liu Bei into coming to Nan Xu in the name of marring him Sun Quan's sister and planed to force Liu to give up Jing Prefecture. But the result was that Zhu Geliang worked out a secret master plan and Dongwu threw the helve after the hatchet.

The Chibi Warfare resulted in the situation of the three kingdoms being nearly equal in power and strategic position. In 108 A.D., Cao Cao led 200,000 soldiers to attack Sun Quan. Though the population of Sun and Liu allied force was only 50 thousand, they defeated Cao forces by adopting the strategy of fire-attack taking the advantages that the Cao force was tired after long march, underestimated the enemy and was not used to sea-fight. This was a famous the-weak-defeating-the-strong battle, and after that the situation of tripartite confrontation was formed.

This set includes 7 kinds of coins: 4 kinds of 27g proof silver coins, one 5 oz. proof silver coin, one 1/2 oz. proof gold coin and one 5 oz. proof gold coin with a common obverse depicting the picture of the portrait of the author Luo Guanzhong, title of PRC, and the issuing year, and with the reverses depicting the pictures of Zhou Yu, Lu Su, Sun Quan, Sun Ce, inter-marriage between Sun and Liu, Chi Bi Warfare respectively and face value.

共同正面

原　大 Full Size

面额（元）	500	50
直径（毫米）	60	27
含纯金（盎司）	5	1/2
成色（%）	99.9	99.9
质量	精制	精制
年号	1997	1997
发行量（枚）	168	3000
铸造单位	上海造币厂	

Face Value (Yuan)	500	50
Diameter (mm)	60	27
Pure Gold Content (oz)	5	1/2
Fineness (%)	99.9	99.9
Quality	Proof	Proof
Issuing Year	1997	1997
Mintage (Pieces)	168	3000
Minted by	Shanghai Mint	

正　面

原　大 Full Size

面额（元）	50	Face Value (Yuan)	50
直径（毫米）	70	Diameter (mm)	70
含纯银（盎司）	5	Pure Silver Content (oz)	5
成色（%）	99.9	Fineness (%)	99.9
质量	精制	Quality	Proof
年号	1997	Issuing Year	1997
发行量（枚）	1500	Mintage (Pieces)	1500
铸造单位	上海造币厂	Minted by	Shanghai Mint

共同正面

原　大 Full Size

面额（元）	10	10	10	10
直径（毫米）	38.6	38.6	38.6	38.6
含纯银（盎司）	0.803	0.803	0.803	0.803
成色（%）	92.5	92.5	92.5	92.5
质量	精制	精制	精制	精制
年号	1997	1997	1997	1997
发行量（枚）	10000	10000	10000	10000
铸造单位	上海造币厂			

Face Value (Yuan)	10	10	10	10
Diameter (mm)	38.6	38.6	38.6	38.6
Pure Silver Content (oz)	0.803	0.803	0.803	0.803
Fineness (%)	92.5	92.5	92.5	92.5
Quality	Proof	Proof	Proof	Proof
Issuing Year	1997	1997	1997	1997
Mintage (Pieces)	10000	10000	10000	10000
Minted by	Shanghai Mint			

Third Set in the Series of
China Silk Road
Gold and Silver Coins

中國貴金屬紀念幣圖鑒

二十一、中国丝绸之路金银币（第3组）

一九九七年

为弘扬中国传统文化，展现古代中国与亚洲、欧洲、非洲政治、经济、文化交流的成果，中国人民银行自1995年开始发行中国丝绸之路金银币，1997年发行了中国丝绸之路金银币第3组。该组金银币由上海造币厂铸造，中国金币总公司总经销。

“丝绸之路”是世界文化之源，在它的东西两端，产生了中国文明、埃及文明、印度文明和美索不达米亚文明、中亚文明、希腊文明等许多古代文明，成为后来世界文明的摇篮。

该组金银币共5个品种，其中1/3盎司精制金币1种，20克精制银币4种。此组金银币正面图案均为国徽、国号、年号，背面图案为法显和尚求经图、礼佛图、宴乐图、捣练图、商贸图及面额。

法显是东晋僧人、旅行家。因慨叹中国律藏残缺，矢志寻求，于东晋安帝隆安三年(399年)，出发西行，前后15年游历30余国，历经艰险，携回许多梵事本经。著有《佛国纪》。

佛陀作为宗教世界精神崇拜的偶像，从它诞生的那天起，就使千百万不同肤色、不同民族的人拜倒、匍匐在它的脚下。礼佛图所绘就是几个风尘仆仆的过客在佛像下面顶礼膜拜的情景，他们虔诚地双手合十，祈祷祝愿。

法显和尚求经图、礼佛图、宴乐图、捣练图、商贸图，从不同侧面表现了丝绸之路上人们的宗教、商贸活动情景以及生活情况，是丝绸之路辉煌时期生活的见证。

To popularize Chinese traditional culture and exhibit the achievements in political, economic and cultural exchanges between Asia, Europe, Africa and China, the People's Bank of China has been issuing the China Silk Road gold and silver coins since 1995, and in 1997 issued the third set, minted by Shanghai Mint and distributed by China Gold Coin Inc..

The Silk Road was the cradle of the cosmopolitan culture and later the cradle of the cosmopolitan civilization. At the eastern and western ends of it, Chinese civilization, Egyptian civilization, Indian civilization, Mesopotamian civilization, Central-Asian civilization, and Greek civilization were fostered.

This set includes 5 kinds of coins: one 1/3 oz. proof gold coin and four kinds of 20g proof silver coins with a common obverse depicting the picture of the national emblem, title of PRC and the issuing year, and with the reverses depicting the pictures of monk Fa Xian Seeking for Buddhist Scripture, worshiping Buddha, feasting and music, beating and washing the wrought thin silk, trade and face value respectively.

Fa Xian, a monk of the Eastern Jin Dynasty and a traveler, struck by the lacking of Chinese Buddhist scriptures of the Disciplines, determined to go westward to seek them in the third year of Long'an period of Emperor An of the Eastern Jin Dynasty (399 A.D.). He had spent about 15 years touring over 30 countries and endured many hardships and dangers. Finally he brought back a lot of original Buddhist scriptures. He had written a book — *Record of the Buddhist Countries.*

Buddha, as a spiritual idol in the religious world, from the very day he was born, made thousands of millions of people from different nationalities prostrate themselves before him. The worshiping Buddha picture depicts the scene of several travel-stained passer-bys prostrating themselves in worship before the Buddha Statue with their palms pressed together piously, praying for happiness.

The pictures of monk Fa Xian seeking for Buddhist scripture, worshiping Buddha, feasting and music, beating and washing the wrought thin silk and trading reflect the religious, trade and commercial activities and the life of people along the Silk Road from different aspects. They are the telling witness of the prosperous period of the Silk Road.

正 面

原 大 Full Size

放 大

面额（元）	50
直径（毫米）	23
含纯金（盎司）	1/3
成色（%）	91.6
质量	精制
年号	1997
发行量（枚）	10000
铸造单位	上海造币厂

Face Value (Yuan)	50
Diameter (mm)	23
Pure Gold Content (oz)	1/3
Fineness (%)	91.6
Quality	Proof
Issuing Year	1997
Mintage (Pieces)	10000
Minted by	Shanghai Mint

共同正面

原　大 Full Size

面额（元）	5	5	5	5
直径（毫米）	36	36	36	36
含纯银（克）	20	20	20	20
成色（%）	90	90	90	90
质量	精制	精制	精制	精制
年号	1997	1997	1997	1997
发行量（枚）	15000	15000	15000	15000
铸造单位	上海造币厂			

Face Value (Yuan)	5	5	5	5
Diameter (mm)	36	36	36	36
Pure Silver Content (g)	20	20	20	20
Fineness (%)	90	90	90	90
Quality	Proof	Proof	Proof	Proof
Issuing Year	1997	1997	1997	1997
Mintage (Pieces)	15000	15000	15000	15000
Minted by	Shanghai Mint			

1997 Shanghai International
Stamps and Coins Exposition
Commemorative Coin

中國貴金屬紀念幣彙鑒

二十二、1997年上海国际邮票钱币博览会纪念币

一九九七年

为纪念1997年上海国际邮票钱币博览会，推动中国邮票钱币事业的发展，中国人民银行发行1997年上海国际邮票钱币博览会纪念币。该币由上海造币厂铸造，中国金币总公司总经销。

1997年上海国际邮票钱币博览会于1997年11月19日～23日在上海展览中心隆重举行。这是中华人民共和国成立以来举办的第二次集钱币、邮票展览和销售于一体的大型展会。这次博览会是一次世界各国、各地区邮票、钱币和制作工艺及其人文历史和风土人情的交流盛会。与会期间还举办了集邮日、集币日、青少年日、国际集邮市场战略研讨会等活动。

1997年上海国际邮票钱币博览会纪念币为1盎司银镶金普制币1种，正面图案为北京天坛祈年殿、国号、年号及“’97上海国际邮票钱币博览会纪念”字样，背面图案为大熊猫、镶嵌的金质小熊猫及面额。

To commemorate 1997 Shanghai International Stamps and Coins Exposition and promote the development of Chinese stamp and coin causes, the People's Bank of China issued the 1997 Shanghai International Stamps and Coins Exposition commemorative coin, minted by Shanghai Mint and distributed by China Gold Coin Inc..

1997 Shanghai International Stamps and Coins Exposition was grandly held at Shanghai Exhibition Center from November 19th to 23rd. This was the second large-scale exhibition involving exhibition and purchase of stamp and coin since the founding of the People's Republic of China. This fair was a grand meeting of stamp, coin, processing technology, human history and customs from areas all over the world. During the exhibition, many activities were held such as stamp-collecting Day, coin-collecting Day, youngsters' Day, and the International Philately Market Strategy Symposium, etc.

The commemorative coin is one 1 oz. bu. silver coin inlayed with gold. The obverse depicts the picture of the Hall of prayer for Good Harvests of the Temple of Heaven in Beijing, title of PRC, issuing year and the characters of ''97 Shanghai International Stamps and Coins Exposition Commemoration'. And the reverse depicts the picture of giant Panda, inlayed gold little panda and face value.

正　面

原　大 Full Size

放　大

面额（元）	10	Face Value (Yuan)	10
直径（毫米）	40	Diameter (mm)	40
含纯银（盎司）	1	Pure Silver Content (oz)	1
成色（%）	99.9	Fineness (%)	99.9
质量	普制	Quality	Bu.
年号	1997	Issuing Year	1997
发行量（枚）	30000	Mintage (Pieces)	30000
铸造单位	上海造币厂	Minted by	Shanghai Mint

中华人民共和国
1995
50元
1996
奥林匹克运动会
纪念
10元
1895 1995
1994
公元1403年
5元
中国抗日战争胜利五十周年纪念
150元

1997 Hong Kong International
Coin Convention
Commemorative Coin

中國貴金屬紀念幣圖鑒

二十三、1997 年香港国际钱币展销会纪念币

一九九七年

为纪念1997年香港国际钱币展销会，中国人民银行发行1997年香港国际钱币展销会纪念币。该币由深圳国宝金币制造厂铸造，中国金币总公司总经销。

1997年香港国际钱币展销会纪念币为1/2盎司普制银币1种，其正面图案为北京天坛祈年殿、国号、年号及“’97香港国际钱币展销会纪念”字样，背面图案为大熊猫及面额。

1997年香港国际钱币展销会于1997年9月5日～7日在香港举办，主办单位为泰星钱币有限公司、中国长城硬币投资有限公司。

To commemorate 1997 Hong Kong International Coin Convention, the People's Bank of China issued 1997 Hong Kong International Coin Convention commemorative coin, minted by Shenzhen Panda Gold Coin Mint and distributed by China Gold Coin Inc..

This commemorative coin is one 1/2 oz. bu. silver coin. The obverse depicts the picture of the Hall of Prayer for Good Harvests of the Temple of Heaven in Beijing, title of PRC, issuing year and the characters of “ ’97 Hong Kong International Coin Convention Commemoration” and the reverse depicts the picture of giant panda and face value.

1997 Hong Kong International Coin Convention was held in Hong Kong from September 5th to September 7th, sponsored by the Tai Xing Money Co. Ltd, and China Great Wall Coins Investments Ltd.

正　面

原　大 Full Size

放　大

面额（元）	5
直径（毫米）	33
含纯银（盎司）	1/2
成色（%）	99.9
质量	普制
年号	1997
发行量（枚）	30000
铸造单位	深圳国宝金币制造厂

Face Value (Yuan)	5
Diameter (mm)	33
Pure Silver Content (oz)	1/2
Fineness (%)	99.9
Quality	Bu.
Issuing Year	1997
Mintage (Pieces)	30000
Minted by	Shenzhen Panda Gold Coin Mint

Series of Chinese Ancient Famous Paintings — *Peacock Displaying Its Fine Tail Feathers* Silver Coin

中國貴金屬紀念幣圖鑒

二十四、中国古代名画系列——《孔雀开屏图》银币

一九九七年

为弘扬传统文化，展示中国古代绘画艺术，中国人民银行曾于1993年发行中国古代名画系列——《孔雀开屏图》金银币，1997年版《孔雀开屏图》银币由上海造币厂铸造，中国金币总公司总经销。

《孔雀开屏图》是清人郎世宁的名作。郎世宁(1688～1766年)，意大利米兰人，于康熙五十四年(1715年)以欧洲耶稣会的传教士身份来到中国。他约于康熙末期进入宫廷供职，经历康、雍、乾三代，在宫中创作了大量人物肖像、历史、花鸟、走兽画，得到皇帝的欣赏，是最著名的宫廷画家之一。

《孔雀开屏图》从题材内容看完全是中国传统的，而在具体描绘上则注重光线明暗和物象立体感的表现。此图构思丰富，虚实处理得当，强调真实描绘，重视形似、质感，有很强的写实能力，堪称绘画中的精品。

该套银币共1个品种，1盎司普制银币1种。正面图案为国号、年号、北京故宫太和殿，背面图案为郎世宁所绘《孔雀开屏图》及面额。

To popularize traditional culture and exhibit Chinese ancient painting art, the People's Bank of China once issued the famous Chinese ancient paintings series — *Peacock Displaying Its Fine Tail Feathers* gold and silver coins in 1993. And the 1997 issue of silver coin were minted by Shanghai Mint and distributed by China Gold Coin Inc..

The picture of *Peacock Displaying Its Fine Tail Feathers* was the masterpiece of Lang Shining in the Qing Dynasty. Lang Shining (1688 ~ 1766), born in Milan, Italy, came to China as a missionary of European Protestantism in the 54th year of Kangxi (1715) of Qing Dynasty. He worked in the court in the last phase of Kangxi's reign and experienced three emperors' reigns, Kangxi, Yongzheng and Qianlong. In the court he created a large number of paintings: figure painting, historical, flower-and -bird, and beast paintings and had won the Emperors' deep appreciation. He was one of the most famous artists of court of the period.

On subject matter, the painting *Peacock Displaying Its Fine Tail Feathers* is absolutely traditional Chinese, meanwhile in the aspect of concrete depicting, it stresses on the contrast between light and shade and the expression of three-dimensional effects of objects. This picture is rich in imagination, proper in the handling of the real and the false. It focuses on real depiction, sharp vividness of forms and the impression of quality. All those above with its strong capability of painting realistically, his works are ranked among the best of Chinese painting.

The 1997 issue of the painting *Peacock Displaying Its Fine Tail Feathers* is a 1 oz. bu. silver coin with the obverse depicting the picture of the title of PRC, issuing year and the Taihe Temple of the Imperial Palace in Beijing, and with the reverse depicting the picture of the painting *Peacock Displaying Its Fine Tail Feathers* and face value.

正　面

原　大 Full Size

放　大

面额（元）	10	Face Value (Yuan)	10
直径（毫米）	40	Diameter (mm)	40
含纯银（盎司）	1	Pure Silver Content (oz)	1
成色（%）	99.9	Fineness (%)	99.9
质量	普制	Quality	Bu.
年号	1997	Issuing Year	1997
发行量（枚）	50000	Mintage (Pieces)	50000
铸造单位	上海造币厂	Minted by	Shanghai Mint

Series of Chinese Modern
Famous Paintings — *Penguins*
Gold and Silver Coins

中國貴金屬紀念幣圖鑒

二十五、中国近代名画系列
——《企鹅图》金银币

一九九七年

为弘扬传统文化，展示中国绘画艺术，中国人民银行发行中国近代名画系列——《企鹅图》金银币。该套金银币由沈阳造币厂铸造，中国金币总公司总经销。

《企鹅图》金银币共2个品种，其中1/2盎司精制金币1种，2/3盎司精制银币1种，其正面图案为国号、年号、中国长城，背面图案均为金鸿钧所绘《企鹅图》及面额。

金鸿钧，1937年9月生于北京，1962年毕业于中央美术学院中国画系，现为中央美术学院中国画系教授。金鸿钧擅长工笔花鸟画、小写意花鸟画，其作品多次参加国内外重大美展，多次在国内获奖，8幅作品被中国美术馆收藏，出版有《工笔花鸟画技法》、《牡丹画谱》、《金鸿钧画集》等。

To popularize traditional culture and show the Chinese painting art, the People's Bank of China issued the series of famous Chinese modern paintings — *Penguin* gold and silver coins, minted by Shenyang Mint and distributed by China Gold Coin Inc.. These coins have 2 kinds: one 1/2 oz. proof gold coin and one proof silver coin with gross weight of 2/3 oz. The common obverse depicts the picture of the title of PRC, issuing year and the Great Wall, and the common reverse depicts the painting Penguin painted by Jin Hongjun and the face value.

Jin Hongjun, who was born in Sep.1937 in Beijing and graduated from the Chinese Traditional Painting Department of the Central Art Academics, is the professor of the university from where he graduated. Mr. Jin is good at fine freehand brushwork of flower-and -bird painting and smaller fine freehand brushwork. His works have been exhibited in important painting exhibitions both at home and abroad for many times and have won several prizes in China. Eight of his works have been stored by the National Art Museum. He has published several books as the *Techniques of Fine Flower-and -Bird-Paintings, A Book on Peony Paintings* and *Collection of Jin Hongjun's Paintings*.

正 面

原 大 Full Size

放 大

面额（元）	100
直径（毫米）	27
含纯金（盎司）	0.458
成色（%）	91.6
质量	精制
年号	1997
发行量（枚）	2800
铸造单位	沈阳造币厂

Face Value (Yuan)	100
Diameter (mm)	27
Pure Gold Content (oz)	0.458
Fineness (%)	91.6
Quality	Proof
Issuing Year	1997
Mintage (Pieces)	2800
Minted by	Shenyang Mint

放　大

正　面

原　大 Full Size

面额（元）	10
直径（毫米）	36
含纯银（盎司）	0.6
成色（%）	90
质量	精制
年号	1997
发行量（枚）	8800
铸造单位	沈阳造币厂

Face Value (Yuan)	10
Diameter (mm)	36
Pure Silver Content (oz)	0.6
Fineness (%)	90
Quality	Proof
Issuing Year	1997
Mintage (Pieces)	8800
Minted by	Shenyang Mint

The Chinese Palace Museum Gold and Silver Coins

中國貴金屬紀念幣考鑒

二十六、中国故宫博物院金银币

一九九七年

为让世界更多地了解故宫，了解中国的古代建筑文化，中国人民银行发行中国故宫博物院金银币。该套币由深圳国宝金币制造厂铸造，中国金币总公司总经销。

故宫位于北京市中心，又名紫禁城，建筑面积15.5万平方米，共有各式宫廷建筑890多座，是中国明、清两朝皇帝的宫殿，也是世界上最大的皇宫。故宫始建于明永乐四年(1406年)，于永乐十八年(1420年)建成。

故宫的主体部分是三大殿：太和殿、中和殿、保和殿，这是朝廷举行大典的地方。“前朝”后面是“内廷”，以乾清宫、交泰殿、坤宁宫为中心，包括两翼的东西六宫，是生活起居用房。乾清宫是皇帝的正式寝宫和日常活动的场所。故宫四周围还有10米高的城墙，墙外有52米宽的护城河环绕，城之四角各有一座华丽奇特的角楼遥遥相望。

故宫的建筑技术和建筑艺术成就都是出类拔萃的，体现了中国古代劳动人民的才智和匠心。

该套金银币共10个品种，其中1/10盎司精制金币1种，1/4盎司精制金币4种，1盎司普制银币5种。其正面图案均为国号、年号、故宫午门，背面图案分别为铜狮、御花园、金水桥、乾清宫、乾清宫内景及面额。

To further inform the world of the Imperial Palace and Chinese ancient architecture, the People's Bank of China issued the Chinese Palace Museum gold and silver coins, minted by Shenzhen Panda Gold Coin Mint, and distributed by China Gold Coin Inc..

The Imperial Palace, also called Forbidden City, is located in the center of Beijing City and covers an area of 155,000 square meters. The Palace, comprising of about 890 various palaces, was the royal palace of Ming and Qing Dynasties and is the largest one all in the world. The Palace was initially built on the 4th year of Yongle 's reign of Ming Dynasty (1406) and was completely finished in the 18th year of that period (1420).

The main body of the Palace includes three halls: Taihe, Zhonghe, and Baohe Halls, where important ceremonies are held. The Inner Court behind the Front Court mainly consists of Qianling Palace, Jiaotai Hall and Kunning Palace, which together with the six palaces on both eastern and western flanks were used as the living rooms. The Qianqing Palace was the emperor's regular resting room and for daily activities, too. Around the city is the ten-meter-high city wall, which is surrounded by the 52-meter-wide moat. In each corner of the city stands a brilliant and peculiar watchtower, facing each other across a distance.

The architectural technology and arts of the Palace are all outstanding and showing the wisdom and genius of Chinese working people in ancient times.

The Chinese Palace Museum gold and silver coins contain 10 kinds: one 1/10 oz. proof gold coin, four kinds of 1/4 oz. proof gold coins, and five kinds of 1 oz. bu. silver coins, with the common obverse depicting the picture of the title of PRC, issuing year and the Front Gate of the Palace, and with the reverses depicting the pictures of bronze lion, royal garden, Gold Water Bridge, Qianqing Palace, interior scenery of Qianqing Palace and face values respectively.

放 大

共同正面

原 大 Full Size

面额（元）	25	25	25	25	10
直径（毫米）	22	22	22	22	18
含纯金（盎司）	1/4	1/4	1/4	1/4	1/10
成色（%）	99.9	99.9	99.9	99.9	99.9
质量	精制	精制	精制	精制	精制
年号	1997	1997	1997	1997	1997
发行量（枚）	4000	4000	4000	4000	11000
铸造单位	深圳国宝金币制造厂				

Face Value (Yuan)	25	25	25	25	10
Diameter (mm)	22	22	22	22	18
Pure Gold Content (oz)	1/4	1/4	1/4	1/4	1/10
Fineness (%)	99.9	99.9	99.9	99.9	99.9
Quality	Proof	Proof	Proof	Proof	Proof
Issuing Year	1997	1997	1997	1997	1997
Mintage (Pieces)	4000	4000	4000	4000	11000
Minted by	Shenzhen Panda Gold Coin Mint				

共同正面

面额（元）	10	10	10	10	10
直径（毫米）	40	40	40	40	40
含纯银（盎司）	1	1	1	1	1
成色（%）	99.9	99.9	99.9	99.9	99.9
质量	普制	普制	普制	普制	普制
年号	1997	1997	1997	1997	1997
发行量（枚）	80000	80000	80000	80000	80000
铸造单位	深圳国宝金币制造厂				

Face Value (Yuan)	10	10	10	10	10
Diameter (mm)	40	40	40	40	40
Pure Silver Content (oz)	1	1	1	1	1
Fineness (%)	99.9	99.9	99.9	99.9	99.9
Quality	Bu.	Bu.	Bu.	Bu.	Bu.
Issuing Year	1997	1997	1997	1997	1997
Mintage (Pieces)	80000	80000	80000	80000	80000
Minted by	Shenzhen Panda Gold Coin Mint				

原　大 Full Size

1997 Munich
International Coin Fair
Commemorative Medals

中國貴金屬紀念幣章鑒

二十七、1997年慕尼黑国际硬币展销会纪念章

一九九七年

为纪念1997年慕尼黑国际硬币展销会这一盛大活动，弘扬世界钱币文化，中国金币总公司特发行1997年慕尼黑国际硬币展销会纪念章，该套纪念章由沈阳造币厂铸造。

该套纪念章共3个品种，其中1/2盎司精制金章1种，1盎司和12盎司精制银章各1种。正面图案：金章为中国长城及中国和德国古钱币，银章为北京天坛祈年殿和慕尼黑风景建筑；背面图案均为母子熊猫食竹图。

To commemorate the grand 1997 Munich International Coin Fair and to promote the world coin culture, China Gold Coin Inc. specially issued the 1997 Munich International Coin Fair commemorative medals, minted by Shenyang Mint.

This set of medals includes three kinds: one 1/2 oz. proof gold medal, one 1 oz. proof silver medal and one 12 oz. proof silver medal. The obverse of the gold medal depicts the picture of the Great Wall and German and Chinese ancient coins. The silver medals have a common obverse depicting the picture of the Hall of Prayer for Good Harvests of the Temple of Heaven in Beijing and Munich scenery and architecture. The gold and silver medals have a common reverse depicting the picture of mother panda and her baby eating bamboo.

正　面

原　大 Full Size

放　大

直径（毫米）	27		Diameter (mm)	27
含纯金（盎司）	1/2		Pure Gold Content (oz)	1/2
成色（%）	99.9		Fineness (%)	99.9
质量	精制		Quality	Proof
年号	1997		Issuing Year	1997
发行量（枚）	880		Mintage (Pieces)	880
铸造单位	沈阳造币厂		Minted by	Shenyang Mint

共同正面

原　大 Full Size

直径（毫米）	80	40
含纯银（盎司）	12	1
成色（%）	99.9	99.9
质量	精制	精制
年号	1997	1997
发行量（枚）	250	1800
铸造单位	沈阳造币厂	

Diameter (mm)	80	40
Pure Silver Content (oz)	12	1
Fineness (%)	99.9	99.9
Quality	Proof	Proof
Issuing Year	1997	1997
Mintage (Pieces)	250	1800
Minted by	Shenyang Mint	

1997 Issue of
the Peony Gold Medal

中國貴金屬紀念幣章圖鑑

二十八、1997年版牡丹花金章

一九九七年

牡丹是中国的特产，其花色泽艳丽，玉笑株香，华贵绝伦，被誉为“花中之王”。牡丹花色较多，有白、绿、红、紫、黄，又各有浓淡深浅之分，花大而香，争奇斗艳，所以也有“国色天香”之称。

牡丹原为野生植物，南北朝时期成为名贵的观赏品，自隋朝开始，牡丹进入皇宫，唐开元年间大盛于长安，由于朝廷带头提倡，牡丹身价百倍。宋代牡丹中心由长安向东转移到洛阳，达到鼎盛时期。到目前为止，中国引进和培育了数百种花大色艳、色彩俱佳的名贵牡丹。

牡丹，是和平、繁荣、吉祥、富贵的象征，被中国各族人民一致推举为国花。

1997版牡丹花金章为1/10盎司普制金章1种，正面图案均为牡丹花，背面图案为龙门奉先寺卢舍那大佛。该章由中国金币总公司发行，由深圳国宝金币制造厂铸造。

Peony is a special flower of China. It is very bright-colored, fragrant and sumptuous, and is eulogized as ‘the Queen of the flowers’. Peony has various kinds of colors including white, green, red, purple, yellow, and the colors are further divided into dark and light colors. The flower is big and fragrant, so it gets another name ‘national beauty and heavenly fragrance’.

Peony was once a kind of wild plant. It became a precious ornamental in the Southern and Northern Dynasties. It had entered the palace since the Sui Dynasty, and had been very popular in Chang’an during the Kaiyuan period of the Tang Dynasty. Because of the advocating of the court of the Song Dynasty, peony had raised suddenly in social status. The center of planting peony was transferred from Chang’an to Luoyang in the Song Dynasty and reached the period of full bloom. Up to now, China has introduced and cultivated hundreds of kinds of rare peony, which are both very big and bright-colored.

Peony, symbolizing peace, prosperity, auspiciousness and, wealth and rank, has been chosen as the national flower by the Chinese people of all nationalities at consensus.

1997 issue of the peony gold medal is one 1/10 oz. bu. gold medal with the obverse depicting the picture of peony, and with the reverse depicting the picture of the statue of Vairocana in the Fengxian Temple of Longmen. This medal was issued by China Gold Coin Inc. and was minted by the Shenzhen Panda Gold Coin Mint.

正 面

原 大 Full Size

放 大

直径（毫米）	18
含纯金（盎司）	1/10
成色（%）	99.9
质量	普制
年号	1997
发行量（枚）	3000
铸造单位	深圳国宝金币制造厂

Diameter (mm)	18
Pure Gold Content (oz)	1/10
Fineness (%)	99.9
Quality	Bu.
Issuing Year	1997
Mintage (Pieces)	3000
Minted by	Shenzhen Panda Gold Coin Mint

The Commemorative
Gold and Silver Stamps
of the Return
of Hong Kong to China

中國貴金屬紀念幣圖鑑

二十九、纪念香港回归祖国金银邮票

一九九七年

1997年7月1日，中英两国政府在香港会展中心举行了交接仪式，香港终于结束了长达一个半世纪的殖民统治，回到了祖国的怀抱。为纪念香港回归祖国，中国金币总公司与中国集邮总公司联合发行纪念香港回归祖国金银邮票，由沈阳造币厂铸造。

纪念香港回归祖国金银邮票共4个品种，其中1/2盎司精制银邮票2种，1种图案为中英联合声明及牡丹花，1种为中华人民共和国香港特别行政区基本法及牡丹花；1盎司精制小型张银邮票1种，图案为邓小平半身像；精制银镶金邮票1种，图案为邓小平半身像及香港风景，为25克银、6克金制。

On July 1, 1997, Chinese and British governments held the hand- over ceremony in Hong Kong Exhibition Center, Hong Kong finally ended its 150-year history of being a colony and came back to the motherland. To commemorate the return of Hong Kong, the return of Hong Kong to China gold and silver commemorative stamps were issued by China Gold Coin Inc. together with C.N.P.C., and were minted by Shenyang Mint.

This set has 4 stamps: two kinds of 1/2 oz. proof silver stamps, one of which with the design of the Joint Declaration of China and U.K. and peony flowers, while the other with design of the Basic Law of Hong Kong Special Administrative Region of P.R.C and peony flowers; one 1 oz. proof small-sized silver stamp with the design of the bust of Deng Xiaoping; one proof silver stamp inlayed with gold (25g silver and 6g gold) with the design of the bust of Deng Xiaoping and Hong Kong scenery.

含纯金（克）	6	
含纯银（克）	25	
含纯银（盎司）		1
成色（%）	99.9	99.9
质量	精制	精制
年号	1997	1997
发行量（枚）	12000	20000
铸造单位	沈阳造币厂	

Pure Gold Content (g)	6	
Pure Silver Content (g)	25	
Pure Silver Content (oz)		1
Fineness (%)	99.9	99.9
Quality	Proof	Proof
Issuing Year	1997	1997
Mintage (Pieces)	12000	20000
Minted by	Shenyang Mint	

含纯银（盎司）	1 /2	1 /2
成色（％）	99.9	99.9
质量	精制	精制
年号	1997	1997
发行量（枚）	20000	20000
铸造单位	沈阳造币厂	

Pure Silver Content (oz)	1 /2	1 /2
Fineness (%)	99.9	99.9
Quality	Proof	Proof
Issuing Year	1997	1997
Mintage (Pieces)	20000	20000
Minted by	Shenyang Mint	

The Commemorative
Gold and Silver Stamps
of the 70th Anniversary
of the Founding
of the People's Liberation Army

中國貴金屬紀念幣圖鑒

三十、纪念中国人民解放军建军70周年金银邮票

一九九七年

1927年8月1日，中国共产党发动和领导南昌起义，打响了武装反抗国民党反动派的第一枪，这个伟大事件标志着中国共产党开始创建自己的军队，中国人民解放军从此诞生。光辉的8月1日，成为中国人民解放军建军纪念日。

为纪念中国人民解放军建军70周年，中国金币总公司与中国集邮总公司联合发行纪念中国人民解放军建军70周年金银邮票。此套金银邮票共2个品种，其中3克精制金邮票1种，2克精制银邮票1种。

On 1st August 1927, the Communist Party of China launched and led the "Na Chang Uprising"firing the first shot against the Kuomintang reactionaries. This event marked the beginning of CCP's establishment of its own revolutionary forces. The people's Liberation Army was hence founded. The glorious date, August 1, became the commemorative day of the founding of PLA.

To mark the 70th anniversary of the founding of PLA, a set of commemorative stamps was issued by China Gold Coin Inc. together with C.N.P.C., including one 3g proof gold stamp and one 2g proof silver Stamp.

含纯金（克）	3
成色（%）	99.9
质量	精制
年号	1997
发行量（枚）	12000

Pure Gold Content (g)	3
Fineness (%)	99.9
Quality	Proof
Issuing Year	1997
Mintage (Pieces)	12000

含纯银（克）	2	Pure Silver Content (g)	2
成色（%）	99.9	Fineness (%)	99.9
质量	精制	Quality	Proof
年号	1997	Issuing Year	1997
发行量（枚）	12000	Mintage (Pieces)	12000

The Year of the Ox
Gold and Silver Stamps

中國貴金屬紀念幣年鑑

三十一、中国丁丑(牛)年金银邮票

一九九七年

1997年为中国农历丁丑(牛)年，中国金币总公司与中国集邮总公司为此联合发行中国丁丑(牛)年金银邮票，该套金银邮票由沈阳造币厂铸造。

牛，性格驯顺，体态雄壮，力大无穷，甘于奉献，是中国古代“六畜”之首。早在新石器时代，中国先民即开始驯牛。随着古代农业的发展，牛更成为人们从事农耕之得力助手。中国先民视牛为予人幸福、吉祥之神兽，且象征智慧。中国人认为牛是人类的忠实伙伴，尤敬其吃苦耐劳、坚韧不拔的奉献精神，认为牛年既是创业、奋进之年，又为事业通达、大获成功之年。

该套金银邮票共2个品种，其中2克精制金邮票和3克精制银邮票各1种，正面图案为同年国家发行的中国牛年生肖邮票图案。

1997 was the year of the Ox according to Chinese lunar calendar. A set of gold and silver commemorative stamps was issued by China Gold Coin Inc. together with C.N.P.C., and was minted by Shenyang Mint.

The meek yet strong ox, powerful and devoting, ranks first in ancient Chinese 'six domestic animals'. As early as in Neolithic Age, Chinese ancients have started to domesticate the ox. With the development of ancient agriculture, the ox has become more and more helpful in farming. Our ancestors regarded the ox as a symbol of wisdom that can bestow happiness and luckiness upon humankind. Chinese people believe that the ox is a faithful companion of humankind, and because of its firm and indomitable spirits, the year of ox is regarded as a year of creation, advancement as well as prosperity and success.

This set contains one 2g proof gold stamp and one 3g proof silver stamp with the common obverse depicting the picture same as that of the stamp of the year of the ox issued in the same year.

含纯金（克）	2	
含纯银（克）		3
成色（%）	99.9	99.9
质量	精制	精制
年号	1997	1997
发行量（枚）	12000	12000
铸造单位	沈阳造币厂	

Pure Gold Content (g)	2	
Pure Silver Content (g)		3
Fineness (%)	99.9	99.9
Quality	Proof	Proof
Issuing Year	1997	1997
Mintage (Pieces)	12000	12000
Minted by	Shenyang Mint	

1998

中國貴金屬紀念幣年鑒

Almanac of Chinesc Precious Metal Commemorative Currencies

1998 Issue of the Chinese Panda Gold and Silver Coin Series

中國貴金屬紀念幣圖鑒

一、1998年版中国熊猫金银币

一九九八年

自1982年起，中国人民银行以大熊猫为题材，每年发行中国熊猫系列金银币。1998年版中国熊猫金银币是中国人民银行发行的第17套熊猫金银币，该套金银币分别由上海造币厂、沈阳造币厂、深圳国宝金币制造厂、中国金币总公司铸造，中国金币总公司总经销。

熊猫又称大熊猫，是中国特有的珍稀野生动物，被称之为“国宝”。熊猫以其温顺的性格、憨态可掬的姿态深受人们喜爱。历年发行的熊猫金银币都是选取不同姿态的熊猫作为背面图案，力求年年有变化，变中有新意，使之更有欣赏价值和升值潜力。

1998年版中国熊猫金银币共10个品种，其中1盎司、1/2盎司、1/4盎司、1/10盎司、1/20盎司普制金币各1种，1/2盎司、1盎司普制银币各1种，1公斤精制银币1种，1盎司、1/2盎司精制彩色银币各1种。正面图案均为北京天坛祈年殿、国号、年号，背面图案均为多种姿态大熊猫及面额。

Since 1982, the People's Bank of China has been issuing the series of panda commemorative coins every year. 1998 issue, the 17th set in this series, was minted respectively by Shanghai Mint, Shenyang Mint, Shenzhen Panda Gold Coin Mint and China Gold Coin Inc., and distributed exclusively by China Gold Coin Inc..

Panda, also called giant panda, is a rare wild animal of China and is called 'National Treasure'. Panda is popular with Chinese people for its meek character and lovely postures. The panda coins issued in different years chose different postures of the panda as reverse pictures, changes were made each year so as to endow these coins with more appreciative value and revaluation potential.

1998 issue of the panda commemorative coin series contains 10 varieties including: 1 oz., 1/2 oz., 1/4 oz., 1/10oz. and 1/20 oz. bu. gold coins, 1/2 oz. and 1 oz. bu. silver coins, 1 kg proof silver coin, 1 oz. and 1/2 oz. proof colorful silver coins. The coins have common obverse depicting the picture of the Hall of Prayer for Good Harvests of the Temple of Heaven in Beijing, title of PRC, and the issuing year. The reverses depict the pictures of different postures of the panda and face value.

正　面

原　大 Full Size

放　大

面额（元）	100
直径（毫米）	32
含纯金（盎司）	1
成色（%）	99.9
质量	普制
年号	1998
发行量（枚）	
铸造单位	上海造币厂 沈阳造币厂

Face Value (Yuan)	100
Diameter (mm)	32
Pure Gold Content (oz)	1
Fineness (%)	99.9
Quality	Bu.
Issuing Year	1998
Mintage (Pieces)	
Minted by	Shanghai Mint Shenyang Mint

共同正面

原　大 Full Size

面额（元）	50	25	10	5
直径（毫米）	27	22	18	14
含纯金（盎司）	1/2	1/4	1/10	1/20
成色（%）	99.9	99.9	99.9	99.9
质量	普制	普制	普制	普制
年号	1998	1998	1998	1998
发行量（枚）				
铸造单位	上海造币厂 沈阳造币厂			

Face Value (Yuan)	50	25	10	5
Diameter (mm)	27	22	18	14
Pure Gold Content (oz)	1/2	1/4	1/10	1/20
Fineness (%)	99.9	99.9	99.9	99.9
Quality	Bu.	Bu.	Bu.	Bu.
Issuing Year	1998	1998	1998	1998
Mintage (Pieces)				
Minted by	Shanghai Mint Shenyang Mint			

正 面

原 大 Full Size

面额（元）	200
直径（毫米）	100
含纯银（公斤）	1
成色（%）	99.9
质量	精制
年号	1998
发行量（枚）	1998
铸造单位	深圳国宝金币制造厂

Face Value (Yuan)	200
Diameter (mm)	100
Pure Silver Content (kg)	1
Fineness (%)	99.9
Quality	Proof
Issuing Year	1998
Mintage (Pieces)	1998
Minted by	Shenzhen Panda Gold Coin Mint

共同正面

原　大 Full Size

面额（元）	10	5
直径（毫米）	40	33
含纯银（盎司）	1	1/2
成色（%）	99.9	99.9
质量	普制	普制
年号	1998	1998
发行量（枚）	250000	200000
铸造单位	上海造币厂 沈阳造币厂	深圳国宝 金币制造厂

Face Value (Yuan)	10	5
Diameter (mm)	40	33
Pure Silver Content (oz)	1	1/2
Fineness (%)	99.9	99.9
Quality	Bu.	Bu.
Issuing Year	1998	1998
Mintage (Pieces)	250000	200000
Minted by	Shanghai Mint Shenyang Mint	Shenzhen Panda Gold Coin Mint

共同正面

放　大

原　大 Full Size

面额（元）	10	5
直径（毫米）	40	36
含纯银（盎司）	1	1/2
成色（%）	99.9	99.9
质量	精制	精制
年号	1998	1998
发行量（枚）	100000	100000
铸造单位	中国金币总公司	

Face Value (Yuan)	10	5
Diameter (mm)	40	36
Pure Silver Content (oz)	1	1/2
Fineness (%)	99.9	99.9
Quality	Proof	Proof
Issuing Year	1998	1998
Mintage (Pieces)	100000	100000
Minted by	China Gold Coin Inc.	

Series of Chinese Twelve
Animals of Lunar Calendar
—The Year of the Tiger
Gold and Silver Coins

中國貴金屬紀念幣圖鑒

二、中国十二生肖系列——戊寅(虎)年金银币

一九九八年

1998年是中国农历戊寅(虎)年，中国人民银行为此发行中国戊寅(虎)年金银币。该套金银币分别由上海造币厂、沈阳造币厂、深圳国宝金币制造厂、中国金币总公司铸造，中国金币总公司总经销。

虎，体态壮美，毛色斑斓，气势威猛，卓而不群。中国先民敬称其为“山之君也”。

在中国古代神话中，虎乃神仙伙伴。国人熟知的财神赵公元帅传说是骑黑虎为人招财进宝，故虎在中国先民心目中又系吉祥、幸福、平安、避邪之神兽，成为供奉于室的守护神。

虎亦颇受历代画家青睐。晋代顾恺之《虎啸图》威猛强健，栩栩如生。现当代画家张善子犹爱画虎，自诩“虎痴”，所绘《虎》图，尽得虎之神韵。画家胡爽庵亦曾绘制《虎》图。

中国人素来视虎为尊贵、威猛、吉祥、强盛的象征，认为虎年是吉祥隆盛、奋发进取、战无不胜之年。

中国戊寅(虎)年金银币共14个品种。其中1盎司普制银币、1盎司精制金币、1盎司精制银币、1盎司精制铂币各1种，正面图案均为国徽、国号、年号，背面图案均为顾恺之所绘《虎啸图》及面额；12盎司精制金币、12盎司精制银币各1种，正面图案均为长城八达岭楼景、国号、年号，背面图案均为胡爽庵所绘《虎》图及面额；1公斤精制金币(梅花型)、1/2盎司精制金币(梅花型)、2/3盎司精制银币(梅花型)、5盎司精制金币、5盎司精制银币各1种，正面图案均为国号、年号、长城八达岭楼景，背面图案均为张善子所绘《虎》图及面额；1盎司精制彩色银币1种，1/10盎司精制彩色金币1种，1/10盎司普制金币1种，正面图案均为国号、年号、长城八达岭楼景，背面图案分别为彩色老虎头像、彩色小老虎、小老虎及面额。

1998 was the year of the tiger according to Chinese lunar calendar, the People's Bank of China issued the year of the tiger commemorative gold and silver coins minted by Shanghai Mint, Shenyang Mint, Shenzheng Panda Gold Coin Mint and China Gold Coin Inc. respectively, and distributed exclusively by China Gold Coin Inc..

Chinese ancestors called this magnificent, multi-colored, powerful and unmatched tiger with respect “the king of the mountains”.

In ancient Chinese legends, tiger was the companion of supernatural beings. It is well known to the Chinese that God of Fortune Marshal Zhao rode on the back of a black tiger to bring in the wealth for people, so in the minds of ancient Chinese people tiger was closely linked with luckiness, happiness, safety and evil-avoiding, and so it became the eudemon worshiped at home.

The tiger is also very popular with painters. Gu Kaizhi, lived in the Jin Dynasty, painted vividly a powerful tiger in his *The Roar of Tiger*. Contemporary painter Zhang Shanzi, favors tiger especially, calls himself ‘lover of the tiger’, whose *Tiger* vividly reproduces the charm of tiger. Another painter Hu Shuang'an once also painted *Tiger*.

Chinese people have long since regarded tiger as a symbol of dignity, might, luckiness and prosperity; the year of tiger is a year of prosperity, advancement and victory.

The year of the tiger gold and silver coins contain 14 varieties: One 1 oz. bu. silver coin, one 1 oz. proof gold coin, one 1 oz. proof silver coin and one 1 oz. proof platinum coin with the common obverse depicting the picture of the national emblem, title of PRC and the issuing year, while the common reverse depicting the picture of the painting of Gu kaizhi's *The Roar of Tiger* and face value; The 12 oz. proof gold coin and 12 oz. proof silver coin have the common obverse depicting the picture of the scene of Badaling of the Great Wall, title of PRC and the issuing year, and with the common reverse depicting the picture of the painting of Hu Shuang' an's *Tiger* and face value; The 1kg proof gold coin (plum flower-shaped), 1/2 oz. proof gold coin (plum-flower shaped), 2/3 oz. proof silver coin (plum-flower shaped), 5 oz. proof gold coin and 5 oz. proof silver coin have a common obverse depicting the picture of the scene of Badaling, title of PRC and the issuing year, and with the common reverse depicting the picture of the painting of Zhang Shanzi's *Tiger* and face value. The 1 oz. proof colorful silver coin, 1/10 oz. proof colorful gold coin and 1/10 oz. bu. gold coin have a common obverse depicting the picture of the scene of Badaling, title of PRC and the issuing year, and with the reverses depict the pictures of the colorful head portrait of tiger, colorful tiger cub, tiger cub and face value respectively.

共同正面

原 大 Full Size

面额（元）	2000	100
直径（毫米）	100	27
含纯金（公斤）	1	
含纯金（盎司）		0.458
成色（%）	99.9	91.6
质量	精制	精制
年号	1998	1998
发行量（枚）	15	2300
铸造单位	上海造币厂	沈阳造币厂

Face Value (Yuan)	2000	100
Diameter (mm)	100	27
Pure Gold Content (kg)	1	
Pure Gold Content (oz)		0.458
Fineness (%)	99.9	91.6
Quality	Proof	Proof
Issuing Year	1998	1998
Mintage (Pieces)	15	2300
Minted by	Shanghai Mint	Shenyang Mint

共同正面

原 大 Full Size

面额（元）	1000	500
直径（毫米）	70	60
含纯金（盎司）	12	5
成色（%）	99.9	99.9
质量	精制	精制
年号	1998	1998
发行量（枚）	99	99
铸造单位	上海造币厂	沈阳造币厂

Face Value (Yuan)	1000	500
Diameter (mm)	70	60
Pure Gold Content (oz)	12	5
Fineness (%)	99.9	99.9
Quality	Proof	Proof
Issuing Year	1998	1998
Mintage (Pieces)	99	99
Minted by	Shanghai Mint	Shenyang Mint

共同正面

放　大

原　大 Full Size

面额（元）	100	10
直径（毫米）	32	18
含纯金（盎司）	1	1/10
成色（%）	99.9	99.9
质量	精制	普制
年号	1998	1998
发行量（枚）	1600	48000
铸造单位	上海造币厂	深圳国宝金币制造厂

Face Value (Yuan)	100	10
Diameter (mm)	32	18
Pure Gold Content (oz)	1	1/10
Fineness (%)	99.9	99.9
Quality	Proof	Bu.
Issuing Year	1998	1998
Mintage (Pieces)	1600	48000
Minted by	Shanghai Mint	Shenzhen Panda Gold Coin Mint

放 大

正 面

原 大 Full Size

面额（元）	10
直径（毫米）	36
含纯银（盎司）	0.6
成色（%）	90
质量	精制
年号	1998
发行量（枚）	6800
铸造单位	沈阳造币厂

Face Value (Yuan)	10
Diameter (mm)	36
Pure Silver Content (oz)	0.6
Fineness (%)	90
Quality	Proof
Issuing Year	1998
Mintage (Pieces)	6800
Minted by	Shenyang Mint

共同正面

原 大 Full Size

面额（元）	100	50
直径（毫米）	80	70
含纯银（盎司）	12	5
成色（%）	99.9	99.9
质量	精制	精制
年号	1998	1998
发行量（枚）	500	1000
铸造单位	上海造币厂	沈阳造币厂

Face Value (Yuan)	100	50
Diameter (mm)	80	70
Pure Silver Content (oz)	12	5
Fineness (%)	99.9	99.9
Quality	Proof	Proof
Issuing Year	1998	1998
Mintage (Pieces)	500	1000
Minted by	Shanghai Mint	Shenyang Mint

共同正面

原　大 Full Size

面额（元）	10	10
直径（毫米）	40	32
含纯银（盎司）	1	1
成色（%）	99.9	99.9
质量	普制	精制
年号	1998	1998
发行量（枚）	50000	8000
铸造单位	上海造币厂	

Face Value (Yuan)	10	10
Diameter (mm)	40	32
Pure Silver Content (oz)	1	1
Fineness (%)	99.9	99.9
Quality	Bu.	Proof
Issuing Year	1998	1998
Mintage (Pieces)	50000	8000
Minted by	Shanghai Mint	

共同正面

放 大

原 大 Full Size

面额（元）	100
直径（毫米）	32
含纯铂（盎司）	1
成色（%）	99.95
质量	精制
年号	1998
发行量（枚）	300
铸造单位	中国金币总公司

Face Value (Yuan)	100
Diameter (mm)	32
Pure Platinum Content (oz)	1
Fineness (%)	99.95
Quality	Proof
Issuing Year	1998
Mintage (Pieces)	300
Minted by	China Gold Coin Inc.

正　面

正　面

原　大 Full Size

原　大 Full Size

面额（元）	10	10
直径（毫米）	18	40
含纯金（盎司）	1/10	
含纯银（盎司）		1
成色（%）	99.9	99.9
质量	精制	精制
年号	1998	1998
发行量（枚）	30000	100000
铸造单位	中国金币总公司	

Face Value (Yuan)	10	10
Diameter (mm)	18	40
Pure Gold Content (oz)	1/10	
Pure Silver Content (oz)		1
Fineness (%)	99.9	99.9
Quality	Proof	Proof
Issuing Year	1998	1998
Mintage (Pieces)	30000	100000
Minted by	China Gold Coin Inc.	

The Centenary of the
Birth of Zhou Enlai
Commemorative Coins

中國貴金屬紀念幣圖鑒

三、周恩来诞辰100周年纪念币

一九九八年

为纪念周恩来诞辰100周年，缅怀革命伟人，中国人民银行发行周恩来诞辰100周年纪念币。该套纪念币由上海造币厂铸造，中国金币总公司总经销。

周恩来(1898年3月5日～1976年1月8日)是中国共产党和中华人民共和国的主要领导人之一，中国人民解放军的创建人之一，中国杰出的无产阶级革命家、政治家、军事家和外交家。原籍浙江绍兴，生于江苏淮安。早年读私塾。1917年毕业于天津南开中学，后赴日本留学。1927年3月，领导上海工人第三次武装起义。同年8月，与贺龙、朱德等领导了震惊中外的南昌起义，开创了中国共产党独立领导革命战争和创建革命军队的新时期。1936年西安事变发生后，全权代表中共中央到西安同蒋介石谈判，为和平解决西安事变，促进抗日民族统一战线的形成和发展，起到了关键性的作用。1945年同毛泽东一起参加重庆谈判。1946年任中国人民解放军总参谋长，参加领导和指挥了辽沈、平津、淮海等战役。

中华人民共和国成立后，周恩来担任政府总理，曾兼任外交部长。"文化大革命"中同林彪、江青集团进行了各种形式的坚决斗争，为保护大批党内外干部作了坚持不懈的努力。他为实现中美、中日关系正常化和恢复中国在联合国的合法席位作出了卓越的贡献。1976年1月8日因病在北京逝世，享年78岁。

几十年来，周恩来为党和人民建立了丰功伟绩，被亿万群众颂扬为"人民的好总理"，赢得了国内外人民的普遍敬重。

周恩来诞辰100周年纪念币共3个品种，其中1/2盎司精制金币1种，1盎司精制银币2种。金币、银币正面图案均为国号、年号、江苏淮安周恩来纪念馆；背面图案使用周恩来不同历史时期的照片，金币背面图案为周恩来头像、海棠花、生辰年代及面额，银币背面图案分别为长征中骑在马上的周恩来像、周恩来在开国大典时的半身像及面额。

To mark the centenary of the birth of premier Zhou Enlai and to commemorate this great revolutionary leader, the People's Bank of China issued the commemorative coins, minted by Shanghai Mint and exclusively distributed by China Gold Coin Inc..

Zhou Enlai (5 March 1898 ~ 8 January 1976), an outstanding revolutionist, statesman, strategist and diplomatist, was one of the major leaders of the Communist Party of China and the People's Republic of China, one of the founders of the Chinese People's Liberation Army. His native home is Shaoxing, Zhejiang province, but Zhou was born in Huai'an, Jiangsu province. In his childhood, he entered an old-style private school. After graduating from Nankai Middle School in Tianjin city in 1917, he went to Japan for further study. In March 1927, he led the third armed uprising of the workers in Shanghai and, in August, he led the world-shaking Nanchang Uprising together with He Long and Zhu De. This event ushered in a new epoch of the independent leadership of CPC in revolution and founding of armed forces. After the Xi'an Incident in 1936, Zhou, on behalf of the CPC, went to Xi'an to negotiate with Jiang Kaishi, and he played a key role in the peaceful solution of the Xi'an Incident and the formation and development of the Anti-Japanese National United Front. Together with Mao Zedong, he attended the Chongqing Negotiation in 1945. He was appointed chief of the general staff in 1946, led and directed Liao Shen, Pingjin and Huaihai Campaigns with other chief leaders.

After the founding of the People's Republic of China, Zhou Enlai acted as the premier of the central government, and once he was the minister of Foreign Ministry at the same time. During the Cultural Revolution he had fought resolutely against the Gong of Four and took great pains to protect some leaders in and out the Party. He had made great contributions to the normalization of the Sino-U.S. and Sino-Japan relationships and the restoration of China's legal position in the United Nations as well. On January 8, 1976, he died in Beijing at the age of 78.

For decades, Zhou Enlai had made great achievements for the Party and the people. He was eulogized as 'good premiere of the people', and won the respect from peoples all over the world.

The commemorative coins include three varieties: 1/2 oz. proof gold coin two kinds of 1 oz. proof silver coins. Both the gold and silver coins have the common obverse depicting the picture of the title of PRC, issuing year and the Zhou Enlai Memorial Hall in Huaian, Jiangsu province. The reverses depict the photos of Zhou of different time. The gold coin has an reverse depicting the head portrait of Zhou, Chinese flowering crabapple, birthday and face value; the silver coins have the reverses depicting the pictures of Zhou riding on a horse during the Long March, the bust of Zhou at the opening ceremony of celebrating the founding of the PRC and face value.

正 面

原 大 Full Size

放 大

面额（元）	50
直径（毫米）	27
含纯金（盎司）	1/2
成色（%）	99.9
质量	精制
年号	1998
发行量（枚）	8000
铸造单位	上海造币厂

Face Value (Yuan)	50
Diameter (mm)	27
Pure Gold Content (oz)	1/2
Fineness (%)	99.9
Quality	Proof
Issuing Year	1998
Mintage (Pieces)	8000
Minted by	Shanghai Mint

共同正面

原　大 Full Size

面额（元）	10	10
直径（毫米）	40	40
含纯银（盎司）	1	1
成色（%）	99.9	99.9
质量	精制	精制
年号	1998	1998
发行量（枚）	38000	38000
铸造单位	上海造币厂	

Face Value (Yuan)	10	10
Diameter (mm)	40	40
Pure Silver Content (oz)	1	1
Fineness (%)	99.9	99.9
Quality	Proof	Proof
Issuing Year	1998	1998
Mintage (Pieces)	38000	38000
Minted by	Shanghai Mint	

The Centenary of the
Birth of Liu Shaoqi
Commemorative Coins

中國貴金屬紀念幣年鑒

四、刘少奇诞辰100周年纪念币

一九九八年

为纪念刘少奇诞辰100周年，缅怀革命伟人，中国人民银行发行刘少奇诞辰100周年纪念币。该套纪念币由上海造币厂铸造，中国金币总公司总经销。

刘少奇(1898年11月24日～1969年11月12日)，中国共产党和中华人民共和国的主要领导人之一，中国杰出的无产阶级革命家、政治家和理论家。生于湖南省宁乡县。1921年在苏联莫斯科东方大学学习期间加入中国共产党。1922年回国后参加领导了粤汉铁路工人大罢工和安源路矿工人大罢工。1934年参加长征，曾任红军第五、第八军团党代表和第三军团政治部主任。1945年在中国共产党第七次全国代表大会上作《关于修改党章的报告》。1947年春开始负责中共中央的日常工作。

1949年中华人民共和国成立后，刘少奇当选为中央人民政府副主席。1959年4月当选为中华人民共和国主席。"文化大革命"中受到错误批判，1969年在河南开封逝世，享年71岁。1980年中共十一届五中全会为其恢复名誉。

几十年来，刘少奇为中国共产党的巩固和发展，为新民主主义革命的胜利，为社会主义革命和社会主义建设事业的胜利，进行了不懈的斗争；在经济建设、政权建设、文化教育事业、外交工作等方面建立了不朽的功绩；对毛泽东思想的形成和发展，作出了杰出的贡献。

刘少奇诞辰100周年纪念币共3个品种，其中1/2盎司精制金币1种，1盎司精制银币2种。金币、银币正面图案均为国号、年号、湖南宁乡刘少奇纪念馆；金币背面图案为长青竹叶环绕的刘少奇头像及面额，两种银币背面图案分别为在第一届全国人民政治协商会议上的刘少奇像、戴红领巾的刘少奇肖像及面额。

To mark the centenary of the birth Liu Shaoqi and to commemorate this great revolutionary figure, the People's Bank of China issued the commemorative coins, minted by Shanghai Mint and exclusively distributed by China Gold Coin Inc..

Liu shaoqi (Nov.24, 1898 ~ Nov.12, 1969), an outstanding revolutionist, statesman and theoretician, was one of the major leaders of CPC and PRC. He was born in Ningxiang county, Hunan province. He joined the Communist Party of China when he studied at Moscow Oriental University in 1921. In 1922, he led the Strike of Yuehan railway workers and the Strike of the miners and railway workers of Anyuan. In 1934, he took part in the Long March and acted as the Party representative for NO. 5 and No. 8 Army Groups and the chief of the Political Department for NO. 3 Army Group. He made a speech on the amendment of the Party Constitution at the 7th National Congress of CPC. In spring, 1947, he started to be in charge of the daily affairs of the Central Committee of CPC.

After the founding of PRC, Liu Shaoqi was elected vice president of the Central Government, and was elected Chairman of the PRC in April 1959. He had been wrongly criticized during the Cultural Revolution and died in Kaifeng, Henan province in 1969 at the age of 71. He was rehabilitated at the 5th plenary session of the 11th Central Committee of CPC.

For decades, Liu made persistent efforts for the consolidation and development of CPC, the victory of New Democratic Revolution and the victory of the socialist revolution and construction. He made great contributions in the fields of economic construction, political power construction, culture and education, foreign affairs and the forming and development of Mao Tse-tung Thought especially.

The commemorative coins contain three varieties: 1/2 oz. proof gold coin and two kinds of 1 oz. proof silver coins with the common obverse depicting the title of PRC, issuing year and the Liu Shaoqi Memorial Hall in Ninginag, Hunan Province. The reverse of the gold coin depicts the picture of the head portrait of Liu surrounded by the evergreen bamboo leaves and face value. The reverses of the silver coins depict the pictures of the head portrait of Liu at the First National People's Political Consultative Conference and the portrait of Liu wearing red scarf and face value respectively.

正 面

原 大 Full Size

放 大

面额（元）	50
直径（毫米）	27
含纯金（盎司）	1/2
成色（%）	99.9
质量	精制
年号	1998
发行量（枚）	8000
铸造单位	上海造币厂

Face Value (Yuan)	50
Diameter (mm)	27
Pure Gold Content (oz)	1/2
Fineness (%)	99.9
Quality	Proof
Issuing Year	1998
Mintage (Pieces)	8000
Minted by	Shanghai Mint

共同正面

原　大 Full Size

面额（元）	10	10
直径（毫米）	40	40
含纯银（盎司）	1	1
成色（%）	99.9	99.9
质量	精制	精制
年号	1998	1998
发行量（枚）	30000	30000
铸造单位	上海造币厂	

Face Value (Yuan)	10	10
Diameter (mm)	40	40
Pure Silver Content (oz)	1	1
Fineness (%)	99.9	99.9
Quality	Proof	Proof
Issuing Year	1998	1998
Mintage (Pieces)	30000	30000
Minted by	Shanghai Mint	

60th Anniversary of the Arrival of Dr. Henry N. Bethune's in China Commemorative Coins

中國貴金屬紀念幣圖鑑

五、白求恩到达中国60周年纪念币

一九九八年

为纪念伟大的国际共产主义战士诺尔曼·白求恩大夫到达中国60周年以及中华人民共和国与加拿大建交28周年，中国人民银行发行白求恩到达中国60周年纪念币。该套纪念币分别由中国深圳国宝金币制造厂和加拿大皇家铸币厂铸造，中国金币总公司总经销。

诺尔曼·白求恩(1890年3月3日～1939年11月12日)，加拿大人，世界反法西斯斗争的英雄，伟大的和平使者，中国人民永远的朋友。出生于加拿大安大略省格雷文赫斯特镇。早年入多伦多大学，攻读生物学。

1937年，为支援中国人民的抗日战争，白求恩受加拿大共产党和美国共产党的派遣，率领一支由加拿大人和美国人组成的医疗队来到中国，并于1938年3月底到达延安。

白求恩把救死扶伤看作医生的最神圣的职责，"一切为伤员着想"，是他工作的出发点。1939年秋，他因手术中不幸手指受伤，导致感染中毒，转为败血症，在河北完县逝世。其遗体解放后安葬在石家庄烈士陵园。

白求恩是一个真正的共产主义者，为国际共产主义事业艰苦卓绝地奋斗了一生。中国人民将世代铭记白求恩的伟大功绩。

该套纪念币共发行2个品种，中方铸造1种、加方铸造1种。中方所铸造的1盎司精制银币正面图案为国徽、国号、年号、梅花，背面图案为松树环绕的白求恩头像、纪念文字、白求恩战地手术的背景图及面额。加方所铸造的1盎司精制银币正面图案为英伊丽莎白女王头像，背面图案为白求恩头像、白求恩在行军途中、延安抗日根据地背景及面额。

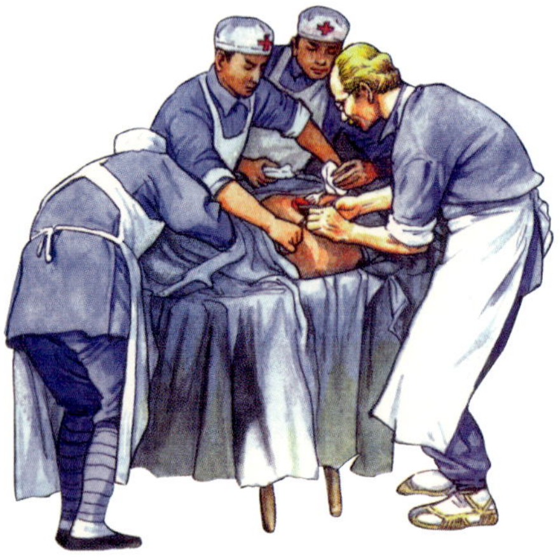

To mark the 60th anniversary of the international communist soldier Doctor Norman Bethune's arrival at China and the 28th anniversary of the establishment of diplomatic relation between China and Canada, the People's Bank of China issued the commemorative coins, minted by Shenzhen Panda Gold Coin Mint and Royal Canadian Mint respectively, exclusively distributed by China Gold Coin Inc..

Norman Bethune (March 3, 1890 ~ Nov12, 1939) was a Canadian anti-fascist hero, a great peace missionary and a life-long friend of Chinese people. He was born in a small town of Canada. He entered Toronto University majoring in biology when he was young.

In 1937, in order to support Chinese people's anti-Japanese war, he was sent by the communist parties of Canada and America leading a medical team made up of Canadian and Americans to China and arrived at Yan'an at the end of March 1938.

Dr. Bethune believed that it's doctor's holy duty to heal the wounded and rescue the dying, and the departure point of his work is to center all the attention in the wounded. In autumn 1939, his finger was injured in an operation and this injury was infected. He died of blood poisoning in Wan County, Hebei province. His remains were buried in the cemetery of revolutionary soldiers of Shi Jiazhang after liberation.

Dr. Bethune was a real communist. He devoted all his life to the cause of international communism. Chinese people will cherish a precious memory of him forever.

This set of commemorative cons includes two varieties: China made one of them, and Canada made the other. The 1 oz. proof silver coins made by China has the obverse depicting the picture of the national emblem, title of PRC, issuing year and the plum flower, and the reverse depicts the picture of the head portrait of Bethune surrounded by pine tress, commemorative words, the background scene of Bethune operating in the battlefield and face value. The 1 oz. proof silver coin made by Canada has an obverse depicting the picture of the head portrait of Queen Elizabeth and a reverse of the head portrait of Bethune, Bethune in marching, the background of Yan'an anti-Japanese base and face value.

正　面

放　大

原　大 Full Size

面额（元）	10
直径（毫米）	40
含纯银（盎司）	1
成色（%）	99.99
质量	精制
年号	1998
发行量（枚）	80000
铸造单位	深圳国宝金币制造厂

Face Value (Yuan)	10
Diameter (mm)	40
Pure Silver Content (oz)	1
Fineness (%)	99.99
Quality	精制
Issuing Year	1998
Mintage (Pieces)	80000
Minted by	Shenzhen Panda Gold Coin Mint

正　面

放　大

原　大 Full Size

面额（元）	5
直径（毫米）	38
含纯银（盎司）	1
成色（%）	99.99
质量	精制
年号	1998
发行量（枚）	80000
铸造单位	加拿大皇家铸币厂

Face Value (Yuan)	5
Diameter (mm)	38
Pure Silver Content (oz)	1
Fineness (%)	99.99
Quality	Proof
Issuing Year	1998
Mintage (Pieces)	80000
Minted by	Royal Canadian Mint

1998 Issue of Ma Zu
Silver Coin

中國貴金屬紀念幣圖鑒

六、1998年版妈祖银币

一九九八年

为了弘扬传统文化，中国人民银行发行1998年版妈祖银币。该币由上海造币厂铸造，中国金币总公司总经销。

妈祖是中国东南沿海著名的海上保护神。传说这位女神曾生活在人间，生时"能言人休咎"、"能知人祸福"，通晓天文气象，擅长海上救护，精通医学，治病防疫，深受爱戴。据说她死后成为海神，继续保佑乡里，感应更为灵验，逐步成为东南沿海百姓共同的保护神。乡人就在湄洲岛上建了一个供奉她的小庙以示感念。

宋元以来，妈祖屡受朝廷赐封，朝廷的赐封进一步扩大了妈祖信仰的区域。

随着移民渡海来到台湾，妈祖的信仰也紧随而来。妈祖在人们心目中是一位慈爱的女神，深得人们信赖。作为从故乡请来的守护神，妈祖信仰也成了人们怀土思乡的重要寄托。

1998年版妈祖银币为1盎司普制银币1种，其正面图案为国号、年号、妈祖庙，背面图案为妈祖像及面额。

In order to promote our traditional culture, the People's Bank of China issued the 1998 issue of Ma Zu silver coins, minted by Shanghai Mint and exclusively distributed by China Gold Coin Inc..

Ma Zu is a well-known protective goddess in the southeast littoral of China. In legend she is said to have been living in our earthly world. In her lifetime she could predict people's birth and death, weal and woe; expert at astronomy and weather, and was good at marine rescue, medicine, sickness-curing and epidemic prevention. Thus she was deeply loved by people. It is said that she became the sea Goddess and went on protecting the land with sharper prognostication after her death. Gradually Ma Zu has become the common protective goddess of the southeast people. The villagers set up a small temple on Meizhou Island dedicated to her to express their gratitude.

The royal courts since the Song and Yuan Dynasties had bestowed glories on Ma Zu. The bestowals helped to enlarge the areas where people worship her.

This belief accompanied the immigrants landing on Taiwan. In these believers' mind, Ma Zu a benevolent goddess and is worthy of their trust. As a protector invited from the native land, this belief in Ma Zu is an embodiment of the homesickness of these immigrants.

1998 issue of Ma Zu silver coin is one 1 oz. bu. silver coin. Its obverse depicts the picture of the title of PRC, issuing year and the Temple of Ma Zu, and the reverse depicts the picture of the portrait of Ma Zu and face value.

正 面

放 大

原 大 Full Size

面额（元）	10
直径（毫米）	40
含纯银（盎司）	1
成色（%）	99.9
质量	普制
年号	1998
发行量（枚）	50000
铸造单位	上海造币厂

Face Value (Yuan)	10
Diameter (mm)	40
Pure Silver Content (oz)	1
Fineness (%)	99.9
Quality	Bu.
Issuing Year	1998
Mintage (Pieces)	50000
Minted by	Shanghai Mint

1998 Issue of the
Avalokitesvara Buddha
Silver Coins

中國貴金屬紀念幣圖鑑

七、1998年版观世音菩萨银币

一九九八年

为使世界了解中国文化传统，中国人民银行自1993年开始发行观世音菩萨银币，1998年版观世音菩萨银币，由上海造币厂铸造，中国金币总公司总经销。

观世音是梵文Avalokites' Vara的意译，据说其可以“观察”世界上的一切声音，所以名为“观世音”菩萨。唐代避李世民之讳，改称观音。

据佛经所载，观世音为了教化不同层次、不同环境的众生，可以化现出三十二种化身及观音本相共三十三身。后来佛教根据观音三十三身的说法，绘制了三十三种观音的画像，即“三十三观音”。

杨柳观音，亦称杨枝观音，手持净瓶、杨枝，为立像。常戴女式风帽，披肩长巾，为民间的标准观音像。

千手观音像有多种形态。有一种是观音端坐于莲花宝座之上，头戴宝冠，身披袈裟，赤双足，臂有千手，手持各种法器，但千手只是概指其手多。

洒水观音，亦名滴水观音，作右手持瓶洒水状。

合什观音，双手常作合掌之像。

其他还有莲座观音、玉露观音、送子观音、玉瓶观音等多种形态。

1998年版观世音菩萨银币共4个品种，其中1盎司普制银币1种，1/2盎司精制银币2种，3.3两精制银币1种。正面图案均为国号、年号、普陀山，背面图案分别为莲座观音像、玉露观音像、合什观音像、千手观音像及面额。

In order to make the world better understand Chinese cultural tradition, the People's Bank of China has been issuing the series of the Avalokitesvara Buddha gold and silver coins since 1993. 1998 issue was minted by Shanghai Mint and exclusively distributed by China Gold Coin Inc..

Guanshiyin is a Chinese transliteration of the Sanskrit word Avalokitesvara. It is said that He could 'observe' all of the sound in the world, and so He is called 'observe the sound in the world' Buddha (Chinese *Guanshiyin*). In the Tang dynasty He was renamed 'observe the sound' (Chinese Guanyin) to avoid the taboo on the personal name of Emperor Li Shimin.

According to the Buddhist scripture, Avalokitesvara could appear as 32 kinds of nirmanakaya (metamorphosic body) and His true body totaling 33 bodies in order to moralize all living creatures of various levels and circumstances. Subsequently Buddhism had drawn 33 kinds of portraits of Avalokitesvara according to this, called '33 Avalokitesvara'.

Willow Avalokitessvara, also called Tender Willow Branch Avalokitesvara, is a standing stature with tender willow branches and clean flask in her hands, wearing woman's funnel cap and long shawl. This is a standard Avalokitesvara image.

There are various postures for the 'Sahasrabhuja-avalokitesvara (Thousand-arm Avalokitesvara). One of which is a sitting Avalokitessvara on a lotus throne wearing a cassock, bare-footed with a crown on his head, holding various musical instruments in his thousand hands. Thousand-hands is a general term not a literal term, just to indicate lots of hands.

Water-spraying Avalokitesvara, also called Water-dripping Avalokitesvara, takes the posture of holding a water flask in her right hand spraying the water from the flask.

Heshi Avalokitesvara takes the posture of putting hands together in prayer.

Other postures include Lotus Throne Avalokitesvara, Jade Dew Avalokitesvara, Birth Giving Avalokitesvara and Jade Flask Avalokitesvara, etc.

1998 issue of the Avalokitesvara Buddha Silver coin series contains four varieties: 1 oz. bu. silver coin, two kinds of 1/2 oz. proof silver, and 3.3 liang (165g) proof silver coin with the common obverse depicting the picture of the title of PRC, issuing year and Putuo Mount. The reverses depict the pictures of the portrait of Lotus Throne Avalokitesvara, Jade Dew Avalokitesvara, Heshi Avalokitesvara, and Thousand-arm Avalokitesvara respectively and face value.

正 面

放 大

原 大 Full Size

面额（元）	50
直径（毫米）	60
含纯银（两）	3.3
成色（%）	99.9
质量	精制
年号	1998
发行量（枚）	5000
铸造单位	上海造币厂

Face Value (Yuan)	50
Diameter (mm)	60
Pure Silver Content (Liang)	3.3
Fineness (%)	99.9
Quality	Proof
Issuing Year	1998
Mintage (Pieces)	5000
Minted by	Shanghai Mint

共同正面

原　大 Full Size

面额（元）	10	5	5
直径（毫米）	40	33	33
含纯银（盎司）	1	1/2	1/2
成色（%）	99.9	99.9	99.9
质量	普制	精制	精制
年号	1998	1998	1998
发行量（枚）	88000	10000	10000
铸造单位	上海造币厂		

Face Value (Yuan)	10	5	5
Diameter (mm)	40	33	33
Pure Silver Content (oz)	1	1/2	1/2
Fineness (%)	99.9	99.9	99.9
Quality	Bu.	Proof	Proof
Issuing Year	1998	1998	1998
Mintage (Pieces)	88000	10000	10000
Minted by	Shanghai Mint		

World Wild Animals
Foundation
Commemorative Coin
(Clouded Leopard
Silver Coin)

中國貴金屬紀念幣圖鑒

八、世界野生动物基金会纪念币
（云豹银币）

一九九八年

世界野生动物基金会于1961年成立，是为保护世界自然环境及生物而建立的资金援助机构。中国于1980年3月加入该机构，接受其在自然保护事业各方面的资金和人才援助。

为了宣传世界野生动物基金会为保护世界范围内野生动物所作出的杰出贡献，中国人民银行1998年发行世界野生动物基金会系列银币之一——云豹银币。该币由上海造币厂铸造，中国金币总公司总经销。

云豹，猫科动物。源于东南亚热带地区，后逐渐北移，现主要分布于亚热带地区，中国浙江、湖南、四川、贵州等南方省市较多。成年云豹毛短，呈浅灰褐色或浅黄色，间有黑斑，身上花纹呈不规则的云块形或荷叶形、龟纹形。每胎多为2～3仔，生产期间须有高度的隐私，否则幼仔不是被母兽吃掉，就是被弃之不顾，是珍贵的野生动物。

该套银币为27克精制银币1种。正面图案为国徽、国号及年号，背面图案为云豹、野生动物基金会WWF标志及面额。

World Wild Animals Foundation, a fund-aid organization, was founded in 1961 for the purpose of protecting the natural environment and wild lives. China joined this organization in March 1980 accepting its financial and personnel help in the field of natural protection.

In order to praise the great contribution that the World Wild Animals Foundation has done to protect the wild lives on world-wide scale, the People's Bank of China issued one of the series of silver coins of World Wild Animals Foundation-clouded leopard silver coin minted by Shanghai Mint and exclusively distributed by China Gold Coin Inc..

Clouded leopard, a kind of felid, originally lived in the tropical zone of Southeast Asia, gradually moved to the north, and now they mainly live in the sub-tropical zone. They mainly distribute over Zhejiang, Hunan, Sichuan and Guizhou provinces. The adult clouded leopard's fur is very short, light brown or light yellow, sometimes spotted with black dots. Its skin pattern resembles cloud, or lotus leaf or turtle's shell. Clouded leopard can give birth to 2～3 baby leopards each time but any disturbance in its reproduction period will result in the eating up of the newly born leopards or the abandonment of them by the mother leopards. Clouded leopard is a kind of rare wild animal.

This set contains one kind of 27g proof silver coin. Its obverse depicts the picture of the national emblem, title of PRC and the issuing year, and the reverse depicts the picture of clouded leopard, logo of WWF and face value.

正 面

放 大

原 大 Full Size

面额（元）	10
直径（毫米）	38.6
含纯银（盎司）	0.803
成色（%）	92.5
质量	精制
年号	1998
发行量（枚）	40000
铸造单位	上海造币厂

Face Value (Yuan)	10
Diameter (mm)	38.6
Pure Silver Content (oz)	0.803
Fineness (%)	92.5
Quality	Proof
Issuing Year	1998
Mintage (Pieces)	40000
Minted by	Shanghai Mint

Series of Chinese Traditional Culture — The Culture of the Dragon Gold and Silver Coins (First Set)

中國貴金屬紀念幣圖鑒

九、中国传统文化系列——龙的文化金银币（第1组）

一九九八年

为弘扬中国传统文化，中国人民银行发行中国传统文化系列——龙的文化金银币(第1组)。该组金银币由深圳国宝金币制造厂铸造，中国金币总公司总经销。

龙，是中华民族自古以来一直崇奉的神异动物，能呼风唤雨、行云播雾，可掌旱涝，是神灵和权威的象征。龙在中国政治、文学、艺术、习俗及信仰中都有鲜明的印迹，成为华夏民族的标志。龙在各类神兽中地位最高，因而自古以来被华夏民族尊为最聪灵的动物，进而被奉为华夏民族的始祖，神龙氏母感神龙而生炎帝的传说由此而来。后来，人们开始将龙喻为杰出之人。龙的形象代表了人类诸多美好品质，集中反映了中华民族的深层心理和审美意识，更反映了中华文明对世界和人生的信念。中华民族作为龙的传人在漫长的世代更替中创造了辉煌灿烂的文化——“龙文化”，即中华民族传统文化。龙文化的创造主体是智慧、勤劳、勇敢、善良的中华民族，龙文化的自然载体是地理景观复杂多样的东亚大陆。古老的龙文化一直保持着自己的本色延续至今，以其固有的特色和顽强的生命力屹立于世界文化之林。

龙的文化金银币(第1组)共2个品种，包括精制金币1种和普制银币1种。正面图案均为国号、年号、商代龙玉珏及建筑。背面图案：金币为人物驭龙图及面额，银币为玉龙(原始社会)、五龙玉璧(战国)、龙纹瓦当(汉代)及面额。

To enhance Chinese traditional culture, the People's Bank of China issued the first set in the series of Chinese traditional culture – the culture of dragon gold and silver coins, minted by Shenzhen Panda Gold Coin Mint and exclusively distributed by China Gold Coin Inc..

Dragon, a supernatural animal, the symbol of dignities and authorities, worshiped by Chinese people from of old, has the ability to summon wind and call for rain, to float the cloud and spread fog, and to control the drought and flood. Dragon, a symbol of Chinese nationality, can find its striking traces in Chinese politics, literature, arts, customs and religious beliefs. Dragon occupies the first position in various kinds of supernatural animals; thus, it is regarded as the cleverest animal and even the ancestor of Chinese. The legend of this miracle dragon's mother giving birth to emperor Yan (Chinese ancestor) finds its origin here. Later, dragon was compared to outstanding figures. The image of dragon embodies many virtues of humankind and it collectively reflects the deeper psychology and aesthetic consciousness and a firm conviction to this world and life of Chinese nationality. As the descendants of dragon, the Chinese Nation has created a splendid culture through centuries – the culture of dragon, that is, the traditional culture of the Chinese Nation. The subject of the creation of the culture is the wise, laborious, brave and kindhearted Chinese nation, and the natural carrier of this culture is the Eastern Asia with complicated and various geographical landscapes. This old culture of dragon with its own characteristics has lasted till now without changes and it will stand among the world culture because of its unique characteristics and vitality.

The first set contains 2 varieties: the proof gold coin and the bu. silver coin with the common obverse depicting the picture of the title of PRC, issuing year, jade dragon and building of the Shang Dynasty. The reverse of the gold coin depicts the picture of a man riding on a dragon and face value, and that of the silver coin depicts the picture of jade dragon (primitive society), five dragons jade bi (a round flat piece of jade with a hole in it, the Warring States period), dragon eaves tile (Han Dynasty) and face value.

正 面

原 大 Full Size

放 大

面额（元）	10
直径（毫米）	18
含纯金（盎司）	1/10
成色（%）	99.9
质量	精制
年号	1998
发行量（枚）	6000
铸造单位	深圳国宝金币制造厂

Face Value (Yuan)	10
Diameter (mm)	18
Pure Gold Content (oz)	1/10
Fineness (%)	99.9
Quality	Proof
Issuing Year	1998
Mintage (Pieces)	6000
Minted by	Shenzhen Panda Gold Coin Mint

正　面

放　大

原　大 Full Size

面额（元）	10
直径（毫米）	40
含纯银（盎司）	1
成色（%）	99.9
质量	普制
年号	1998
发行量（枚）	100000
铸造单位	深圳国宝金币制造厂

Face Value (Yuan)	10
Diameter (mm)	40
Pure Silver Content (oz)	1
Fineness (%)	99.9
Quality	Bu.
Issuing Year	1998
Mintage (Pieces)	100000
Minted by	Shenzhen Panda Gold Coin Mint

Hong Kong's New Look
Silver Coin

中國貴金屬紀念幣章鑒

十、中国香港新貌银币

一九九八年

中国人民银行于1998年发行中国香港新貌银币，该币由上海造币厂铸造，中国金币总公司总经销。

1997年7月1日，中英两国政府在香港会展中心举行了交接仪式，香港终于结束了长达一个半世纪的殖民统治，回到了祖国的怀抱。回归祖国以后，香港在“一国两制”的大框架下，各方面都在继续发展。随着21世纪的来临，香港这颗东方明珠将放射出更加绚丽的光芒。

中国香港新貌银币共1个品种，由4枚方形银币(均为2盎司精制)连续组成，其正面图案均为国号、年号、国旗、香港特别行政区区旗、紫荆花，背面图案为香港会展中心、天坛大佛、青马大桥、九龙海景连续组成的香港新貌图及面额。

In 1998, the People's Bank of China issued the Hong Kong's new look silver coin, minted by Shanghai Mint and exclusively distributed by China Gold Coin Inc..

On July 1, 1997, the hand-over ceremony held in Hong Kong Exhibition Center between China and U.K. put an end to the colonial rule of Hong Kong for one and a half centuries, and at last it was returned to China. After the hand over, Hong Kong continues to develop in all respects under the framework of 'One country, two systems'. As the 21st century drawing near, Hong Kong, an'oriental pearl' will be more prosperous.

The Hong Kong's new look silver coin is made up of four conjoint square silver coins (2 oz. each). The common obverse depicts the picture of the title of PRC, issuing year, national flag, regional flag of Hong Kong Special Administrative Region and the flower of Chinese redbud, and the reverse depicts the picture of the new look of Hong Kong made up of the Exhibition Center, the Statue of Buddha in Temple of Heaven, Qingma Bridge and the sea scene of Kowloon and face value.

放　大

正　面

原　大 Full Size

面额（元）	20(×4)
规格（毫米）	55 × 36(×4)
含纯银（盎司）	2(×4)
成色（%）	99.9
质量	精制
年号	1998
发行量（枚）	11800(×4)
铸造单位	上海造币厂

Face Value (Yuan)	20(×4)
Size (mm)	55 × 36(×4)
Pure Silver Content (oz)	2(×4)
Fineness (%)	99.9
Quality	Proof
Issuing Year	1998
Mintage (Pieces)	11800(×4)
Minted by	Shanghai Mint

Second Set in the Series of the Return of Macao to China Commemorative Coins

中國貴金屬紀念幣章鑒

十一、澳门回归祖国纪念币（第2组）

一九九八年

为纪念澳门回归祖国，中国人民银行特发行澳门回归祖国纪念币1套，共3组，第1组和第2组分别于1997年12月、1998年12月发行。澳门回归祖国纪念币(第2组)由沈阳造币厂铸造，中国金币总公司总经销。

澳门自古就是中国领土。澳门在公元前3世纪，即秦始皇第一次统一中国时期，已正式归入中国版图。1535年葡萄牙人贿赂广东地方官取得在澳门码头停靠船舶进行贸易的权利，1557年开始在澳门长期居住。1840年鸦片战争后，葡萄牙殖民主义者又侵占氹仔岛和路环岛。1887年葡萄牙强迫清政府先后签订了《中葡会议草约》和《中葡北京条约》，从此，葡萄牙一直霸占澳门。

中华人民共和国成立后，中国政府多次发表声明：澳门历来是中国领土，澳门问题属于历史的遗留问题。经过多次谈判，中葡两国政府于1987年签署联合声明，中国政府将于1999年12月20日对澳门恢复行使主权，澳门将成为中国特别行政区。

澳门回归祖国纪念币(第2组)共4个品种，其中1/2盎司、5盎司精制金币各1种，1盎司、5盎司精制银币各1种。其正面图案均为国号、年号、天安门、牡丹花，背面图案均为中华人民共和国澳门特别行政区基本法、装饰图案、背景图和中、英、葡文字样及面额。

To commemorate the return of Macao to China, the People's Bank of China specially issued the series of commemorative coins including 3 sets. The first and second sets were issued in December 1997 and December 1998 respectively. The second set was minted by Shenyang Mint and exclusively distributed by China Gold Coin Inc..

Macao has been Chinese territory from time immemorial. In the 3rd century B.C., Macao was formally included in Chinese territory by Emperor Qinshihuang of Qin Dynasty, who united China for the first time in Chinese history. In 1535, the Portuguese, by offering bribes to the local officials in Guangzhou acquired facilities of port calls at Macao dock and the right to conduct trade there. In 1557 they began to settle in Macao. After the Opium War in 1840,Portugal colonists forcibly occupied the Taipa and Coloane Islands. In 1887 they compelled the Qing government to sign on the *Draft Treaty of the Sino-Portugal Meeting* and the *Treaty of Peking of China and Portugal*. Since then Portuguese have been occupying Macao till now.

After the founding of PRC, the government has on many occasions expounded its position on the question of Macao, that is, Macao has been part of Chinese territory and the question of Macao is left over from history. The government of China and that of Portugal signed a joint declaration in 1987, after several rounds of negotiations, which stipulates that Chinese government will resume the exercise of sovereignty over Macao with effect from 20 December 1999. Macao will become a special administrative region of China.

The second set in the series of the return of Macao to China commemorative coins contains 4 kinds: 1/2 oz. proof gold coin, 5 oz. proof gold coin, 1 oz. proof silver coin, and 5 oz. proof silver coin. The coins share a common obverse depicting the picture of the title of PRC, issuing year, Gate of Heavenly Peace and peony flower. The reverses all depict the picture of the Basic Law of Macao Special Administrative Region, decorative patterns, Chinese, English and Portuguese words and face value.

共同正面

原　大 Full Size

面额（元）	500	50
直径（毫米）	60	27
含纯金（盎司）	5	1/2
成色（%）	99.99	99.9
质量	精制	精制
年号	1998	1998
发行量（枚）	228	11800
铸造单位	沈阳造币厂	

Face Value (Yuan)	500	50
Diameter (mm)	60	27
Pure Gold Content (oz)	5	1/2
Fineness (%)	99.99	99.9
Quality	Proof	Proof
Issuing Year	1998	1998
Mintage (Pieces)	228	11800
Minted by	Shenyang Mint	

共同正面

原 大 Full Size

面额（元）	50	10
直径（毫米）	70	40
含纯银（盎司）	5	1
成色（%）	99.9	99.9
质量	精制	精制
年号	1998	1998
发行量（枚）	5000	88000
铸造单位	沈阳造币厂	

Face Value (Yuan)	50	10
Diameter (mm)	70	40
Pure Silver Content (oz)	5	1
Fineness (%)	99.9	99.9
Quality	Proof	Proof
Issuing Year	1998	1998
Mintage (Pieces)	5000	88000
Minted by	Shenyang Mint	

China International
Aviation & Aerospace
Fair of 1998
Commemorative Coin

中國貴金屬紀念幣圖鑑

十二、1998年中国国际航空航天博览会纪念币

一九九八年

为纪念1998年中国国际航空航天博览会，中国人民银行发行1998年中国国际航空航天博览会纪念币。该币由上海造币厂铸造，中国金币总公司总经销。

1998年中国国际航空航天博览会于1998年11月15日～22日在广东珠海隆重举行。这是中国举办的第二届中国国际航空航天博览会。此次航展共22个国家和地区的500多家厂商前来参展，其中包括世界排名前20位的航空航天厂商，如波音、空中客车、戴姆勒·克莱斯勒、法国宇航，参展飞机100多架。此次博览会，从参展的企业、展示的档次、产品的分类；到飞行表演所展现的装备性能和驾驶技术，都代表了当今航空航天事业发展的主流和水平。

该套纪念币为1盎司普制银币1种，正面图案为国号、年号、北京天坛祈年殿，背面图案为大熊猫及镀金博览会会标。

To mark 1998 China International Aviation & Aerospace Fair, the People's Bank of China issued the China International Aviation & Aerospace Fair of 1998commemorative coin minted by Shanghai Mint and exclusively distributed by China Gold Coin Inc..

China International Aviation & Aerospace Fair was held in Zhuhai, Guangdong Province during Nov. 15~22, 1998. This was the second China International Aviation & Aerospace Fair. More than 500 manufacturers from 22 countries and regions attended this fair including some of the world top 20 manufacturers, such as Boeing, Air Bus, Daimule Kelaisle and French Aircraft. Over 100 planes were on display. Those on display stand for the mainstream and technical level in the development of aviation and aerospace industries from the angle of the participating manufacturers, grade of the plane, classification of the products, equipment function and driving technique showed in the flight performances.

The commemorative coin is one 1 oz. bu. silver coin with the obverse depicting the picture of the title of PRC, issuing year and the Hall of Prayer for Good Harvests of the Temple of Heaven in Beijing, and with the reverse depicting the picture of panda and the gilded mark of this fair.

正　面

放　大

原　大 Full Size

面额（元）	10
直径（毫米）	40
含纯银（盎司）	1
成色（%）	99.9
质量	普制
年号	1998
发行量（枚）	50000
铸造单位	上海造币厂

Face Value (Yuan)	10
Diameter (mm)	40
Pure Silver Content (oz)	1
Fineness (%)	99.9
Quality	Bu.
Issuing Year	1998
Mintage (Pieces)	50000
Minted by	Shanghai Mint

Chinese Traditional
Auspicious Picture
— *All Things Take On A New Aspect*
Gold and Silver Coins

中國貴金屬紀念幣[illegible]鑒

十三、中国传统吉祥图
——《万象更新》金银币

一九九八年

为弘扬中华传统文化，中国人民银行发行中国传统吉祥图——《万象更新》金银币。该套金银币由沈阳造币厂铸造，中国金币总公司总经销。

古人以象为吉祥。吉祥图《万象更新》是一个传统吉祥纹样：在象的背上驮一盆万年青，寓意为“万象更新”，旁边画一童子，手拿花瓶，锦团簇绣，更增添了喜庆、吉祥气氛，表达了人们美好的祝愿和无限的希望。

《万象更新》金银币共5个品种，其中普制银币2种，精制彩色金币1种，精制彩色银币2种。正面图案均为国号、年号、华表，背面图案均为中国传统吉祥图案《万象更新》及面额。

In order to enhance the traditional culture, the People's Bank of China issued the Chinese traditional auspicious picture — *All Things Take On A New Aspect* gold and silver coins, minted by Shenyang Mint, exclusively distributed by China Gold Coin Inc..

Ancient Chinese believed that elephant could bring luckiness. The auspicious picture — *All Things Take On A New Aspect* is of traditional design: a basin of evergreen tree on the back of an elephant means everything taking on a completely new look, beside the elephant, there is a child with a vase full of flowers in his hands, which further strengthens the happy and lucky airs. This vivid picture expresses people's good wishes and great expectations.

This set of coins contains five varieties: two kinds of bu. silver coins, two kinds of proof colorful silver coins and one kind of proof colorful gold coin. The common obverse of these coins depicts the picture of the title of PRC, issuing year and the ornamental columns, and the common reverse depicts the tradition auspicious picture — *All Things Take On A New Aspect* and face value.

共同正面

放　大

原　大 Full Size

面额（元）	10	5
直径（毫米）	40	33
含纯银（盎司）	1	1/2
成色（%）	99.9	99.9
质量	普制	普制
年号	1998	1998
发行量（枚）	80000	80000
铸造单位	沈阳造币厂	

Face Value (Yuan)	10	5
Diameter (mm)	40	33
Pure Silver Content (oz)	1	1/2
Fineness (%)	99.9	99.9
Quality	Bu.	Bu.
Issuing Year	1998	1998
Mintage (Pieces)	80000	80000
Minted by	Shenyang Mint	

正　面

放　大

原　大 Full Size

面额（元）	10
直径（毫米）	18
含纯金（盎司）	1/10
成色（%）	99.99
质量	精制
年号	1998
发行量（枚）	20000
铸造单位	中国金币总公司

Face Value (Yuan)	10
Diameter (mm)	18
Pure Gold Content (oz)	1/10
Fineness (%)	99.99
Quality	Proof
Issuing Year	1998
Mintage (Pieces)	20000
Minted by	China Gold Coin Inc.

共同正面

放　大

原　大 Full Size

面额（元）	10	5
直径（毫米）	40	36
含纯银（盎司）	1	1/2
成色（%）	99.9	99.9
质量	精制	精制
年号	1998	1998
发行量（枚）	100000	100000
铸造单位	中国金币总公司	

Face Value (Yuan)	10	5
Diameter (mm)	40	36
Pure Silver Content (oz)	1	1/2
Fineness (%)	99.9	99.9
Quality	Proof	Proof
Issuing Year	1998	1998
Mintage (Pieces)	100000	100000
Minted by	China Gold Coin Inc.	

1998 Issue
of Spring-hugging
Gold and Silver Coins

中國貴金屬紀念幣圖鑑

十四、1998年版迎春金银币

一九九八年

为弘扬传统文化，中国人民银行发行1998年版迎春金银币。该套金银币由上海造币厂铸造，中国金币总公司总经销。

迎春图是中国民间传统的吉祥图，画面上三个童子，憨态可掬，稚拙可爱，他们正在欢呼着放风筝。风筝，亦称纸鸢，战国时期已出现，是中国民间传统的游乐工具。每年到了春天，尤其是三月三这一天，到处都是放风筝的孩子，天上飘满造型各异、精工绝伦的风筝，煞是好看。这已成了中国的习俗，风筝也成了春天先行者，向人们传达着春的信息。风筝飘入辽远的碧空，带着人们的希望和祝福，而人们用线控制着风筝，似乎就象征着人们抓住了希望和幸福。图中还画有鱼的图案，鱼者“余”也，寓喜庆、吉祥之意。

1998年版迎春金银币共5个品种，其中5盎司精制金币及1/4盎司、1/10盎司普制金币各1种，5盎司精制银币、1盎司普制银币各1种。其正面图案均为国号、年号、宫灯，背面图案均为迎春图“放风筝”及面额。

To popularize the traditional culture, the People's Bank of China issued the 1998 issue of Spring-hugging gold and silver coins, minted by Shanghai Mint and exclusively distributed by China Gold Coin Inc..

The picture of *Spring-hugging* is a Chinese traditional auspicious picture. Three children, charmingly naive and lovely innocent, are flying kites in the picture cheerfully. The kite, also called paper hawk, made its appearance as early the Warring States period, which is a traditional amusement. Children fly various kinds of exquisite kites every spring, especially on March 3 of the lunar calendar. The sky dotted with these kites is very beautiful. Flying kites has found its way into Chinese customs and kites have become the pioneer of spring that foretells the coming of spring. Kites with people's hopes and wishes fly in the sky while people flying it with a spread seem to indicate that people hold hopes and happiness in hand. There's fish in the picture too. Fish, means surplus, symbolizes happiness and luckiness.

1998 issue of the spring-hugging gold and silver coins contains 5 varieties: 5 oz. proof gold, 1/4 oz.bu. gold and 1/10 oz. bu. gold coins each,5 oz. proof silver and 1 oz.bu. silver coins each, with the common obverse depicting the picture of the title of PRC, issuing year and the palace lantern, and with the common reverse depicting the picture of *Flying Kites* and face value.

共同正面

原　大 Full Size

面额（元）	500	25	10
直径（毫米）	60	22	18
含纯金（盎司）	5	1/4	1/10
成色（%）	99.9	99.9	99.9
质量	精制	普制	普制
年号	1998	1998	1998
发行量（枚）	128	10000	60000
铸造单位	上海造币厂		

Face Value (Yuan)	500	25	10
Diameter (mm)	60	22	18
Pure Gold Content (oz)	5	1/4	1/10
Fineness (%)	99.9	99.9	99.9
Quality	Proof	Bu.	Bu.
Issuing Year	1998	1998	1998
Mintage (Pieces)	128	10000	60000
Minted by	Shanghai Mint		

共同正面

原　大 Full Size

面额（元）	50	10
直径（毫米）	70	40
含纯银（盎司）	5	1
成色（%）	99.9	99.9
质量	精制	普制
年号	1998	1998
发行量（枚）	1500	80000
铸造单位	上海造币厂	

Face Value (Yuan)	50	10
Diameter (mm)	70	40
Pure Silver Content (oz)	5	1
Fineness (%)	99.9	99.9
Quality	Proof	Bu.
Issuing Year	1998	1998
Mintage (Pieces)	1500	80000
Minted by	Shanghai Mint	

1998 Beijing
International Coin
Exposition
Commemorative Coin

中國貴金屬紀念幣圖鑑

十五、1998年北京国际钱币博览会纪念币

一九九八年

为纪念1998年北京国际钱币博览会的举行，推动国际、国内钱币事业的发展，中国人民银行发行1998年北京国际钱币博览会纪念币。该币由上海造币厂铸造，中国金币总公司总经销。

1998年北京国际钱币博览会于1998年11月6日~8日在北京国际贸易中心举行。此次博览会由中国金币总公司、中国印钞造币总公司和中国钱币学会联合举办。参加此次博览会的有近20个国家和地区的造币厂和钱币经销公司。中国包括香港特别行政区在内的一些造币厂和钱币经销公司也参加了此次盛会。此届博览会展销结合，以展为主，展出了116个国家的现行货币，旨在弘扬钱币文化，促进中外钱币文化的交流，同时为广大钱币收藏家、爱好者提供一次难得的鉴赏、选购的机会。

1998年北京国际钱币博览会纪念币为1盎司普制镀金熊猫银币1种。银币正面图案为国号、年号、北京天坛祈年殿及展销会纪念文字，背面图案为镀金的大熊猫及面额。

To mark '98 Beijing International Coin Exposition and push forward the development of the cause of coin both at home and abroad, the People's Bank of China issued 1998 Beijing International Coin Exposition commemorative coin, minted by Shanghai Mint and exclusively distributed by China Gold Coin Inc..

Beijing International Coin Exposition was held in Beijing International Trade Center during Nov.6 ~ 8 1998. China Gold Coin Inc. and China Banknote Printing & Minting Corp. together with China Numismatic Society held this exposition. Mints and coin distributing companies from over 20 countries and regions attended this exposition. Some mints and coin distributing companies of China including Hong Kong also attended this exhibition. While centering in the display, this exposition combined display with sale. It displayed the current coins of 116 countries for the purpose of promoting coin culture and the coin culture exchange. At the same time it provided a precious opportunity for the coin collectors and coin lovers to appreciate and purchase the coins.

1998 Beijing International Coin Exposition commemorative coin is a 1 oz. bu. gilded panda silver coin. The obverse depicts the picture of the title of PRC, issuing year, Hall of Prayer for Good Harvests of the Temple of Heaven in Beijing and the commemorative words of the exposition, and the reverse depicts the picture of the gilded panda and face value.

共同正面

放　大

原　大 Full Size

面额（元）	10
直径（毫米）	40
含纯银（盎司）	1
成色（%）	99.9
质量	普制
年号	1998
发行量（枚）	30000
铸造单位	上海造币厂

Face Value (Yuan)	10
Diameter (mm)	40
Pure Silver Content (oz)	1
Fineness (%)	99.9
Quality	Bu.
Issuing Year	1998
Mintage (Pieces)	30000
Minted by	Shanghai Mint

NEC

1998 Hong Kong
International Coin
Exhibition Fair
Commemorative Coin

中國貴金屬紀念幣圖鑒

十六、1998年香港国际钱币展销会纪念币

一九九八年

为纪念1998年香港国际钱币展销会，中国人民银行发行了1998年香港国际钱币展销会纪念币。该币由深圳国宝金币制造厂铸造，中国金币总公司总经销。1998年香港国际钱币展销会纪念币为1/2盎司普制熊猫加字银币1种，正面图案为北京天坛祈年殿、国号、年号及展销会纪念文字，背面图案为中国大熊猫及面额。

1998年香港国际钱币展销会于1998年9月4日～6日在香港举行，由泰星钱币有限公司、中国长城硬币投资有限公司主办。

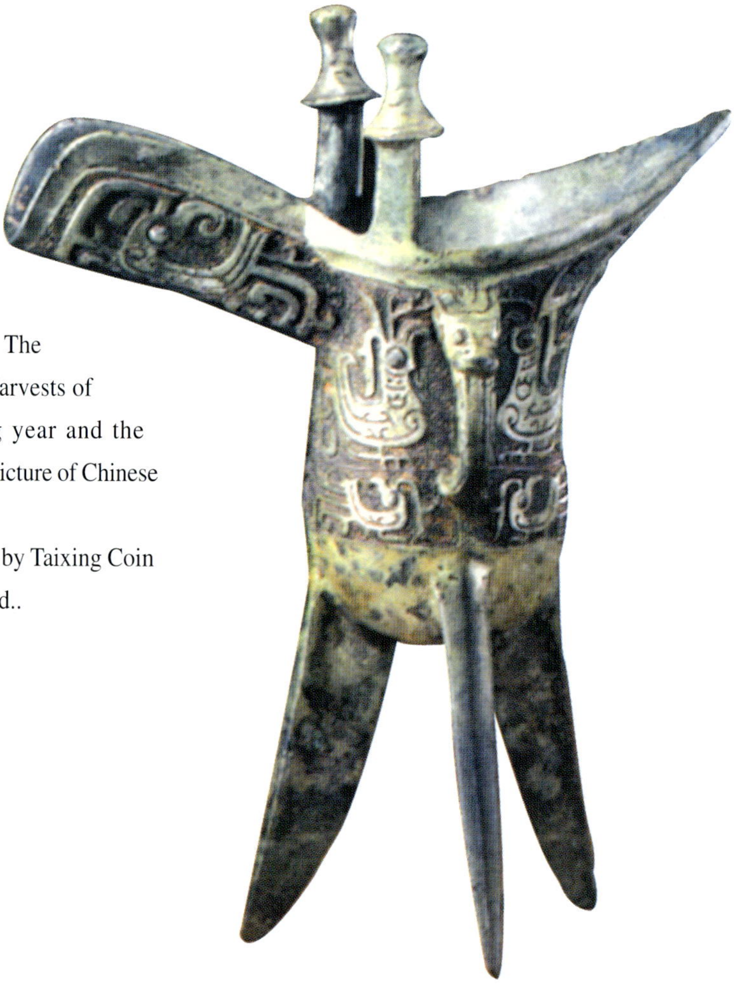

To mark 1998 Hong Kong International Coin Exhibition Fair, the People's Bank of China issued the 1998 Hong Kong International Coin Exhibition Fair Commemorative Coin, minted by Shenzhen Panda Gold Coin Mint and exclusively distributed by China Gold Coin Inc.. It is a kind of 1/2 oz. bu. panda plus words silver coin. The obverse depicts the picture of the Hall of Prayer for Good Harvests of the Temple of Heaven in Beijing, title of PRC, issuing year and the commemorative words of this fair, and the reverse depicts the picture of Chinese panda and face value.

This fair was held in Hong Kong during Sept.4 ~ 6, 1998 by Taixing Coin Corporation Ltd. and China Great Wall Coins Investments Ltd..

正　面

原　大 Full Size

放　大

面额（元）	5
直径（毫米）	33
含纯银（盎司）	1/2
成色（%）	99.9
质量	普制
年号	1998
发行量（枚）	30000
铸造单位	深圳国宝金币制造厂

Face Value (Yuan)	5
Diameter (mm)	33
Pure Silver Content (oz)	1/2
Fineness (%)	99.9
Quality	Bu.
Issuing Year	1998
Mintage (Pieces)	30000
Minted by	Shenzhen Panda Gold Coin Mint

Series of Chinese
Ancient Famous
Paintings — *Qing Ming*
Shang He Tu
Silver Coin

中國貴金屬紀念幣存鑒

十七、中国古代名画系列
——《清明上河图》银币

一九九八年

为弘扬传统文化，中国人民银行发行中国古代名画系列之一 ——《清明上河图》银币。该币由上海造币厂铸造，中国金币总公司总经销。

宋人张择端的精品名作——《清明上河图》，在中国绘画史上是一幅历史性的代表作，是中国绘画艺术的瑰宝。《清明上河图》产生于12世纪初的中国宋代，这决不是偶然的，它是在中国古代城市发展至宋代这个历史转折时期产生的。北宋首都东京(又称汴，即今河南开封)，是中国封建社会由封闭型向敞开型转化的典型城市，它的出现深刻地反映了中国古代封建社会内部的商品经济有了巨大的发展，并且影响到社会生活的各个方面，这是宋代市肆风俗画得以兴起的经济基础。

《清明上河图》全幅画长一丈六尺五寸，高七尺六寸。该图共绘各种人物810多个、牲畜94头、树木170多棵，把汴京郊外的菜园风光、汴河上繁忙的交通运输、船夫们紧张的劳动、士大夫们的闲暇自得等，一一勾画得惟妙惟肖。其直观效果强烈感人，具有不可估量的艺术价值。

该套币共1个品种，由6枚长方形银币(均为2盎司精制)连续组成，其正面图案均为国号、年号、开封名胜风景及面额，背面图案为由6枚银币连续组成的张择端所绘《清明上河图》。

To popularize the traditional culture, the People's Bank of China issued one of the series of famous Chinese ancient paintings (painters) commemorative coins — *Qing Ming Shang He Tu* silver coin, minted by Shanghai Mint and exclusively distributed by China Gold Coin Inc..

Qing Ming Shang He Tu is a famous painting drawn by Zhang Zedan of the Song Dynasty, which is a masterpiece in the history of Chinese painting and a treasure of Chinese painting art. Appearing in 12th century of the Song Dynasty, this painting was not an accidental product but a product of the development of cities in Song Dynasty that was a turning point in history. Dongjing, capital of Song Dynasty, also called Bian, that is, the Kaifeng City of Henan Province, was a typical city in the transformation from close type to open type in feudal society. The appearance of this painting shows that market-oriented economy had developed rapidly in feudal society and had affected every aspect of the social life. This market-oriented economy laid an economic foundation for the flowering of city-based genre painting.

Qing Ming Shang He Tu is 528cm long and 24.8cm wide. There are more than 810 persons, 94 domestic animals and 170 trees in this painting. Zhang vividly painted the scene of vegetable plots in the environs of Dongjing, the busy traffic in River Bian, the hard-working boatmen and the carefree and content officials. This painting is of strong intuitive effect and inestimable art value.

Qing Ming Shang He Tu silver coin is made up of 6 conjoint rectangular silver coins (all 2 oz. proof silver). The obverse depicts the picture of the title of PRC, issuing year, the scenic spots of Kaifeng and face value. The reverse depicts the picture of *Qing Ming Shang He Tu* made up by the 6 conjoint coins.

放　大

面额（元）	20(× 6)	Face Value (Yuan)	20(× 6)
规格（毫米）	55 × 36(× 6)	Size (mm)	55 × 36(× 6)
含纯银（盎司）	2(× 6)	Pure Silver Content (oz)	2(× 6)
成色（%）	99.9	Fineness (%)	99.9
质量	精制	Quality	Proof
年号	1998	Issuing Year	1998
发行量（枚）	18800(× 6)	Mintage (Pieces)	18800(× 6)
铸造单位	上海造币厂	Minted by	Shanghai Mint

中华人民共和国
1998
20元
中华人民共和国
1998
20元
中华人民共和国
1998
20元

.999 Ag 2oz
.999 Ag 2oz
.999 Ag 2oz

共同正面

原　大 Full Size

Series of Chinese Ancient
Famous Paintings
— *Tang Dai Shi Nu Tu*
(Ladies of the Tang Dynasty)
Silver Coin

中國貴金屬紀念幣圖鑒

十八、中国古代名画系列
——《唐代仕女图》银币

一九九八年

为弘扬传统文化，中国人民银行发行《唐代仕女图》彩色银币，该币由中国金币总公司铸造、总经销。

《唐代仕女图》(即《簪花仕女图》)是中唐罗绮人物画派名家周昉的作品。《簪花仕女图》描绘的是五个宫廷贵族妇女在庭院中游乐的场面。春夏之交，牡丹花竞开，一群插戴玉簪、珍珠、荷花、牡丹花而服饰华丽奢艳的嫔妃在游戏取乐，有的手持拂子，逗引小狗戏闹；有的手拈红花，举目欣赏，凝神屏息，正欲将其插上发鬓，以至无暇顾及从身边走过的白鹤；有的从远处姗姗而来……图中仕女形象皆脸颊丰腴而圆润，体现了唐代仕女画的鲜明特点。作者采用了以透明的纱衫半罩半露的手法表现了仕女丰满的前胸和圆润的臂膀；在色彩上，运用不透明的石质颜料与透明的植物质颜料，通过冷色与暖色、深色与浅色的对比关系，相互衬托。这一切，都产生了真实可信、含蓄而又丰富的艺术效果。图中这种“浓丽丰肥之态”的“罗绮人物”成为唐代仕女的典型形象。

《唐代仕女图》银币为5盎司精制彩色长方型银币1种，正面图案为国号、年号、唐代长安大明宫含元殿，背面图案为唐代周昉所绘《簪花仕女图》(彩色)及面额。

To enhance the traditional culture, the People's Bank of China issued the *Tang Dai Shi Nu Tu* (Ladies Of the Tang Dynasty) colorful silver coin, minted and exclusively distributed by China Gold Coin Inc..

Tang Dai Shi Nu Tu (Ladies Wearing Hairpins) was a masterpiece of Zhou Fang, a famous painter of the School of Figure in Silk of the mid-Tang Dynasty period. This painting presents a scene of five royal ladies playing in the courtyard. At the end of spring and the beginning of summer while peonies bloom, a group of ladies elegantly attired with jade hairpins, pearls, lotus flowers and peony in their hair play in the courtyard; some with a fan in hand playing with dogs; some with red flowers in hand appreciating attentively and about to wear it in the hair while white crane flying past them drawing no attention of them and some walk leisurely toward this yard. All ladies in this painting have full and round faces, which is a striking feature of the paintings of figures of ladies of Tang Dynasty. Zhou had his figures wear semi-transparent yarn dress to show their plump breasts and shoulders. Zhou used non-transparent stony colors and transparent botanic colors, and through the contrast of the cold color and warm color, deep color and light color to set off each other. All these produce a real, trustworthy, implicit and rich artistic effect. The full and round elegantly attired figures in silk became typical images of ladies of Tang Dynasty.

Tang Dai Shi Nu Tu silver coin is a kind of 5 oz. rectangular colorful proof silver coins. The obverse depicts the picture of the title of PRC, issuing year and the Hanyuan Hall of Daming Palace in Chang'an, and the reverse depicts the colorful painting of *Tang Dai Shi Nu Tu* drawn by Zhou Fang and face value.

正　面

原　大 Full Size

面额（元）	50
规格（毫米）	90 × 40
含纯银（盎司）	5
成色（%）	99.9
质量	精制
年号	1998
发行量（枚）	18800
铸造单位	中国金币总公司

Face Value (Yuan)	50
Size (mm)	90 × 40
Pure Silver Content (oz)	5
Fineness (%)	99.9
Quality	Proof
Issuing Year	1998
Mintage (Pieces)	18800
Minted by	China Gold Coin Inc.

The Scenery
of Guilin, China
Gold and Silver Coins

中國貴金屬紀念幣圖鑒

十九、中国桂林山水金银币

一九九八年

为让世人更多地了解奇山秀水的桂林风景，中国人民银行发行中国桂林山水金银币。该套金银币由沈阳造币厂铸造，中国金币总公司总经销。

桂林是广西壮族自治区东北部著名的风景城市，所谓“桂林山水甲天下”，正是对它的赞美。由于桂林的地形是典型的溶岩地形，因而使桂林山水别具一格。桂林的山，多从平地拔起，巍然耸立，形态万千，而且有很多曲折深邃的岩洞，洞内遍布各种形态的石钟乳，玲珑剔透，色彩缤纷。无数的奇峰异洞和环城的碧流相辉映，形成了“山青、水秀、洞奇、石美”的绮丽景色。桂林市中心有独秀峰、花桥、象鼻山、榕湖和杉湖；北面有叠彩山和伏波山两个主要风景区；西面有隐山、西山和桃花江；西北有著名的芦笛岩风景区。从市中心向东通过解放桥，便到达风景点集中的七星公园，这里有花桥、普陀山、七星岩、骆驼山、月牙山、龙隐洞和桂海碑林。漓江是桂林山水的主要组成部分，它发源于桂林东北兴安县的猫儿山，流经桂林、阳朔，在梧州市汇入西江，全程437公里。漓江蜿蜒于群山之中，处处奇峰挺拔，秀水萦回，田野似锦，江山如画。

中国桂林山水金银币共有2个品种，1种由4枚方形金币(均为1/2盎司精制)连续组成，1种由4枚方形银币(均为2盎司精制)连续组成。金银币图案相同，其正面图案分别为国号、年号以及桂林象鼻山、花桥、独秀峰、南溪山，背面图案均为桂林山水图及面额。

To make the world better understand the beautiful sceneries of Guilin, the People's Bank of China issued the Guilin scenery gold and silver coins minted by Shenyang Mint and exclusively distributed by China Gold Coin Inc..

Guilin, a beautiful city in the northeastern part of Guangxi Zhuang Nationality Autonomous Region, enjoys the fame of ‘Guilin's scenery is the best in the world ’. Because Guilin's terrain is the typical Karst terrain, the scenery of Guilin forms a class by itself. The hills of Guilin rising from the ground are of many shapes with lots of deep solution caves, where are various shapes of stalactite, multi-colored and exquisitely carved. Numerous wonderful peaks and caverns and the clear flow of water round the city form the beautiful scenery of 'Green hills, clear water, wonderful caverns and beautiful rocks.' In the center of Guilin are Duxiu peak, Flower Bridge, Trunk Mount, Rong lake and Shan Lake; in the north are Diecui Mount and Fubo Mount; in the west are Yin Mount, West Mount and Peach Blossom River; in the northwest is the scenic spot of Ludi Rock.From the center of the city, we go along the Liberation Bridge and reach the scenic spots centered at the Seven Star Park. Here are Flower Bridge, Putuo Mount, Seven-Star Rock, Camel Mount, New-moon Mount, Longyin Cavern and Guihai Forest of Steles.The Li River is a major part of Guilin scenery. It rises in Maoer Mount in Xing'an county northeast of Guilin, and runs through Guilin, Yangshuo and finally runs into the West River in Wuzhou city. It covers a length of 437 kilometers. Li River runs through mountains on both sides of the mountains, in which are wonderful peaks, beautiful fields.

Guilin Scenery gold and silver coins contain two varieties: one is made up of 4 square consecutive 1/2 oz. proof gold coins and the other is made up of 4 square consecutive 2 oz. proof silver coins. The obverses all depict the picture of the title of PRC, issuing year, Trunk Mount, Flower Bridge, Duxiu Mount and Nanxi Mount, and the reverses all depict the picture of Guilin scenery and face value.

正 面

原 大 Full Size

放 大

面额（元）	50 (× 4)	Face Value (Yuan)	50 (× 4)
规格（毫米）	19 × 29(× 4)	Size (mm)	19 × 29(× 4)
含纯金（盎司）	1/2(× 4)	Pure Gold Content (oz)	1/2(× 4)
成色（%）	99.9	Fineness (%)	99.9
质量	精制	Quality	Proof
年号	1998	Issuing Year	1998
发行量（枚）	1600(× 4)	Mintage (Pieces)	1600(× 4)
铸造单位	沈阳造币厂	Minted by	Shenyang Mint

正　面

原　大 Full Size

面额（元）	20(×4)	Face Value (Yuan)	20(×4)
规格（毫米）	36×55(×4)	Size (mm)	36×55(×4)
含纯银（盎司）	2(×4)	Pure Silver Content (oz)	2(×4)
成色（%）	99.9	Fineness (%)	99.9
质量	精制	Quality	Proof
年号	1998	Issuing Year	1998
发行量（枚）	18800(×4)	Mintage (Pieces)	18800(×4)
铸造单位	沈阳造币厂	Minted by	Shenyang Mint

The Exorcising and Commemorative Coins of the Southern Tang Dynasty Gold and Silver Coins

中國貴金屬紀念幣圖鑒

二十、大唐镇库金银币

一九九八年

为弘扬中国古代钱币文化，中国人民银行发行大唐镇库金银币。该币由上海造币厂铸造，中国金币总公司总经销。

镇库钱，一般是指在正式开炉铸钱之初，特意制造的一种大钱。它的质地考究，制作精美，为纪念和辟邪之用，放在库里，不作正式货币参与流通。大唐镇库钱是南唐所铸。大唐镇库是历代钱币中以“镇库”为钱名之第一钱。不过，在历代钱币中，虽然不铸镇库二字，实际上也有镇库性质的大型钱币。

大唐镇库金银币共有4个品种，包括1/10盎司普制金币1种，1盎司普制银币1种，1公斤精制金币、银币各1种。正面图案均为国号、年号、唐草装饰图案及面额，背面图案均为“大唐镇库”字样。

To popularize Chinese ancient coin culture, the People's Bank of China issued the Zhen Ku Coins (Exorcising and Commemorative Coins) of the Southern Tang Dynasty gold and silver coins, minted by Shanghai Mint and exclusively distributed by China Gold Coin Inc..

The so-called Zhen Ku coin is a kind of deliberately madc big coins before the beginning of real coinage. It is of high quality and elegantly made for the purpose of commemoration and exorcising. It was put in the national treasury and didn't enter into the circulation. The Zhenku coin of Tang Dynasty was made in the Southern Tang Dynasty. It was the first of this kind using the name of Zhen Ku meaning safeguard the national treasury. However, in history, though there was no casting name for such kind of coins, there were coins made for the purpose of safeguarding national treasury.

This set contains four varieties: 1/10 oz. bu. gold coin, 1 oz. bu. silver coin, 1kg proof gold coin and silver coin each. The common obverse depicts the picture of the title of PRC, issuing year, decorative Tang Dynasty grass and face value, and the common reverse depicts the Chinese characters da tang zhen ku (Tang Dynasty Safeguard).

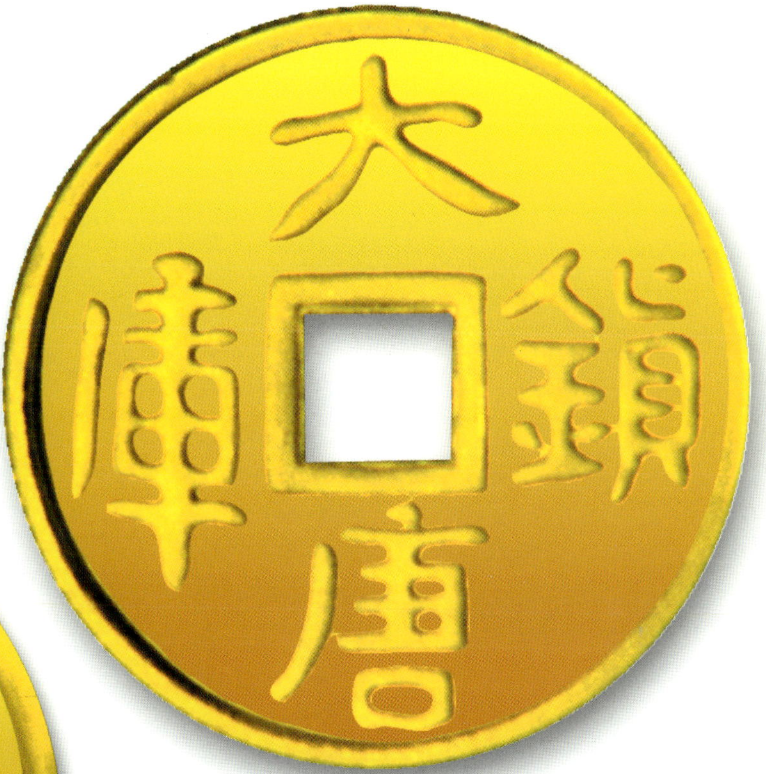

正　面

原　大　Full Size

正　面

面额（元）	2000	10
直径（毫米）	100	18
含纯金（公斤）	1	
含纯金（盎司）		1/10
成色（%）	99.9	99.9
质量	精制	普制
年号	1998	1998
发行量（枚）	68	60000
铸造单位	上海造币厂	

Face Value (Yuan)	2000	10
Diameter (mm)	100	18
Pure Gold Content (kg)	1	
Pure Gold Content (oz)		1/10
Fineness (%)	99.9	99.9
Quality	Proof	Bu.
Issuing Year	1998	1998
Mintage (Pieces)	68	60000
Minted by	Shanghai Mint	

正　面

原　大 Full Size

正　面

面额（元）	200	10
直径（毫米）	120	40
含纯银（公斤）	1	
含纯银（盎司）		1
成色（%）	99.9	99.9
质量	精制	普制
年号	1998	1998
发行量（枚）	2800	100000
铸造单位	上海造币厂	

Face Value (Yuan)	200	10
Diameter (mm)	120	40
Pure Silver Content (kg)	1	
Pure Silver Content (oz)		1
Fineness (%)	99.9	99.9
Quality	Proof	Bu.
Issuing Year	1998	1998
Mintage (Pieces)	2800	100000
Minted by	Shanghai Mint	

The Year of the Tiger
Gold and Silver Stamps

中國貴金屬紀念幣章鑒

二十一、中国戊寅(虎)年
金银邮票

一九九八年

1998年是中国农历戊寅(虎)年，中国金币总公司为此与中国集邮总公司联合发行中国戊寅(虎)年金银邮票。

中国十二生肖以虎与地支“寅”相配，其最早的文献记载，见于1975年湖北云梦睡虎山出土的秦简《日书》中。

在中国古代神话中，虎乃神仙伙伴。国人熟知的财神赵公元帅传说中骑黑虎为人招财进宝，故虎在中国先民心目中又系吉祥、幸福、平安、避邪之神兽，成为供奉于室的守护神。

中国人素来视虎为尊贵、威猛、吉祥、强盛的象征，认为虎年是吉祥隆盛、奋发进取、战无不胜之年。

中国戊寅(虎)年金银邮票共有2个品种，包括2克精制金邮票和2克精制银邮票各1种，图案为国家同年发行的虎年生肖邮票。

1998 was the year of the tiger, China Gold Coin Inc. together with C.N.P.C., specially issued the year of the tiger gold and silver stamps.

In Chinese Twelve Animals Cycle, tiger is matched with *Yin* of the twelve Earthly Branches. The first match can be traced back to *Rishu* (Day Book) of the Qin period unearthed in Shuihudi of Yunmeng, Hubei Province.

In ancient Chinese legends, tiger was the companion of supernatural beings. It is well known to the Chinese that God of Fortune Marshal Zhao rode on the back of a black tiger to bring in the wealth for people, so in the minds of ancient Chinese people tiger was closely linked with luckiness, happiness, safety and evil-avoiding, and so it became the eudemon worshiped at home.

Chinese people have long since regarded tiger as a symbol of dignity, might, luckiness and strength, and they think the year of tiger is a year of prosperity, advancement and victory.

The year of the tiger gold and silver stamps contain 2 varieties including one 2g proof gold stamp and one 2g proof silver stamp. The designs are the same as that of the year of tiger stamps issued in the same year.

含纯金（克）	2
成色（%）	99.9
质量	精制
年号	1998
发行量（枚）	12000

Pure Gold Content (g)	2
Fineness (%)	99.9
Quality	Proof
Issuing Year	1998
Mintage (Pieces)	12000

含纯银（克）	2
成色（%）	99.9
质量	精制
年号	1998
发行量（枚）	12000

Pure Silver Content (g)	2
Fineness (%)	99.9
Quality	Proof
Issuing Year	1998
Mintage (Pieces)	12000

中国金币总公司各特约经销部通讯录　（1～56）

1. 中国金币深圳经销中心

地址：深圳市解放西路188号农行大厦18楼
邮编：518001
电话：0755-5590734　5590699
传真：0755-5590775
法人代表：王　喆
联 系 人：井　军

2. 北京开元中国金币经销中心

地址：北京海淀区西三环北路100号金玉大厦12层
邮编：100037
电话：010-68727609
传真：010-68727612
法人代表：黎昌国
联 系 人：李殿霄

3. 北京华银金饰品公司

地址：北京市西城区新康街甲1号
邮编：100088
电话：010-62385151
传真：010- 62061773
法人代表：李月明
联 系 人：张继成　黄　斌

4. 北京京宝金店

地址：北京市前门西河沿9号
邮编：100051
电话：010-63014671
传真：010-63151302
法人代表：王志成
联 系 人：张　尧　李京成

5. 北京人银科工贸集团

地址：北京市西城区新文化街甲58号
邮编：100031
电话：010-66053032
传真：010-66053036
法人代表：徐金元
联 系 人：谭天农

6. 北京金博仑金银珠宝公司

地址：北京市 建国门大街15号妇联大厦 11 层
邮编：100730
电话：010-65221133-3135
传真：010-65221133-3133
法人代表：邢树尧
联 系 人：邓一明

7. 北京金大来金银珠宝行

地址：北京市 西城区太平桥大街250号
邮编：100032
电话：010-66069726　66065421
传真：010-66065421
法人代表：贡 强
联 系 人：贡 强

8. 天津宝华金店

地址：天津河西区绍兴道元兴里10号楼4门首层
邮编：300041
电话：022-23257168
传真：022-23257088　23280551
法人代表：郭　元
联 系 人：徐承玺　王学杰

9. 山西万泉钱币有限公司

地址：太原市迎泽大街135号
邮编：030001
电话：0351-4069842　4042314
传真：0351-4069842
法人代表：崔　青
联 系 人：任虎英

10. 大同银星金店

地址：山西大同市大东街8号
邮编：037004
电话：0352-2050918　2044332
传真：0352-2047160
法人代表：苏裕田
联 系 人：王美元

11. 石家庄宝源金银币经销部

地址：河北 石家庄市中山东路61号
邮编：050000
电话：0311-6087838　6032231
传真：0311-6087838
法人代表：李小平
联 系 人：李小平

12. 内蒙古银泉钱币经销部

地址：内蒙古 呼和浩特南马路26号
邮编：010050
电话：0471-6918866-8002
传真：0471-6918866-8001
法人代表：王喜文
联 系 人：王维平

13. 沈阳造币厂 金银币经销部

地址：沈阳大东区大东路113号
邮编：110042
电话：024-24311412
传真：024-24315297
法人代表：刘传升
联 系 人：刘传升

14. 长春金行

地址：长春市解放大路111号(邮寄址)
邮编：130021
电话：0431-8969429　8968987
传真：0431-8968987　8946961
法人代表：崔振山
联 系 人：崔振山

15. 吉林省集币有限责任公司

地址：长春市人民大街87号
邮编：130021
电话：0431-8949372
传真：0431-8949373
法人代表：许俊奇
联 系 人：许俊奇　朱　玲

16. 哈尔滨丰顺钱币有限公司

地址：黑龙江哈尔滨道里区兆麟街9号
邮编：150036
电话：0451-4610796
传真：0451-2308626
法人代表：迟庆山
联 系 人：李纯栋

17. 中国金币总公司上海特约经销部

地址：上海市南京西路801号
邮编：200041
电话：021-62551239
传真：021-62551239
法人代表：杜文孝
联 系 人：朱爱球　陶　涌

18. 上海瑞祥金饰品公司

地址：上海市普陀区长寿路295弄8号9楼G室
邮编：200060
电话：021-62997885
传真：021-62997624　62989647
法人代表：王　瑛
联 系 人：王　瑛　张　磊

19. 上海申泉金银制品总汇

地址：上海市 北京西路1804号
邮编：200042
电话：021-62530437　62405178
传真：021-62538310
法人代表：朱伟春
联 系 人：皮　民

20. 山东省金泉纪念币有限公司

地址：济南市大纬二路23号院
邮编：250001
电话：0531-6058992
传真：0531-6058992
法人代表：崔兆森
联 系 人：崔兆森　李影星

21. 江苏东方钱币经销中心

地址：南京市建邺路88号
邮编：210004
电话：025-4790159
传真：025-4412643　4790157
法人代表：郑如虎
联 系 人：郑如虎

22. 南京宝祥金店

地址：南京市夫子庙贡院西街35号
邮编：210001
电话：025-2201370　6626961
传真：025-6626961
法人代表：刘志荣
联 系 人：刘志荣

23. 上海造币厂南京特约经销部

地址：江苏南京市中山东路1号
邮编：210005
电话：025-4710097
传真：025-4728192
法人代表：胡居友
联 系 人：胡居友

24. 无锡金银制品公司（无锡宝泉珍品销售部）

地址：江苏无锡市五爱路33号
邮编：214031
电话：0510-2700674
传真：0510- 2730134
法人代表：杨 革
联 系 人：杨 革　华 群

25. 常州金店

地址：江苏常州市延陵西路7号楼
邮编：213003
电话：0519-6635260
传真：0519- 6680334
法人代表：李慧君
联 系 人：李慧君

26. 扬州金店

地址：江苏扬州汶河路67号
邮编：225002
电话：0514-7313600　7346314
传真：0514-313600
法人代表：何秀珍
联 系 人：何秀珍

27. 涂州金店

地址：江苏徐州中山南路91号
邮编：221003
电话：0516-3813355
传真：0516-3813355
法人代表：侯英武
联 系 人：侯英武

28. 镇江恒祥金银珠宝有限责任公司
（镇江恒祥金店）

地址：江苏镇江中山东路[illegible]号[illegible]幢[illegible]楼
邮编：212001
电话：0511-501[illegible]　50[illegible]
传真：0511-5035299
法人代表：杨树明
联 系 人：杨树明　钱 勇

29. 昆山金银珠宝行

地址：江苏昆山市人民路126号
邮编：215300
电话：0520-7553941
传真：0520-7305462
法人代表：沈丽霞
联 系 人：蒋建刚

30. 浙江省金银饰品经销公司

地址：浙江杭州市中山北路267号
邮编：310003
电话：0571-7822608
传真：0571-7823808
法人代表：赵祖馨
联 系 人：赵祖馨　祝 梅

31. 宁波市金鑫金银饰品公司

地址：浙江宁波市中山西路215号
邮编：315010
电话：0574-7294893
传真：0574-7374406
法人代表：陈海涌
联 系 人：陈海涌

32. 杭州市金银制品厂

地址：浙江杭州市中河路161号
邮编：310001
电话：0571-7028109
传真：0571-7028109
法人代表：周家洪
联 系 人：周家洪

33. 安徽银海实业公司

地址：合肥市金寨路188号
邮编：230022
电话：0551-3632684　3633001
传真：0551-3632910
法人代表：孙 诚
联 系 人：黄向卿

34. 江西省赣昌金银制品厂
赣昌金银饰品店

地址：江西南昌市中山路233号
邮编：330008
电话：0791-6623649　6624079
传真：0791-6624079
法人代表：高 江
联 系 人：张 洁

35. 福州闽鑫金银特艺制品有限公司

地址：福州市五四路220号
邮编：350003
电话：0591-7854131　7850142
传真：0591-7827894
法人代表：刘维惠
联 系 人：刘维惠

36. 泉州宝辉钱币经销中心

地址：福建泉州市新华南路人行泉州中心支行院内
邮编：362000
电话：0595-2370921
传真：0595-2384597
法人代表：蔡长华
联 系 人：蔡长华

37. 陕西金店

地址：西安市解放路159号
邮编：710004
电话：029-7427389　742691-4311
传真：029-7428170
法人代表：王增强
联 系 人：李占华

38. 甘肃省集币公司

地址：兰州市城关区静宁路53号
邮编：730030
电话：0931-84[illegible]5746
传真：0931-8430881　8435746-201
法人代表：王成顺
联 系 人：王成顺　牛 卫

39. 中国金币公司宁夏特约经销部

地址：银川市解放东街11号
邮编：750004
电话：0951-6022326　6022033
传真：0951-6023292
法人代表：杜汉平
联 系 人：常海燕

40. 新疆天宝珠宝金饰品公司

地址：新疆乌鲁木齐市人民路20号
邮编：830002
电话：0991-2821227
传真：0991-2821227
法人代表：胡 伟
联 系 人：孙本强

41. 青海恒泰钱币经销中心

地址：西宁市东关大街228号
邮编：810000
电话：0971-8143825　8134654
传真：0971-8134654
法人代表：朱立国
联 系 人：王 麟

42. 河南省钱币开发总公司

地址：河南省郑州市经五路20号附1号
邮编：450002
电话：0371-5715467　5719045
传真：0371-5715462
法人代表：崔建伟
联 系 人：崔建伟

43. 广西桂盈实业有限公司

地址：广西南宁市教育路15号桂银大酒店第21层
邮编：530021
电话：0771-2828884
传真：0771-2827284
法人代表：刘大任
联 系 人：章士琦

44. 桂林黄金首饰公司

地址：桂林市中山中路348号
邮编：541001
电话：0773-2822255　2800169
传真：0773-2822255
法人代表：董爱群
联 系 人：秦德超

45. 湖南省钱币公司

地址：长沙市蔡锷中路24号
邮编：410005
电话：0731-4301689　4301054
传真：0731-4301689
法人代表：田金凤
联 系 人：陈义亚

46. 湖北金银首饰公司

地址：武汉市汉口中山大道633-635号
邮编：430022
电话：027-82817180　82811402
传真：027-82821004
法人代表：胡菊莲
联 系 人：张 轶

47. 武汉汉银金饰珠宝公司

地址：武汉市江汉路19号
邮编：430014
电话：027-82838817　82815925
传真：027-82851448
法人代表：王玉霞
联 系 人：杜世平

48. 广东粤宝金银珠宝有限公司
（[illegible]）

地址：广州市沿江西路1[illegible]号
邮编：510120
电话：020-83313019　83313020
传真：020-81921039　81845383
法人代表：甄伟钢
联 系 人：阮瑞英

49. 汕头汕银金银珠宝首饰公司

地址：广东汕头市外马路25号
邮编：515011
电话：0754-8273959
传真：0754-8291950
法人代表：蔡 迅
联 系 人：蔡 迅

50. 佛山市宝华金饰公司

地址：佛山市汾江南路83号
邮编：528000
电话：0757-3336985
传真：0757-3337486
法人代表：周燕芬
联 系 人：周燕芬

51. 海口鑫鑫金店

地址：海口市滨海大道花园新村2号
邮编：570105
电话：0898-6764977
传真：0898-6773396
法人代表：刘兆英
联 系 人：刘兆英

52. 中国金币总公司成都特约经销部

地址：成都市锦江区北新街26号
邮编：610016
电话：028-6678662　6659408
传真：028-6673750
法人代表：蒋卓民
联 系 人：蒋卓民

53. 重庆钱币公司

地址：重庆市渝中区新华路74号
邮编：400011
电话：023-63830160
传真：023-63830160
法人代表：宋光节
联 系 人：徐 怡

54. 西藏银桥发展总公司

地址：拉萨市夺底路1号银桥饭店1408房
邮编：850000
电话：0891-6336327　6326898
传真：0891-6336896
法人代表：何荣才
联 系 人：何荣才

55. 云南银泉工贸有限公司

地址：昆明护国路192号
邮编：650021
电话：0871-3167586
传真：0871-3167586
法人代表：程建华
联 系 人：程建华

56. 贵州筑金钱币公司

地址：贵阳市富水中路28号天业大厦B座五楼
邮编：550001
电话：0851-5812762
传真：0851-5812762
法人代表：张 琍
联 系 人：张 琍

中国金币总公司国外主要经销商名单（按字母顺序）

1. 中国长城硬币投资有限公司

CHINA GREAT WALL COINS
INVESTMENTS LTD
UNIT 4101，41/F.,
COSCO TOWER,
183 QUEEN'S ROAD
HONG KONG
TEL: (+852) 2543 3199

2. 中国长城硬币（欧洲）有限公司

CHINA GREAT WALL
COINS (EUROPE) GMBH
OVERSTOLZENSTR. SA
50677 KOLN
GERMANY.
TEL: (+49) 221 3363 968

3. 中国长城（美国）硬币投资有限公司

CHINA GREAT WALL (US) COINS
INVESTMENTS LTD.
225 WEST WACKER DRIVE, SUITE 1550
CHICAGO, IL 60606
U. S. A.
TEL: (+1) 312 372 0600

4. 中国金币代理有限公司

CHINA COINS AGENCY (HK) LTD.
701-2 CHINA INSURANCE GROUP BLDG.,
141 DES VOEUX ROAD, CENTRAL,
HONG KONG
TEL: (+852) 2545 0083

5. MTB 银行

MTB BANK
90 BROAD STREET
NEW YORK,
NY 10004 - 2290
U. S. A.
TEL: (+1) 212 858 3309

6. 美国熊猫钱币公司

PANDA AMERICA CORP
3460 TORRANCE BLVD. STE 100
TORRANCE, CA 90503
U. S. A.
TEL: (+1) 310 378 6024

7. 德国理查德·鲍瑞克公司（MDM）

RICHARD BOREK GMBH
D - 38090 BRAUNSCHWEIG
THEODOR - HEUSS - STRASSE 7
GERMANY
TEL: (+49) 531 205 1251

8. 日本泰星钱币公司

TAISEI COINS CORPORATION
FUJILIGHT SHINKAWA BLDG.,
5F 1-22-11 SHINKAWA
CHUO-KU TOKYO 104, JAPAN
TEL: (+81) 3 3297 8222

1996～1998年中国贵金属纪念币设计、生产人员

（以姓氏笔画为序）

生产组织： 王　忠　王生龙　王景琴　车宏伟　兰士贤　石　瑛　田继新　宁应成　孙凤全　孙宝根　江　涛　华　蔚　任军传　张玉勉　张健建　刘英武　张维斌　刘晓静　许淑兰　吴　伟　宋　翔　陈剑峰　邵哲雷　杨学玉　郝和铭　郝建中　钱　亮　高礼红　徐铁峰　费良汗　董　江　彭书开　黎昌国　魏立营

生产顾问： 赵孝经　高礼红

工艺设计： 王丽云　方茂森　刘大力　刘　强　刘现轻　刘耀光　宋　飞　何　伟　时　晓　李学飞　林兰英　杨明志　赵丕信　崔宝玉

美工设计： 王云野　王亚莉　王福德　白　牧　白文均　白立梅　艾　松　叶柏林　申宪章　张　江　张文竞　张春晔　孙嘉英　向黎明　刘鸿鹏　陈　坚　陈丹丹　余　敏　李继峰　谷英斌　金刚山　郁友奎　周　静　罗永辉　岳俊峰　赵　力　赵　青　赵　樯　骆行沙　胡福庆　晏景奎　俞霞薇　顾杏宝　常　欢　童友明　曾成沪　温海东　储　巍　富丽丽　蔡寅昱

List of Designers and Producers of 1996~1998 Chinese Precious Metal Commemorative Currencies

Organized by

Wang Zhong, Wang Shenglong, Wang Jingqin, Che Hongwei, Lan Shixian, Shi Ying, Tian Jixin, Ning Yingcheng, Sun Fengquan, Sun Baogen, Jiang Tao, Hua Wei, Ren Junzhuan, Zhang Yumian, Zhang Jianjian, Liu Yingwu, Zhang Weibin, Liu Xiaojing, Xu Shulan, Wu Wei, Song Xiang, Chen Jianfeng, Shao Zhelei, Yang Xueyu, Hao Heming, Hao Jianzhong, Qian Liang, Gao Lihong, Xu Tiefeng, Fei Lianghan, Dong Jiang, Peng Shukai, Li Changguo, Wei Liying

Advised by

Zhao Xiaojing, Gao Lihong

Technological Designers

Wang Liyun, Fang Maosen, Liu Dali, Liu Qiang, Liu Xianqing, Liu Yaoguang, Song Fei, He Wei, Shi Xiao, Li Xuefei, Lin Lanying, Yang Mingzhi, Zhao Pixin, Cui Baoyu

Art Designers

Wang Yunye, Wang Yali, Wang Fude, Bai Mu, Bai Wenjun, Bai Limei, Ai Song, Ye Bailin, Shen Xianzhang, Zhang Jiang, Zhang Wenjing, Zhang Chunye, Sun Jiaying, Xiang Liming, Liu Hongpeng, Chen Jian, Chen Dandan, Yu Min, Li Jifeng, Gu Yingbin, Jin Gangshan, Yu Youkui, Zhou Jing, Luo Yonghui, Yue Junfeng, Zhaoli, Zhao Qing, Zhao Qiang, Luo Xingsha, Hu Fuqing, Yan Jingkui, Yu Xiawei, Gu Xingbao, Chang Huan, Tong Youming, Zeng Chenghu, Wen Haidong, Chu Wei, Fu Lili, Cai Yinyu

编 后 记

中国现代金银纪念币发行20年来，得到了海内外众多热心朋友的支持与厚爱。我们以此书的出版表示由衷的感谢。

《中国贵金属纪念币年鉴》是一部具有极高权威性和重要史料价值的工具书。为了编好此书，我们专门组织人员搜集、整理了公开发行的金银纪念币背景资料，以便在更宽广的层面上对金银纪念币的纪念价值和文化内涵作更全面、更贴切的诠释，其中许多资料、数据和制作背景情况是首次向社会公布。

为保证《中国贵金属纪念币年鉴》(1996～1998)编制的质量，并充分体现其权威性、知识性、史料性和艺术性的完美统一，在半年多的时间里，编辑组全体工作人员孜孜以求，全力以赴，付出了大量的辛勤劳动，务求使本书成为具有收藏价值的珍品。在整个编辑出版过程中，得到了中国人民银行办公厅、货币金银局领导的大力支持。在收集资料过程中，上海造币厂、沈阳造币厂、深圳国宝金币制造厂给予了积极的协助。参与编辑工作的人员还有：刘晓静、兰士贤、金刚山、周洋、周静、邵军志、林虹、肖仙。另外在拍摄样币中，我们还得到了中国金币总公司北京开元中国金币经销中心有关人员的大力协助。在此，我们一并表示衷心的感谢。

编　者

二〇〇〇年三月

ACKNOWLEDGMENTS

A great number of warm-hearted friends have contributed to the issue of Chinese modern gold and silver commemorative coins during the past 20 years, to whom we wish to express our utmost gratitude.

Almanac of Chinese Precious Metal Commemorative Currencies is an authoritative reference book that has important historic values. In order to compile this volume, we specially organized personnel to collect and sort out the background data of the publicly issued gold and silver commemorative coins. We wish this work would help readers to understand the commemorative values and cultural traits of the gold and silver commemorative coins from wider and more proper aspects. Many materials, data and the productive backgrounds are the first time to be publicized.

To ensure the quality of this book and to fully reflect the perfect unity of its authority, knowledge, history and artistry, the stuff of the editorial department spared no effort in the past half year. We hope that this book deserves collecting. The leaders of the People's Bank of China Governer's Office and the Currency, Gold & Silver Bureau have offered their great support. Shanghai Mint, Shenyang Mint and Shenzhen Panda Gold Coin Mint have greatly assisted in collecting material. Their help are appreciated. The other personnel who have also participated in compiling this book are: Liu Xiaojing, Lan Shixian, Jin Gangshan, Zhou Yang, Zhou Jing, Shao Junzhi, Lin Hong and Xiao Xian. We are particularly grateful for the assistance of the staff of the Beijing Kai Yuan China Gold Coin Trade Center of China Gold Coin Inc. in photographing model coins.

2000 . 3